The Medical Assault on the American Brain

The Medical Assault on the American Brain

Vaccination, Social Violence, and Criminality

Harris L. Coulter

Skyhorse Publishing, Inc.
New York, NY

Skyhorse Publishing books may be purchased in bulk at special discounts for sales promotion, corporate gifts, fund-raising, or educational purposes. Special editions can also be created to specifications. For details, contact the Special Sales Department, Skyhorse Publishing, 307 West 36th Street, 11th Floor, New York, NY 10018 or info@skyhorsepublishing.com.

Skyhorse® and Skyhorse Publishing® are registered trademarks of Skyhorse Publishing, Inc.®, a Delaware corporation.

Visit our website at www.skyhorsepublishing.com.

10 9 8 7 6 5 4 3 2 1

Library of Congress Cataloging-in-Publication Data is available on file.

Print ISBN: 978-1-5107-8528-1
eBook ISBN: 978-1-5107-8555-7

Cover design by Brian Peterson

Printed in the United States of America

Table of Contents

Introduction:
"The Most Immunized Child in History!"

The twentieth century is the age of vaccination. Edward Jenner's 1798 discovery that cowpox inoculation prevents later infection with smallpox was the start of a new science. Now called "immunology," it has been adorned by such historic names as Louis Pasteur, Robert Koch, Emil von Behring, Jonas Salk, Albert Sabin, and many others less prominent.

After cowpox came vaccines against rabies (1885), typhoid (1911), tuberculosis (1921), diphtheria (1925), tetanus (1925), yellow fever (1937), influenza (1943), poliomyelitis (1954 and 1956), and others.

Most have been beneficial, especially those against the great epidemic diseases which once ravaged Africa, Asia, and Latin America—bubonic plague, yellow fever, cholera, typhus, and poliomyelitis. In the nineteenth century no European or American could visit the African or Asian continents without risking a potentially fatal illness. British, French, and Portuguese diplomats and colonial administrators perished in large numbers.

Even today, travel or business in most parts of the Third World would be impossible without vaccines.

These triumphs of immunology are undisputed, and no criticism is made of them in the following pages. Tuberculosis, for instance, even in the early twentieth century, carried off thousands every year; today deaths from this disease have been sharply reduced, thanks, in part, to the vaccine.

According to the World Health Organization, the smallpox eradication campaign has completely rid the world of this once-feared epidemic disease.

However, as so often happens in human affairs, success led to excess. After taming these ancestral scourges, physicians sought new challenges and, in due course, directed their attention to the common diseases of childhood.

The first such vaccine was for whooping cough (pertussis) in 1925. A vaccine for measles followed in 1960, for German measles (rubella) in 1966, and for mumps in 1967. A vaccine against chicken-pox is under preparation today.

Researchers and physicians, however, gave insufficient thought to the difference between the fully grown adult and the newborn baby. Even in the former, the injection of toxic proteins carries a measure of risk. Injecting the same material into small babies is far more dangerous. The adult immune system has been toughened and can withstand the stress of vaccination. The two-month-old baby is inconceivably more vulnerable. But that is when immunization commences in the United States.*

The consequences are described in the following pages.

Vaccination programs commenced in earnest during and after World War II. In the 1960s persuasion became obligation as the shots were made compulsory in most states. Today nearly every American child is vaccinated against whooping cough, German measles, poliomyelitis, diphtheria, mumps, measles, and tetanus. (Western Europe, in contrast, requires only tetanus and oral polio vaccinations.)

The list is open-ended, however, as enterprising manufacturers prepare more and more substances for injection into the arms and thighs of our children, as though every conceivable illness could be warded off by timely administration of the appropriately prepared disease protein.

The campaigns are hard to resist. Vaccines have for decades been in the vanguard of medical progress. What mother will not protect her baby from a bacterial or viral menace? What working parent can afford the inconvenience of staying home for days or weeks with a

---

*The rule that vaccination should start at two months—earlier in the United States than in any other country—is designed mainly for the convenience of pediatricians (see Coulter, H. and Fisher, B., 32).

convalescing schoolchild?

No nights at the cradle side. No missed days at school!

The convenience extends also to the physician or pediatrician. No more house visits. No phone calls at midnight, with a distraught or outraged parent at the other end of the line! Instead, a nice steady stream of infants and mothers coming to the office for "well-baby visits" and the obligatory "shots."

And, of course, a much-reduced danger of children dying or suffering brain damage from the encephalitis which sometimes occurs in more severe cases of measles, mumps, or whooping cough.

In recent years a common advertisement for vaccines in American medical journals has featured a rosy-cheeked youngster extolled as "the most immunized child in history!"

It announces that nearly every child born in the United States will have been immunized against seven or eight diseases by the age of two.

The manufacturer sponsoring this publicity is proud of his vaccines, seeing them as unquestioned successes of modern medicine.

Nearly everyone else will agree—the physicians who administer them, the medical organizations which promote them to the public and to state legislatures, and most parents of the ultimate consumers of these products.

The consensus is that childhood vaccinations confer major health benefit at minimal cost.

Rare is the discordant voice in this almost-unanimous chorus of self-congratulation.

Indeed, the benefits of childhood vaccination are seemingly so self-evident that hardly anyone gives thought to a possible negative side.

No one has suggested, for instance, that the threat of encephalitis is hardly mitigated by a vaccine which causes encephalitis.

Little or nothing has been published about adverse reactions. But such reactions are, in fact, widespread.

In 1985 Barbara Fisher and I wrote *DPT: A Shot in the Dark*—the first critical scrutiny of this most sacred cow of American medicine.* We described the typical side effects of the DPT (diphtheria-pertussis-tetanus) shot which nearly every American baby receives starting at two months. We estimated that 1000 babies, at a minimum, die from this vaccine every year while 12,000 are permanently damaged.

Our figures have never been challenged by the medical establishment, although these numbers were far more pessimistic than previous assessments.

And the Congress agreed with our conclusions. In December 1986, it adopted the National Childhood Vaccination Compensation Law authorizing payment of damages to children harmed by an immunization.

Vaccine damage is now a legitimate topic of public debate. Adverse reactions have been discussed on radio and television programs and in the press. Growing awareness of vaccination risk has made parents more willing to sue vaccine producers.

One manufacturer, Lederle Laboratories, informed physicians in 1987 that "a significant portion" of the price of vaccines was being reserved to pay future damage awards.

A national parents' organization has been formed: Dissatisfied Parents Together (DPT), headquartered in Washington, D.C. Mothers who must make decisions about their children's health are striving to become better informed. More and more are refusing to submit their children to the shots, even when they are a prerequisite for school entry.

Professional medical organizations have not responded to these developments. Instead of recognizing that vaccines are dangerous and taking the needed measures to reduce the risk, the American Medical Association and the American Academy of Pediatrics have seen fit to maintain silence, hoping that the tumult will die down and that vaccination as usual can continue.

There has been no official reaction to the very serious charges made in *DPT: A Shot in the Dark.*

When accused of participating in a "conspiracy of silence," a

---

* New York: Harcourt Brace Jovanovich, 1985. Revised, 1991, Avery Publishing Group, Inc., Garden City Park, New York.

physician prominent in the Immunization Division of the Centers for Disease Control answered: "It is not feasible to respond to every document that deals with vaccines . . ."—as if our 439-page book, containing more than 100 interviews with families of vaccine-damaged children, had the status of an article in the *National Enquirer.*

But ostrich-like refusal to examine the data is not an appropriate response. Officers of the Centers for Disease Control, the Public Health Service, the Food and Drug Administration, and the National Institutes of Health are themselves public servants, working for the taxpayers who pay their salaries. When a responsible critique of vaccination appears, they are obligated to give it an honest hearing.

DPT: A Shot in the Dark described the effects of vaccination on babies and small children. In the present work we follow these children into adolescence and adulthood.

We show that long-term effects of vaccination are far more common than has ever been suspected. These disabilities have been ascribed to other causes, and the connection with vaccination has been systematically ignored.

The American Psychiatric Association publishes a guide to mental illnesses in this country, the *Diagnostic and Statistical Manual,* which devotes seventy pages to "Disorders Usually First Evident in Infancy, Childhood, or Adolescence."*

These disorders have received the appellation "developmental disabilities." Probably the leading one is "dyslexia," also called "minimal brain damage." Another prominent one is "autism." But there are many others: "hyperactivity," "reactive attachment disorder of infancy," "oppositional disorder," "identity disorder," "functional enuresis," and so on.

Probably twenty percent of American children—one youngster in five—suffers from a "developmental disability." This is a stupefying figure. If some foreign enemy had inflicted such damage on our

---

*Third Edition, Revised, 1987. The second edition in 1968 dealt with these disorders in only 3½ pages. The first edition, 1952, did not mention them at all. "Disorders Usually First Evident in Infancy, Childhood, or Adolescence" are clearly mushrooming.

country, we would declare war. But, as the following pages demonstrate, we have inflicted it on ourselves. And we persist in it to this very day.

The following pages show that "developmental disabilities" are nearly always generated by encephalitis. And the primary cause of encephalitis in the United States and other industrialized countries is the childhood vaccination program.*

To be specific, a large proportion of the millions of U.S. children and adults suffering from autism, seizures, mental retardation, hyperactivity, dyslexia, and other shoots and branches of the hydra-headed entity called "developmental disabilities," owe their disorders to one or another of the vaccines against childhood diseases.

The so-called "sociopathic personality," which is at the root of the enormous increase in crime of the past two decades, is also largely rooted in vaccine damage.

Thus the vaccination program has served to undermine the American school system—which is in collapse through inability to cope with the one-fifth or one-quarter of students who will never be able either to read or to perform simple arithmetical calculations.

And it has contributed to the wave of violent crime which is turning our cities into jungles where the strong and the vicious prey upon the weak and unprotected.

The effects of vaccination have altered the very tone and atmosphere of modern society. Because the changes are so insidious and widespread, and because we lack perspective, they have been largely overlooked. It is not easy to discern the outlines of the incubus which the vaccination program has loosed upon us.

Every day this program continues, hundreds of normal healthy babies are turned into defective goods: mentally retarded, blind, deaf, autistic, epileptic, learning-disabled, emotionally unstable, future juvenile delinquents, and career criminals.

This may seem a wild exaggeration, but it is a sober conclusion based on the evidence collected in the following pages.

---

*Encephalitis can arise in other ways: from trauma to the head, from a severe burn, or from an infectious disease, but these are comparatively rare occurrences.

Whoever doubts that so much evil could flow from the point of a hypodermic needle has only to read on.

*   *   *

A word about the research method.

We have drawn primarily on the specialized literature about autism, developmental disabilities, encephalitis, and vaccination. When read with sufficient care, these books and articles prove unexpectedly revealing.

We have made heavy use of direct quotation, partly for its intrinsic interest and partly because the following pages are not only an analysis of the childhood vaccination programs but also a history of medical views and opinions. Doctors change their minds, express puzzlement, contradict one another, sometimes talk nonsense. These human aspects of the physician's *persona* are brought out more graphically by direct quotation.

Another body of information quoted copiously in these pages is drawn from three sets of interviews with parents of neurologically damaged children.* One series of 100 cases is made up of parents we contacted when writing *DPT: A Shot in the Dark*. Their children had reacted violently to the DPT shot, and the parents blamed their later disabilities on this vaccine. The second and third series, about sixty cases in all, consist of families interviewed by me to ascertain if their neurologically damaged child was a victim of vaccination.

The three series are thus complementary, illuminating the relationship between vaccination and neurological disabilities from the two ends of the causal chain. The parents in the first series knew that their child had reacted violently to vaccination and suspected it to be the cause of the subsequent disability. The parents in the second and third series examined the possibility that their child's otherwise unexplained neurologic damage was really due to a childhood vaccination.

Here also we make heavy use of direct quotation. When parents discuss their children, their language is vivid; they pick the precise word to describe some particular quirk of personality or behavior;

---

*See Appendix.

their way of expressing themselves can hardly be improved upon, and direct quotation merely does justice to the depth and intensity of their feelings.

The three series are not to be considered "scientific" samples. The interviews with parents serve only to illustrate the argument drawn from the specialized literature on autism, developmental disabilities, encephalitis, and criminal behavior.

*   *   *

The following pages contain much implicit, and some explicit, criticism of the medical profession. This is not unreasonable since who else, if not the physicians themselves, must bear responsibility for the calamity visited upon this country by the vaccination programs?

This does not mean, of course, that every physician is deserving of censure. Doctors are human like the rest of us, with the same weaknesses and strengths. Most entered medicine in the first place with the intention of helping the afflicted. They have been caught up in a world made by others and must abide by rules which they never formulated. In that sense, it would not be fair to hold each one personally responsible.

But the organized profession—which was granted a legal monopoly on "health care" in the 1920s—together with groupings such as the American Medical Association and the American Academy of Pediatrics, the major medical journals, the professors of pediatrics and immunology at the country's medical schools, the congeries of drug and vaccine manufacturers, hospitals, state and local medical societies, and other appanages and fiefdoms which together make up the "new medical-industrial complex" must shoulder a large measure of blame. For decades it has stifled voices within and outside the profession warning against impending catastrophe.

The insulation of organized medicine from public opinion and from pressure by its own members has kept such knowledge from becoming known and from influencing policy.

If catastrophes such as the vaccination program are not to be repeated *ad nauseam* in the future, the legally privileged position of the medical profession must be modified.

This is discussed further in Chapter VI.

I

Autism

The first victims of the medical assault on the American brain were the autistic children.

In a now-legendary 1943 article the world's best-known child psychiatrist, Leo Kanner, described eleven cases of a new mental illness in young people which he called "inborn autistic disturbances of affective contact."[1]

"The condition differs," he wrote, "markedly and uniquely from anything reported so far. . . ."

It soon came to be known as "early infantile autism" or simply "autism."[2]

No one at the time, or for many decades thereafter, noted that the first cases of autism emerged in the United States at a time when vaccination against whooping cough was becoming increasingly popular and widespread.

Alienation

The outstanding feature of the autistic child was self-absorbed aliention ("autism" is from the Greek *auto*, meaning "self"). Kanner noted "the children's inability to relate themselves in the ordinary way to people and situations from the beginning of life . . . From the start an *extreme autistic aloneness*. . . ."[3] There was "no felt need for communication."[4]

These infants did not "reach out" to their parents when picked up and would not mold themselves to fit into the mother's arms.

They played by themselves without demanding attention: "he walks as if he is in a shadow, lives in a world of his own where he cannot be reached."[5] They were "detached" and "inaccessible." They could not, or would not, smile; refused to be touched, even by their parents, and were "nervously hostile" with strangers.

They suffered from "emotional blunting," "affective isolation," "a syndrome of affective inadequacy."[6]

I remember him especially sitting inside a circle of toys, as if to block out the rest of the world.*

Her response to us seemed fleeting and transient, not pronounced or vigorous. It took a real effort to get her to smile or to pay attention. She would stare blankly into space.

I remember saying to people, "He's so aloof! What a snob!" Even when he was tiny, I used to say, "He's my aloof baby, no interest in people."

Their aloneness stemmed from inability to empathize with others, to sense what they were thinking and feeling. A British medical group seeking to define autism found "gross and sustained *impairment of emotional relationships* with people. This includes the more usual aloofness and the empty clinging (so-called symbiosis): also abnormal behavior towards other people as persons, such as using them, or parts of them, impersonally. Difficulty in mixing and playing with other children is often outstanding and long-lasting."[7] They are unsuited to "adaptive social behavior," do not recognize the "emotional significance of persons or events," and show "lack of concern for others." They cannot judge another's emotional state by the facial expression.[8]

Jerry Goldsmith, an eighteen-year-old near-normal autistic, is described as follows: "functions 'like a machine,' without emotion, and has only intellectual appreciation of environment . . . intellectual but emotionally empty awareness of social interaction." When he was fourteen, he went with his family to a Mexican border town

---

*Unattributed quotations (in italics) are taken from the author's interviews with families (see Appendix). The names used are fictitious (Harvey Jackson, Jr., Tammy Garrett, etc.).

where, not liking the smell of the market, he disappeared and walked the ten miles back to the motel without telling his parents, leaving them to search frantically for him all day. "He did not understand that his family might be concerned by his disappearance and so had not told anyone he was leaving. Of all his problems, this lack of sympathy, illustrated in this vignette, seemed to be his greatest deficiency. He simply could not appreciate how other people felt, and so could not respond appropriately. Indeed, lacking an empathic sensitivity to the feelings of others, he could not even predict how they would behave and so seemed ever surprised and puzzled by their actions. This made life within his family difficult and life outside his family impossible."

> The major defect that has affected Jerry throughout his entire life (and is a prominent symptom in all autistic individuals) is a glaring lack of empathic relatedness . . . This fundamental interpersonal bond appears to have always been lacking, and thus the world of humans, in contrast to that of inanimate objects, has always seemed puzzling and frightening. Even as an adult Jerry appears, at times, to understand intellectually how another person might feel, but he does not seem to be able to automatically sense in himself another's inner state. He remains an isolated, mechanical being, unable to intuit the social nuances of behavior and is therefore forced to retreat from a world that is persistently surprising and lacking in regularity.[9]

Ego Weakness

Kanner and others were quick to note the *ego weakness* of the autistic child. At best, he felt vulnerable, inept, and inferior to others; in an extreme case there was:

> *apparent unawareness of . . . personal identity* to a degree inappropriate to his age. This may be seen in abnormal behavior towards himself such as posturing or exploration and scrutiny of parts of his body.[10]

This seems a paradox: how is ego-weakness reconciled with total self-absorption?

The answer is simple. Lacking any sense of self, the autistic child identifies with the whole world:

They say he doesn't know where he stops and someone else begins.

He thinks the world revolves around him. He sees himself as the center of the universe. Anything that happens, he wants to know how it will affect him.

Ronald, a moderately autistic adult, states:

"I really didn't know there were people until I was seven years old. I then suddenly realized there were people. But not like you do. I still have to remind myself that there are people."

This need to remind himself was apparent in his relations. He would walk past a person as if he did not exist, or fade off while talking to someone as if the other person had simply died.[11]

But this self-absorption cannot withstand exposure to reality. The adolescent autistic realizes how different he is.[12] He understands that the outside world is uncooperative and hostile. His grandiose view of himself, his ego, shrinks to nothing. If he cannot identify with the whole world, he has very little left.

This is manifested in a number of ways. One is *inability to handle criticism* or even a sharp word.

He responds well to praise. They don't have to discipline him much at school. All they have to do is to praise him enough. He is very pleased with himself when he does something right, but he is very sensitive to criticism and would cry right away if you said something to him. We never had to discipline him in any other way . . . If another boy knocked him down, he would just lie there and cry.

The autistic child is often *unable to say "yes"*; assenting to an offer or proposition would require an awareness of self, of the existence of a person with a will or willingness to agree, and this is beyond the powers of most of them. Agreement is often signified by repeating the question.

Ego weakness can be manifested as *inability to look another in the eye*, and autistic children are famous for their "sidelong glances." Tammy Garrett is "afraid of people's eyes. She is afraid she will fall into someone's eyes."

Lack of ego integration is seen also in the autistic's inability to use personal pronouns correctly. In particular, he *cannot under-*

stand the significance of "I." The child does not refer to himself voluntarily in any way, does not call himself "I," and does not point.[13] Personal pronouns are repeated just as heard, with no change to suit the altered situation. "The child, once told by his mother, 'Now I will give you your milk,' expresses the desire for milk in exactly the same words. Consequently, he comes to speak of himself always as 'you,' and of the person addressed as 'I'."[14]

Ego weakness is also manifested by *fear of taking initiative*, lack of spontaneity, even in conversation.[15]

> *He would answer questions but never initiate speech. You couldn't have a conversation with him.*

"Sometimes I hear them playing," says the mother of two daughters, one autistic. "Fran takes Beth's part in the conversation. It makes you kind of sad, you know, that she doesn't have a sister to talk to."[16] The mother of another autistic boy complained: "The only spontaneous thing my son has ever done was to introduce himself to someone at a party."[17]

Ego weakness is seen in *unawareness of risk*. The autistic child walks out into traffic and along the edges of roofs, climbs up drainspouts, tight-rope walks on clotheslines, nonchalantly dives off the high board, etc.:

> Unable to comprehend danger, he showed no change in expression as cars screeched to a halt in front of him. Heights also captivated him at one time, and we often found him standing on a second-storey window ledge, staring down at the cement below.[18]

Fear and Anxiety

Another manifestation of ego weakness is diffuse, undirected fear and anxiety. These children's faces betray "an anxious tenseness, probably because of the uneasy anticipation of possible interference. . . ."[19] They are afraid of everything: dogs and other animals, loud noises, guns, the refrigerator, a furnace, flashing lights, a spot on the wall, and especially of the dark—"night terrors."

Tony M., a near-normal autistic, wrote in a short autobiography:

I was living in a world of daydreaming and fear revolving about myself. I had no care about human feelings or other people. I was afraid of everything! I was terrified to go in the water swimming, and of loud noises; in the dark I had severe repetitive nightmares and occasionally hearing electronic noises with nightmares. I would wake up so terrified and disoriented I wasn't able to find my way out of the room for a few minutes. It felt like I was being dragged to Hell. I was afraid of simple things such as going into the shower, getting my nails clipped, soap in my eyes, rides in the carnival . . . I was horrified the first time I saw my own blood—cut. I also was very hard to assure or convince and always needed reassurance and still do today. I don't or didn't trust anybody but myself—that still is a problem today. And I was and still am very insecure . . . and was very nervous about everything, and feared people and social activity greatly.[20]

Jerry Goldsmith exhibited "profound feelings of inadequacy" and pervasive anxiety when interviewed at age twenty-two:

His childhood experiences could be summarized as consisting of two predominant experiential states: confusion and terror. The recurrent theme that ran through all of Jerry's recollections was that of living in a frightening world presenting painful stimuli that could not be mastered . . . everything was unpredictable and strange . . . Dogs were remembered as eerie and terrifying. As a child, he believed that they were somehow humanoid (since they moved of their own volition, etc.), yet they were not really human, a puzzle that mystified him . . . He was also frightened of other children, fearing that they might hurt him in some way. He could never predict or understand their behavior. Elementary school was remembered as a horrifying experience. The classroom was total confusion, and he always felt he would "go to pieces."[21]

Leonard, a moderately severe autistic occupied in a menial and highly structured job, responded to his father's request that he move up a little in life:

"I can imagine myself doing it, my mind wanders in the air, and I can imagine doing it—getting a job, driving a car. But it will be quite some time. You know, last year I had dreams of going to another city, but nothing like that is possible for me." When

asked why he couldn't do what he wished, he would answer:
"I simply couldn't drive. Even the littlest things make me
too anxious, too panicked. Unmistakably, unquestionably, if I
tried to drive, I would just certainly fall apart."[22]

"The Refrigerator Mother"

Frustrated by their inability to help, or even to explain autism (no
cure has ever been found), psychiatrists and psychoanalysts concluded that the parents, especially the mother, were to blame for
the child's alienation, self-absorption, ego weakness, and anxiety.
Kanner's discovery marked the start of an orgy of speculation which
has not quite run its course even today.

Kanner himself was at first influenced by prevailing theories
of psychoanalysis and took the lead, writing in 1944 that the parents
of autistics are rarely "warmhearted."

For the most part the parents, grandparents and collaterals are persons strongly preoccupied with abstractions of a scientific, liter-
ary, or artistic nature and are limited in genuine interest in people.
Even some of the happiest marriages are rather cold and formal
affairs. The question arises whether or to what extent this fact has
contributed to the condition of the children.[23]

In a 1949 article he described a family's visit to the psychiatrist:

As they come up the stairs, the child trails forlornly behind the
mother, who does not bother to look back. The mother accepts
the invitation to sit down in the waiting room, while the child sits,
stands, or wanders about at a distance. Neither makes a move
toward the other. Later, in the office, when the mother is asked
under some pretext to take the child in her lap, she usually does
so in a dutiful, stilted manner, holding the child upright and using
her arms solely for the mechanical purpose of maintaining him
in his position. I saw only one mother of an autistic child who
proceeded to embrace him warmly and bring her face close to his.[24]

Kanner's views may have been influenced by the public he was
dealing with. His early patients were from the upper and upper-middle
classes of Baltimore, Maryland, who are restrained in their display
of emotion. To a compassionate East European Jew their reticence

might have seemed inordinate inhibition. In any case, these observations led to his "refrigerator mother" theory of autism—"the emotional refrigeration which the children experience from such parents cannot but be a highly pathogenic element in the patients' early personality development."[25] When exposed to "prolonged affective deprivation," children display antisocial and psychopathic behavior:

> It is difficult to escape the conclusion that this emotional configuration in the home plays a dynamic role in the genesis of autism.[26]

The finding that autism affects males four or five times as often as females added fuel to the general assault on the American mother who, as it were, could rear her daughters successfully but not her sons.

But Kanner was an observant clinician, and he soon started hedging his theory, writing as early as 1944 that these children often show symptoms "from the beginning of life," making it hard to blame the parents' rearing practices.[27] And why did autistic children often have normal brothers and sisters? Finally, some parents with frigid personalities reared normal children who, "far from withdrawing autistically, responded with restless aggressiveness. It is not easy to account for this difference of reaction."[28]

In 1954 he raised the possibility of a biological abnormality in the children, causing an autistic reaction to the "refrigerator mother."[29] In 1955 he noted that about ten percent of parents did not fit the stereotype.[30] And in 1971 he admitted that the whole theory of the "refrigerator" or "psychotoxic" mother had been a blunder.[31]

In the meantime, however, others had taken it up. This was the era of Freud's dominance of the treatment of mental illness. To psychoanalysts mesmerized by the dynamics of ego, superego, and id, autism presented a rich field for speculation.

They usually selected one aspect of the autistic child's behavior and on it erected an ideological structure reflecting Freud's tripartite theory.

The poor ego development of autistic children, in particular, opened almost limitless vistas. It was usually taken as the initial cause of the condition and was, of course, blamed on the mother.

A generation of American moms was accused of subconsciously hating their children and thus undermining their egos:

The fact that parents can be sick emotionally without being aware of it and can have their pathological symptoms brought to light in the setting of parenthood with such tragic effects on the child is shocking and challenging . . . the negative mother does not truly want her child. She has little capacity to devote herself to him, and this fact comes to light very clearly in the way she handles the infant. Her mothering is a duty and often produces a negative response in the baby, who is made uneasy by her ministrations . . . It seems to me that the mother of the child who develops autistic behavior is an extreme case of this negative woman, and unfortunately the infant is the first to sense her unconscious hostility.[32]

A 1949 article about autistic children opined that the ego, which serves to defend the individual against external stimuli, must itself be developed in an orderly fashion. This is the task of the mother, who can err in two ways. Either she fails to give the child sufficient stimulus, leading to "delayed and possibly all-too-delayed ego formation." Or, and this is almost worse, she overstimulates—causing a "substitute" ego to be hastily erected. But this "premature ego organization" provides only a "weak protective barrier against stimuli" and then breaks down—meanwhile having inhibited the formation of a mature ego organization. "Parents and others concerned with the welfare of these children would have to protect these children thoroughly from intensive stimulation until such time as the child's ego might be able to take over this function without strain."[33]

This analysis may well have been based on the psychoanalyst's correct observation that autistic children are often hypersensitive to sensory impressions.

Another group of researchers held that defective ego development in the first five years of life results in a libidinal (id-derived) surge threatening the ego structure. "In a desperate attempt to maintain a hold on reality the child relates to its less threatening aspects: objects and parts, rather than to its more dangerous aspects: persons and wholes. Then the mental function of symbolization fails to develop."[34]

Autistic children do indeed relate to bits and pieces of their environment and have difficulty with symbolization, but why "libidinal"? In any case, this daring conjecture was criticized on the ground that it "begs the question as to what leads to the original [ego] defect and what is its nature."

A penetrating observation, but the author's own proposal was hardly an improvement:

> This writer would like to postulate that, as we move in our spectrum of schizoid phenomena toward the more virulent and morbid extreme, autism increases and that at one point of loading it becomes the primary defect. The writer would place the pathological locus of this manifestation at the level of the mysterious translation of "organic" perceptions (the result of "mechanical" stimuli from the inner and outer physical worlds) into meaningful and integrated psychic experiences. . . . [??!]³⁵

Psychoanalysts could sometimes make correct observations—such as that autism is associated with ego weakness and the need to protect it—but these were then inundated by a flood of hypotheses about psychological causes:

> Ego safety is achieved by an active and automatic pattern of self-inhibition and withdrawal which raises an autistic barrier between himself and others, designed to conceal his vulnerability and resulting in the characteristic psychological isolation. By withdrawing from emotional contact with others, the patient not only achieves ego safety but also succeeds in frustrating the attempts of others to relate themselves to him and so retaliates in a measure by sabotaging the effectiveness of the "influencing" pressures which he resents. His ego safety and his retaliation—both accomplished by the pattern of withdrawal—are purchased, however, at the price of emotional frustration, loneliness, and the negation of further ego growth . . . etc. etc.³⁶

Why, in any case, was the American mom so inattentive or uninterested in her son? What induced her to block his ego development in this systematic way? J. Louise Despert, professor of clinical psychiatry at Cornell University Medical College, presented a case in which the mother supposedly rejected her son through identifying him with an incident of attempted rape by her cousin when she was four years old. Thus the boy was

> involved in a conflict which made sex powerfully tabooed and childbirth in a sense illegitimate (recall the involved fantasy

regarding sex, rape, and illegitimacy). The sensuous pleasures associated with infant care, which mothers usually reveal in indirect statements in their accounts of the baby's first year, are here forbidden . . . Although no deep analysis of this mother's sexual conflict was made, the nature of the conflict, even in its more superficial aspects, is so significant that conclusions regarding its bearing on the rejection of motherhood are inescapable.[37]

Of all the fault-finders and critics of the American mother the most pertinacious by far was Bruno Bettelheim, who had spent several years in an Austrian concentration camp (which he called the "turning point" in his life) and later interpreted the parent-autistic-child relationship in terms of camp-guards and inmates. His book, *The Empty Fortress*, which appeared in 1967, remained influential for a decade or more and delayed a correct understanding of autism for the same length of time. Assuming *a priori* that the parents were guilty, he laid down the rule in his Orthogenic School at the University of Chicago that "the patient is always right." By extension the parent was always wrong. Even the staff of the Orthogenic School was wrong in any conflict with an autistic child—who was seen as willing himself to be sick in revenge for lack of attention from his parents.[38] Thus, if the child was beating on a chair with a stick, the interpretation was: "He's symbolically punishing his mother for rejecting him."

But, as one such mother pointed out with at least equal plausibility, "Billy could just as well be punishing *you* for taking him away from his beloved mother for this silly therapy hour."[39] Other parents have described similar experiences:

If assistance *was* offered, it was on the basis of a correction of causative and contributing factors in the parents *first*; then and *if* this were accepted, treatment of the child followed. The parents went from being hostages of the child to hostages of the system. This attitude among professionals has not died out completely [1978] in dealing with the families of autistic children. Unfortunately, we see it resurfacing in small communities where the only psychiatrist in town is "king," his word is law, and you had better hope he is not an admirer of Bettelheim.[40]

They never were interested in really seeing the child, but they had my husband and I come in forever—really doing the trick on us.

> We both thought we loved each other before we went there, but after that things have never been the same—even though it was fifteen years ago . . . But I never accepted Bettelheim. No. Nobody ever loved anything or anybody like I love this kid. I would gladly, at a moment's notice, give my life for the slightest improvement in him—I mean that. I'm doing it every day.[41]

Psychiatrists and psychoanalysts criticized in the gravest terms the inexplicable unwillingness of mothers to be treated for their supposed sexual frustrations and blockages so as to cure their child of autism.

> They reject treatment for themselves; and when it is possible to link them actively to the therapeutic process, their participation remains one of contribution to the child's treatment rather than any involvement in their own personal difficulties. They see the problem outside of themselves; they are victims of, rather than contributors to, the misfortune that has befallen them . . . Although it is reported that they felt responsible for their child's illness, that they had scrutinized their own background and their handling of the child, there is no indication that they revealed the kind of persons they themselves were, the kind of emotional and sexual adjustment they themselves had made.[42]

Bettelheim's thesis had, in fact, been demolished even before it appeared—by Bernard Rimland's 1964 *Infantile Autism—the Syndrome and Its Implications for a Neural Theory of Behavior.* Rimland went through the arguments for the psychoanalytic theory of causation and picked them apart one by one. There was no evidence that even severe maternal rejection of a child, or maternal deprivation, could cause a syndrome as severe as autism. Children can withstand very severe treatment and still come out normal. Kanner's data never suggested deprivation or rejection. At worst, the mothers performed like "overconscientious gasoline-station attendants."[43]

The child's withdrawal and other phenomena of autism must be seen as *symptoms* of an underlying condition rather than as part of the causal process.

In any case, as Rimland noted, parents often seemed a little cool to the psychiatrist's suggestions because they sensed he was blaming them for their child's condition.

They protested in vain that their attitude *resulted* from their child's illness rather than *causing* it. As one mother said, "It is very hard to keep trying to make a relationship with a child who doesn't know you exist."[44]

They could never make clear to psychiatrists that aloofness, and even occasional hostility, toward an autistic child were the natural outcome of having to spend twenty-four hours a day, 365 days a year, with an individual who was totally unresponsive, probably mentally defective, possibly incontinent, often hyperactive, and even violently aggressive.

When asked how these supposedly inadequate parents could raise other children successfully, psychiatrists pointed out, "A mother, biogenetically identical for all her children, may nevertheless psychogenetically differ widely from one child to another."[45] In normal language: she treats different children differently, causing some to be normal and others to be autistic. [!!]

The major argument advanced by Bettelheim and others to support their "emotional" thesis (and still advanced today!) was that psychotherapy helps in the treatment of autism. If psychotherapy could cure, they claimed, the cause must be psychological or "emotional." But Kanner disputed this, stating that the children who receive the most intensive psychiatric care show poorer records of recovery than those provided little or no professional treatment, while those who have recovered sufficiently to go to school "are children who have not had anything that is regarded as good psychotherapy or as psychotherapy at all."[46]

This remains true today. The millions of hours of psychiatric and psychoanalytic counseling of autistics and their parents during the past several decades have produced little or no benefit. A small proportion of autistics seem to improve marginally with age, but this is due to the self-healing capacity of the developing nervous system.[47]* Autistics can sometimes be trained but cannot be cured.

The "refrigerator mother" or "psychogenetic" theory of autism, and the turmoil it engendered, these "decades of psychotoxic

---

*See discussion of demyelination and autism in Chapter IV.

theorizing," have been described as "a black mark in the history of medicine."[48] It led to immeasurable "shame, guilt, inconvenience, financial expense, and marital discord," as Rimland put it. Indeed, it has been estimated that more than half of families with autistic children end in the divorce courts. Rimland, who himself has an autistic son, wrote:

> The damage and torment this practice has wrought upon parents whose lives and hopes have already been shattered by their child's illness is not easy to imagine nor pleasant to contemplate. To add a heavy burden of shame and guilt to the distress of people whose hopes, social life, finances, well-being, and feelings of worth have been all but destroyed seems heartless and inconsiderate in the extreme. Yet it is done . . .[49]

This was in 1964. Things have gotten a little better today, but not much, and attempts to trivialize autism crop up at regular intervals. Nikolaas Tinbergen, professor of animal behavior at Oxford, received the 1973 Nobel Prize in Physiology and Medicine, and used the platform provided by his Prize Lecture to revive this largely discredited hypothesis. He propounded, or repropounded, the thesis that autism is essentially an "emotional disturbance," an "anxiety neurosis which prevents or retards normal affiliation and subsequent socialization." It is due not to "genetic abnormalities or to gross brain damage, but to early environmental influences. The majority of autistics, as well as their parents, seem to be genuine victims of environmental stress." Therapy thus must "aim at the reduction of anxiety and at a restarting of proper socialization." Tinbergen mentioned favorably a therapist in Australia who "considers the restoration of initially defective affiliation with the mother as the first goal of the treatment of autism . . . She does this by provoking in the mother an increase in maternal, protective behavior. . . ."[50]

A 1980 textbook on "emotional disorders in children and adolescents" reads: "The initial treatment plan for this [autistic] child focussed on both child and parents. The child was assigned to a warm mothering child-care worker on a 1:1 basis, and parents were worked with as a couple at first to support them *and further delineate their problems* [emphasis added], following which they sought individual treatment."[51]

A parent's-eye view of this sort of program (1984):

> Evaluations at the handicapped center were unfortunately carried out by psychologists trained in the outmoded parental causation theory of autism. Treatment, therefore, was based on that premise, and we were made to feel ashamed and guilty. . . We pressed for a specific diagnosis, only to be told that Brian was a "very unhappy little boy." . . . In the ensuing months Brian was labelled as "emotionally disturbed," "mentally retarded," "neurologically impaired," and as having "minimal brain dysfunction" . . . Could we possibly have brought on such a reaction in a little child who had been loved and wanted from the beginning? Our every comment seemed to be twisted to fit the Bettelheim mold. . . .[52]

Robert Cancro in 1981 levelled a critique at the whole decades-long endeavor to treat serious mental illness psychiatrically; his words apply *a fortiori* to Bettelheim's management of autism:

> As so often happens following a "hard sell," the initially convinced customer is left with a significant level of disappointment, if not rage. Thus it was with psychiatry, which could not deliver the cornucopia of benefits that were promised and in fact found great difficulty in even reducing the anguish of the chronically psychotic. After riding off madly in all directions, psychiatry did grievous if not mortal injury to its credibility.[53]

A Neurologic Theory of Autism

Rimland's work sparked a reevaluation of autism and a new departure. The "refrigerator mother" theory had had a long run, doing incalculable harm to autistic children and their families in the process, but it was largely laid to rest (except at the Orthogenic School in Chicago) while researchers started looking at the data neurologically.

Physicians and scientists eventually came to appreciate that autistics ordinarily suffer from a multitude of other disorders—mental retardation, epilepsy, cerebral palsy, and others—which are clearly of neurologic origin. This strengthened the arguments of those who had called autism a neurologic disorder all along.

The relationship with mental retardation was the first to attract attention. Kanner had thought that autistic children were of at least

normal intelligence but suffered from an "innate inability to form
. . . affective contact with people."[54] Indeed, encounters with individuals possessing "splinter skills"—powerful memories, extraordinary imitative abilities, remarkable musical talent—convinced him
that autistics, by and large, were of superior intellectual ability.
Later research, however, has revealed that three-quarters are mentally retarded, while forty percent have an IQ lower than 50.[55]

It is not always possible even to distinguish autism from retardation.[56] William and Marian DeMyer wrote in 1984: "No specific
cutoff exists between 'mental retardation' and autism. In fact, the
rule is that the more retarded the child, the more 'autistic' features
he or she will display."[57]

For that matter, "mental retardation" itself has no clear
definition.[58]

Just as there is much mental retardation among autistics, so the
incidence of "autism" among children labelled "mentally retarded"
is three to four times higher than in the general population.[59]

Another major finding was the close association between autism
and seizure disorders. Kanner in 1943 mentioned a case with an
abnormal EEG and seizures but did not view this as significant.[60]
In 1963 Richard J. Schain and Herman Yannet of the Yale Medical
School investigated fifty autistics from a Connecticut mental hospital and found, to their "distinct surprise," that the children suffered
disproportionately (twenty-one cases) from epilepsy and other seizure
disorders—in addition to their autistic symptoms. They observed,
"Our review of the literature dealing with autism gave no indication
of such an association . . . Other authors have not commented to
our knowledge on an association between a history of seizures and
the autistic syndrome."[61]

Some twenty to thirty percent of autistics are now known to
have a seizure disorder: convulsions, fits, clonic spasms, infantile
spasms, hypsarrhythmia, temporal lobe epilepsy, psychomotor
epilepsy, "strange quivering tensing of all muscles in a kind of passing paroxysm," grand mal, petit mal, "absence seizures" or "staring
spells," and combinations of all of these.[62]

Sometimes these develop only in adolescence.

Seizures, furthermore, are almost universal in autistics with an

IQ lower than 50, while rare in those of normal intelligence. In other words, autism, mental retardation, and seizure disorders tend to cluster in the same child.[63]

Autistics have problems with muscular control: motor disorders, paralyses, cerebral palsies, paraplegia (paralysis of the lower limbs), hemiplegia (paralysis of one side of the body), hemiparesis (slight paralysis of one side of the face or body), hypotonia (muscular weakness), Duchenne's muscular dystrophy, spasticity, etc.

Peggy Napear's *Brain Child: A Mother's Diary* is an account of a cerebral palsy child with autistic features.[64]

Autistics have a sixty-five percent incidence of abnormal EEG readings, also a high incidence of "soft" neurological signs: too little muscle tone (hypotonia) or too much (hypertonia, hyperreflexia), poor coordination, clumsiness, hyperactive knee jerks, ankle clonus, and others.[65]

Kanner had noted in 1943 that "several of the children were somewhat clumsy in gait and gross motor performances," but had not thought more of it.

A quite common symptom of hypotonia in autistics, often noted by parents in the very young child, is reluctance to use the hands and arms: the baby will reach for objects with his toes, not his hands; the child will refuse to throw or catch a ball.

I did notice that he would never squeeze my hand, even as a small baby. Even when I would take his hand to go somewhere, it was like his hand was just there. At some point I noticed that he didn't use his hands in this normal way.

As they get older, they are reluctant to shake hands: "The extremely handsome, almost cherubic-looking twenty-one-year old approached me slowly and revealed his hand like a flag furled in a breeze. I shook his hand and thought that it had little relation to any hand I'd ever touched."[66] Others have noted the autistic child's "curious, slipping handclasp."[67]

Here, however, as in many other aspects of autism, opposites meet. While some autistics can do nothing with their hands, others have remarkable control. Some autistic toddlers can consistently throw a ball within an inch of someone's hand across a large room.[68]

These children have difficulty crawling when small. Some never crawl but only start to walk, usually later than normal. Many walk on their toes for years—indicating a general tension of the muscular system.

The sensation of pain may be severely diminished, and even the sense of touch may be absent. "Objects placed in the hand may be allowed to fall away as if they made no tactile representation. Painful stimuli are often ignored; the children may not notice painful bumps, bruises, cuts, or injections."[69] The child plays outdoors in the winter without mittens or jacket, is impervious to hot or cold water in his bath, or, alternately, is very sensitive to heat and insists only on lukewarm baths.

The prevalence of left-handedness and ambidexterity in the autistic population (common also in the epileptic and the mentally retarded) has long excited comment.[70]

Autistics are prone to a number of sleep disturbances and do not observe the normal day-night rhythm. Even in the first year the child "turns night into day and day into night." But sometimes the child sleeps normally for the first year or eighteen months and develops irregular sleeping habits later.[71]

Sleeping difficulties continue into adolescence, often accompanied by night terrors:

> It is not uncommon to hear that parents spell each other during the night when their autistic child screams unceasingly for several hours. Often it is the mother who stays up or stays in the basement with the child "because Daddy has to go to work in the morning."[72]

These children may grind their teeth while asleep, and sometimes during the day as well.[73]

Cranial Nerve Palsies

Finally, the neurologic interpretation was able to account for that hallmark of autism—the child's "alienation" from his surroundings.

It was now seen to reflect impairment of the cranial nerves, which run from the eyes, ears, nose, vocal cords, mouth, and muscles of the face, over the skull to the "brainstem," at the back of the neck, between the spinal cord and the brain.

These nerves convey information to the brain and help effect control by the brain over the respective sensory organs and muscles.

In the autistic child the sensory organ itself is sometimes defective, but more often there is impairment (palsy) of one or more of the cranial nerves. The sensory organ itself functions but for some reason cannot transmit information to the brain.

When this happens, the individual is to that extent isolated from his surroundings.

To survive and prosper we must absorb and process information from the environment. Data are perceived through the sensory organs and processed in the brain. Making sense of information in this way enables us to function in life, and when we cannot gather this information, we are *ipso facto* diminished as human beings.

Autistic children suffer from a large range of cranial nerve disorders.

Take, for instance, the vision. There may be pathology of the eyeball itself, or of the muscles which regulate its movements. Blindness is not uncommon. The eyes may be crossed (strabismus). The normal visual reflexes may be diminished (known as decrease or absence of postrotatory nystagmus), or the cornea may be deformed (keratoconus). Kanner reported a case of "conjugate deviation of the eyes to the right."[74] There may be problems with spatial perception. These children tend to look to the side of the object regarded, or beyond it, and refuse to make eye contact; on the other hand, they sometimes stare so intently as to raise a question of absence seizures.

They may be unable to control the movement of their eyes—the "lazy eye syndrome."

Others have better than perfect sight. Harvey Jackson, Jr., had the "vision of a hawk."

Often the eyeball is intact, but information is not processed from the eyes to the brain, as in autistics who are dyslexic.

A related disorder is hyperlexia: the child reads fluently but without any comprehension.[75]

He reads anything you put in front of him. He doesn't understand it but he reads it.

The same variety of disorders is found with the hearing, ranging from total deafness to various degrees of impairment.

Autistics suffer frequently from otitis media and other ear infections; these are likely to be more serious in the more seriously autistic child, less pronounced in the mildly autistic.[76]

Otitis, of course, may be partially responsible for the hearing loss.

It may be difficult, however, to determine if the hearing defect is in the eardrum or somewhere in the brain. As already noted with the eyes, the eardrum itself may be normal and function normally part of the time, but then "switch off"; for instance, the child has normal hearing when tested through the audiometer but cannot comprehend words.

In 1951 Isaac Karlin called attention to a phenomenon which he called "congenital word deafness," describing, for example, a boy with an apparent ninety-eight percent hearing loss who could still distinguish the sounds identifying certain preferred toys; he had learned to speak in simple sentences, even though this should have been impossible with a ninety-eight percent hearing loss.[77]

Other children are seemingly deaf to some sounds, such as the mother's voice or a door slamming right behind them, but can hear others, such as a cellophane candy-bar wrapper being removed, a vending machine delivering chewing gum, or a favorite TV commercial.

He can hear the higher pitch, the higher ranges, but he can't process the low voice ranges, such as my voice.

"Word deafness" can be called by such names as peripheral processing defect, central processing defect, etc. It signifies inability to extract meaning, to make sense, of what is heard—i.e., a "central defect in the processing of any sort of coded, meaningful, or temporally patterned stimuli."[78]

Other autistics have hyperacute hearing (hyperacusis) and may be pathologically reactive to sounds which normal persons do not notice at all: the slamming of a door, the buzz of a hairdryer, or the noise of a crowd.

He is terribly sensitive to loud noises and will put his hands over his ears. Once at a basketball game he sat with his hands over his ears because of the crowd noises.

This is due to the child's inability to filter useful information out of background noise. All their channels are open, and they are confused by extraneous inputs.

Music, however, is different, presumably because of its inherent structure. The great majority of autistics are entranced by music, and often display amazing abilities.

Some memorize TV jingles and popular songs, reciting them back faultlessly after hearing them once or twice. Some have perfect pitch. One legendary case could sing scales "with extraordinary accuracy of pitch" at fourteen months, at seventeen months spontaneously repeated in full an aria from *Don Giovanni* after hearing his parents sing it once, and by age three could sing entire symphonies by Mozart and Haydn, songs by Schubert and Brahms, selections from *Carmen*, a Tchaikovsky piano concerto, as well as "diversified well-known songs."[79]

More often, however, the voice and speech are impaired, due to delayed or nonexistent development of the nerves governing the mouth, throat, and vocal cords. The baby starts to burble, gurgle, and chatter, and then, usually before age two, loses this ability and lapses into muteness. About half of autistics remain completely mute throughout life (if the IQ is high enough, they may learn sign language). Or they develop speech late and progress only to a certain level, well below their chronological age.

Sometimes the child can speak but prefers not to (elective mutism). Or he uses an almost inaudible whisper:

Leonard . . . could not speak in a tone of voice louder than a conversational one. "This is going to sound really foolish to you," he said. "but I just can't talk any louder. I have to talk the way I am now."[80]

Or she will shout for help in an emergency but otherwise remain mute: "When one patient was receiving an injection, she clearly said that she wanted to go home, virtually her first sentence."[81]

Or he will have severe speech difficulties: "Paul, ten, seems to be trying hard to speak, without success so far except for a few unintelligible sounds and a clear 'Mommie' recorded recently on tape."[82] The moderately autistic child may have a terrible stutter.

On the other hand, he may be capable of speech and chatter nonstop, but without making any sense (hyperlalia), or may limit himself to parrotlike repetition of phrases heard in other conversations (delayed echolalia)—even with the precise intonation; or there will be rote enumerations (stereotyped utterances) of rhymes, lists of names, and other "semantically useless exercises" (as Kanner called them).[83]

Thus, even when the child can speak, he will not use language for communication. He may have a fairly large vocabulary but be unable to convey meaning. Some autistics can mimic another's voice or some other sound to perfection. One remarkable child spoke French, Spanish, Japanese, Arabic, Hebrew, and several other languages but could not say an original sentence in any of them.[84]

Truly spontaneous and unconstrained conversation is essentially impossible for an autistic; there is flat intonation with no variation of tone or pitch, little or no use of gesture, no communication through facial expression, no interaction with others.

The tone of the voice may be unnaturally high, described as a "screech" or "high-pitched" (palsy of the twelfth cranial nerve).[85]

In these speech disorders autism overlaps with what is called "developmental aphasia" or "dysphasia," defined as "disorder of speech due to a brain lesion" in a child. Researchers have asked whether these two groups really are different or, alternatively, part of the same continuum.

Such comparisons stand or fall on the definition of "autism" selected. Existing definitions are artificially restrictive. Once autism is understood to be a one-sided exacerbation of a larger condition—the post-encephalitic syndrome discussed below in Chapter III—this latter syndrome becomes the principal object of investigation. Aphasia, dysphasia, autism itself, and many other syndromes and conditions will take their places as parts of the post-encephalitic syndrome.

The salivary glands are regulated by derivatives of the cranial nerves and are thus affected by the same palsies. The tendency of autistics to salivate, drool, and spit indicates damage to these nerves.

Another set of cranial nerves governs the facial muscles. When these nerves are impaired, the face takes on an unnaturally rigid look (known as "rigid *facies*" or "Moebius Syndrome").

These failures of sensory communication may be compensated by apparent over-development of the senses of taste and smell. Autistic children often smell, lick, and mouth objects and people— to extract at least some meaning from their environment. They can be extraordinarily sensitive to smells and extremely fussy about their food.[86]

One theory holds that taste and smell are preserved unimpaired in autistics because these cranial nerves, unlike the others, are not myelinated. If, as we suspect, autism is related to demyelination of the cranial nerves, those which are not myelinated in the first place might be relatively immune.

Another important cranial nerve is the vagus or pneumogastric, providing the regular neural impulse to the lungs that stimulates the breathing process. Future autistics have sometimes been noted to suffer from "asthma" in infancy, but this relationship has been insufficiently stressed.

Many kinds of breathing difficulties are common in autism. Called "stereotyped respiratory maneuvers" or "compulsive respiratory stereotypies," these include breath-holding attacks, hyperventilation, deep inspiration followed by a grunting exhalation, "Valsalva Maneuver" (trying to exhale while keeping the mouth and nose closed), exhalation without inhaling (causing a fainting fit); and the like. Often these are confused with seizures and may, in fact, have a seizure component.[87]

Harvey Jackson, Jr., is a classic case. According to his father's diary, at age three months his breathing stopped altogether—thirty-six hours after his second DPT shot. The father describes this occurrence:

I'm looking at the shot record now, and it states that on January 13, 1972, Harvey was given a DPT shot. I then looked at my diary, since this is an event you can never forget. Saturday morning, January 15, 1972, I wrote: "A difficult and frightening day. Harvey had been wheezing loudly since the morning, and by one to two P.M. he was so severely tried in his breathing that I became terribly alarmed. He had to be held upright so he could breathe. Once, possibly twice, as I held him, he stopped breathing, only to start again after being thrown over my shoulder and hit on the back. We then saw a doctor —the backup doctor for the regular pediatrician—who said to take him to Children's Hospital. He was admitted at 5:15 P.M., and we anxiously awaited news of him. By the next day he was much better, and his color was back to pink. He was born in October, so he was three months and a few days old."

Harvey, Sr., believes that Harvey, Jr., narrowly escaped "sudden infant death." The boy grew up to be moderately autistic.

Thus autism and SIDS appear to be generated in the same way—by an encephalitis most commonly caused by vaccination. Breathing difficulties of various kinds ensue, and during one such "breath-holding attack" the infant simply expires. The child who would have grown up autistic dies instead of "sudden infant death syndrome" (SIDS).

A Neurologic Basis for Alienation and Ego Weakness

The emerging neurologic theory of autism was reinforced by Stella Chess's 1971 observation that children with "congenital rubella" frequently displayed classic autistic features. These children suffered, in particular, from "multiple sensory disabilities," and it gradually became clear that the autistic's characteristic alienation, withdrawal, and ego weakness—initially seen as causal—were actually the effects of disorders of sense percerception. The autistic child lacks the instruments—the five senses in proper running order—that would enable him to extract meaning from the external world. Unable to extract meaning, he is lost in the swirl of events. M. Rutter and L. Bartak suggested very accurately in 1971, ". . . a central deficit in processing of symbolic or sequence information is likely to prove the basic defect . . . in infantile autism."[xx]

Once we have received information through the senses, we extract meaning and organize it in the form of concepts or ideas.

These are stored in the memory and recalled when necessary. In this way sense-perception and memory help us acquire *experience*.

This the autistic cannot do. He cannot receive sensory information in an orderly fashion. He cannot distinguish impulses, sensations, and other mental contents which originate inside from those which originate outside the self.[89] He cannot generate order out of himself and impose it on his surroundings. One investigator wrote: "Severely autistic children exhibit a preoccupation with the sensory impressions stemming from the world about them, but seem unable to organize perceptions into functional patterns."[90]

Weakness of memory adds to their problems. Rimland has written:

> *The child with early infantile autism is grossly impaired in a function basic to all cognition: the ability to relate new stimuli to remembered experience.* The vital connections between sensation and memory can be made only with difficulty. New sensation can be related only to sharply limited fragments of memory. The child is thus virtually divested of the means for deriving meaning from his experience.[91]

Observers have been fooled by the startling capacities manifested by these "sharply limited fragments of memory" (already noted in connection with the musical abilities of autistics). One mother interviewed claimed that her autistic son could remember events occurring when he was six months old!!

But these mnemonic talents, however striking, are nonetheless fragmentary. In the broader sense the autistic has a weak memory. He cannot recall, compare, and process a broad range of information. Sensory experience reaches the child's mind as if phrased in a foreign language whose words and syntax he will never master.

Furthermore, the process of maturing involves moving beyond the concreteness of sense perception into the world of abstraction—of symbols. During evolution the human brain acquired a capacity to abstract—located in the frontal and temporal lobes—which is not found in animals. Researchers have found autism to be associated with immature development and organization of the brain, specifically, of the frontal and temporal lobes.[92]

Hence the autistic cannot create and manipulate the *symbols* which normal people use to represent and act upon external reality.

Neurologic testing of autistics has disclosed evidence of damage to the brainstem and cranial nerves. Student and Sohmer in 1978 investigated the brainstem and auditory nerve in a group of fifteen autistic children, finding organic lesions seemingly related to "immaturity in the development of certain brainstem mechanisms."[93] Rosenblum and coworkers repeated these tests with the same results, concluding that the immaturity was due to defective myelination of these nerves.*[94] Tanguay and Edwards in 1982 agreed that autistic children have a "generalized lower brainstem dysfunction":

> Brain development involves differentiation of systems or parts of systems that mature at very different rates. . . In the human it would appear that the period between approximately ten and twenty months of age is a particularly critical period in development, where the neural organization responsible for internal cognitive operations is reaching a functional state.[95]

This neurological research demonstrates that the "developmental delay" or "maturational delay" associated with autism reflects an actual biological delay in maturation of the brain and nervous system. Other phenomena such as "failure to develop abstract reasoning and concepts," "absent or limited symbolic capacities," or "relative inability to process symbolic information," are the consequences.[96]

Hence autistics do poorly on IQ tests "demanding symbolic or abstract thought and sequential logic."[97]

> In spite of his interest in reading, [Ronald] could neither formulate his thoughts in language nor provide an extended oral report of his daily activities; nor could he write in anything more than a laborious slow manner . . . In a characteristic incident of that period [age fifteen], Ronald became panicked in a theater when he realized that he could not follow the lines being spoken by the actors. On another occasion, he recognized how he became blank and incomprehending when asked the directions in a city that he could easily navigate using guide books.[98]

---

*The myelination of the brain and nervous system during the first year or two of life, and the impact of vaccination on this process, are discussed below in Chapter IV.

By the same token the autistic has trouble with comparisons. As Kanner noted, "Though he could speak of things as big or pretty, he was utterly incapable of making comparisons ('Which is the bigger line? Prettier face?' etc.)."[99]

He is unable to "play," since play, like speech, is a largely symbolic activity.

He has little or no sense of humor.[100] He can read atlases and encyclopedias but cannot understand fiction. He is "restricted, literal, and concrete in his thinking."[101] Kanner wrote:

> His father said something about the pictures they have at home on the wall. This disturbed John somewhat. He corrected his father. "We have them *near* the wall" ("on" apparently meaning to him "above" or "on top").[102]

Unwillingness to use the word "yes"—analyzed above as signifying ego weakness—also reflects inability to abstract. "Yes," indicating abstract assent, is a concept the autistic may take years to acquire. Normally he indicates "yes" by repeating the question. One child learned to say "yes" when his father rewarded him by putting him on his shoulders. Thereafter the word meant only the desire to be put on his father's shoulders, and it took months before he could detach it from this specific situation.[103]

This combination of inability to cope with new stimuli, disturbances of perception, and lack of ability to abstract and conceptualize severely restricts their relations with others and even with themselves, making them aware that they are both different from others and less worthy.

They live in the world without acquiring experience of the world; their awareness of being cut off in this way, of being alienated from the world, deprives them of self-confidence and ego strength.

This generates their pervasive fear and anxiety—which at length deteriorate into paranoia and depression.[104]

> In the hospital and to others he reported, "I'm no good" and "I don't know what's the matter with me." He thought about committing suicide.[105]

At the age of thirteen years he believed that other children in his
class were talking about him and trying to influence his thoughts.
He was agitated and belligerent with those he believed were per-
secuting him.[106]

Jerry Goldsmith exhibited some incipient paranoid distortions; for
example, if he found any of his possessions missing he would
automatically assume that one of the other children had stolen
them.[107]

Thus research since the late 1960s has shown that the typical
"emotional" symptoms of autism—the alienation, ego-weakness,
lack of a sense of humor, and paranoia—as well as the "mental"
ones—inability to symbolize and memory weakness—are all rooted
in actual neurologic deficiencies.

Appetite, Digestive, and Bowel Disturbances

With the progress of research in autism, other constellations of
symptoms became associated with this condition. While usually
labelled "emotional" at their first appearance, these symptoms are
recognized today as neurologic.

Autistics have many abdominal pains and appetite disturbances
and are often described as "feeding problems."[108] Six of Kanner's
first eleven cases had serious difficulties with nursing, taking the
bottle, changing formulas, and the like. Take John F., for instance:

The father said: 'The main thing that worries me is the difficulty
in feeding. That is the essential thing, and secondly his slowness
in development. During the first days of life he did not take the
breast satisfactorily. After fifteen days he was changed from breast
to bottle but did not take the bottle satisfactorily. There is a long
story of trying to get food down. We have tried everything under
the sun . . . There were frequent hospitalizations because of his
feeding problem.'[109]

One three-year old would eat nothing but baby foods; another,
at the age of one year, "began to starve himself"; the mother of a
third "first suspected a problem at age five months because of chok-
ing and gagging with feeding."[110]

At one year I couldn't get her to eat. She was real skinny and existed almost entirely on nursing. She didn't lose weight, but she didn't keep pace either.

Another autistic child was described as follows:

At seven years of age the patient began to vomit each night at bedtime . . . the pediatrician diagnosed "psychosomatic hyperemesis." At the age of nine years . . . his pediatrician reported "deteriorating behavior" and reappearance of regurgitation. By ten years of age the parents sought psychiatric help. Episodic vomiting reappeared, behavior deteriorated, and he was mumbling to himself incoherently.[111]

This behavior is sometimes labelled *anorexia nervosa* (literally: "nervous loss of appetite"):

In school S. refused to take certain previously eaten foods, saying she could no longer eat them because she did not like the way they tasted—a similar pattern occurred at home. . . . She would attempt to eat with prompting but would often gag and spit up. Large quantities of milk or water were used to help her wash down small amounts of food. S. stated that she could not eat because food would make her sick. During the third week of May, S. became physically ill and vomited at the sight of some foods and refused to eat them. Subsequently, on three consecutive mornings she vomited breakfast on the bus en route to school. By this time S.'s symptoms were strongly indicative of *anorexia nervosa*. She had a noticeable weight loss . . . a distorted perception of eating . . . and vomiting.[112]

Alternatively, these children can have tendencies to bulimia, being "indiscriminate" about what they eat—meaning not only food but such substances as sawdust, dog turds, dirt, and the like.[113]

He would eat his own feces if you didn't watch him. It didn't bother him a bit.

Christopher Gillberg, a leading Swedish researcher, in 1985 found a link between autism and *anorexia nervosa*, noting that such an association had never previously been recorded.[114]

"Rumination," meaning the regurgitation, sucking, and reswallowing of partially digested food, is associated with autism and severe developmental disorders and falls into the same category of gastrointestinal disorders.[115]

Soviet researchers have found a tendency to obesity in autistic children, and Gillberg found that one-third of a group of autistics grew "coarser and plumper" with age.[116] Although no systematic data exist on the weights of autistics in the United States, their numerous disturbances of appetite function suggest the possibility of long-term anorexia or excessive weight gain.

The food, once eaten, is digested with difficulty. Autistics suffer frequently from colic and other gastrointestinal pains. The baby may cry with pain or arch his back. Studies of autistic children often find a past history of gastrointestinal symptoms, "abdominal pain," "recurrent gastrointestinal upsets," etc.

This may be associated with chronic constipation or acute diarrhea; the bowel movements of the autistic baby may have a sour, acid, or musty smell. Autistics suffer with abnormal frequency from celiac disease. And their non-autistic siblings seem also to have an unusual incidence of abdominal pains and gastrointestinal disorders.[117]

They have difficulty with bowel and bladder control (enuresis and encopresis) at night and even during the day. Or they may have had bowel control early in infancy, only to lose it at about eighteen months.

Difficulties with elimination foster an inordinate interest in urine and feces and a tendency to smear them around:

He developed an obsession about feces, would hide it anywhere (for instance, in drawers), would tease me if I walked into the room: "*You* soiled your pants, now *you* can't have your crayons!"

As a result, he is still not toilet trained [age 4½]. He never soils himself in nursery school, always does it when he comes home. The same is true of wetting. He is proud of wetting, jumps up and down in ecstasy, says, "Look at the big puddle *he* made!"[118]

Headaches, Head-Banging

Severe headaches are a feature of autistic pathology which has been commented on anecdotally but never given sustained attention.[119]

Bernard Rimland, whose San Diego-based Institute for Child Behavior Research has files on 10,000 autistic children, feels that they do indeed suffer disproportionately from headaches.[120]

Harvey Jackson, Jr., had frontal headaches painful enough to cause nausea. And Tony W.'s autobiographical account speaks of "pounding hard migraine headaches."[121]

Of course, if the headache is being experienced by a very small baby, he cannot describe it in words. What he will do is rock back and forth, roll his head from side to side, or bang it against the cradle, walls, or floor, pick at his hair or ears, arch his back, or extend his neck ("hyperextension")—all of which are common in autistics and suggest ways of coping with head pain.

In 1982 Norman Geschwind and Peter Behan published their finding of an association among autism, celiac disease, dyslexia, stuttering, migraine headaches, developmental disabilities, and left-handedness—i.e., all features which we here discuss as part of the post-encephalitic syndrome. Their article caused a sensation in scientific circles because of inability to imagine what the connecting thread among these disparate conditions could be.[122]

We feel that Geschwind and Behan's findings were a preliminary outline of the correlations presented in this book. And the connecting thread is found in the childhood vaccination program.

Defining Autism: Rett Syndrome, Asperger's Syndrome

The discovery that autism is accompanied by neurologic symptoms never included in Kanner's first definition showed the condition to be unexpectedly complex. In 1971, checking up on the eleven children from his first group, Kanner found outcomes ranging "all the way from complete deterioration to a combination of occupational adequacy with limited though superficially smooth social adjustment" and commented, "In medicine . . . any illness may appear in different degrees of severity, all the way from the so-called *forme fruste* to the most fulminant manifestation. Does this possibly apply also to early infantile autism?"[123]*

Forme fruste: the patient manifests few or no symptoms.

A decade later Rimland gave a striking demonstration of the complexity of autism: he compared the original diagnoses of 445 autistic children with a "second opinion" and found no trace of a positive correlation between them!! The relationship between the two diagnoses was practically random.[124]

Rimland's finding has been confirmed repeatedly. Almost as many criteria are in use today for diagnosing autism as there are writers on the subject.[125]

Autism cannot easily be distinguished from such "overlapping" neurologic conditions as mental retardation, cerebral palsy, and epilepsy.[126] Hetzler and Griffin wrote in 1981: "The extremely heterogeneous autistic population may represent a variety of central nervous system dysfunctions resulting in overlapping overt behavioral manifestations."[127] Deborah Fejn in the same year: "There is considerable disagreement about which symptoms should be considered as necessary and sufficient for the diagnosis of autism . . . There is also considerable uncertainty about the degree of symptom overlap between autism and other severe developmental disabilities, and probably for this reason, the reliability of diagnoses within the general category of 'childhood psychosis' or 'severe developmental disability' is poor."[128]

The arbitrariness of the diagnostic process was encapsulated by W. and M. DeMyer, who wrote in 1984, "It seems that each investigator looks through his own peephole, finds an abnormality, and thus confirms his preconceptions."[129]

While this confusion and disagreement about the diagnosis of autism has sometimes been blamed on "the inexperience or lack of scholarly rigor of diagnosticians," it would be more reasonable to admit that autism does not exist as an independent entity.

It is only a piece of the post-encephalitic syndrome. That the diagnosis should be continually contaminated by other bits and pieces of this syndrome is hardly unexpected.

Why, then, do specialists insist that autism is unique and unrelated to other neurologic diseases and disorders? The answer was given by a speaker at the 1980 Conference of the National Society for Autistic Children:

Autism is not a specific disorder. I think that makes a lot of us uncomfortable because it's the banner under which we rally, it's what brings us all together, it's what we all share in common, and it's rather threatening for someone to say that what we are rallying around is less than real. We need to think about what that means. It's not that anyone is saying that the disorder does not exist. That we have disturbed children is rather apparent. But the trap we can fall into is thinking about autism as if it were a disease which is going to lend itself to a singular remedy . . . These are the myths that we get caught up in . . . We are really talking about a spectrum.[130]

Insistence on the autonomous status of autism reflects to some degree the organizational or class interest of the physicians, psychologists, psychoanalysts, psychiatrists, and other medical professionals who make a living diagnosing, treating, and writing about autism, and for whom its existence is a vital necessity.

The ensuing definitional fuzziness is overcome by adopting the "Chinese Restaurant menu" approach—"two dishes from Group A and three from Group B, etc." A checklist compiled in 1971 listed fourteen items and concluded, "For a diagnosis of autism at least seven of these criteria should be present. . ."

The 1987 edition of the *Diagnostic and Statistical Manual* used the same technique:

[For a diagnosis of autism] at least eight of the following sixteen items are present, these to include at least two items from A, one from B, and one from C.[131]

If this approach is accepted, two individuals can have totally different patterns of symptoms, eight each out of the total of sixteen, and both be diagnosed as autistic!!

No single symptom is indispensable. Michael Rutter and Eric Schopler wrote in 1987 that differentiation of autistic cases "could only truly be based on some unequivocal indication of some specifically and uniquely autistic feature. Such a feature has yet to be identified."[132]

Only when autism is recognized as merely one particular configuration of the hundreds of symptoms included in the post-encephalitic syndrome will physicians be able to discard these fruitless efforts to pin it down more precisely.

For, just as autism cannot readily be demarcated from other neurologic states, so it often cannot be distinguished from psychological (emotional!) normality.

As early as 1964 Rimland claimed that some children meeting Kanner's original "essential diagnostic criteria . . . extreme aloneness and a desire for the preservation of sameness," were quite normal in other respects and in no way autistic.[133]

In 1981 the DeMyers noted: "A continuum exists among the behaviors of typical autistic children, other retarded children without overtly or numerous autistic traits, and even normal children."[134]

Such diagnoses as "autistic-like," "with strong autistic features," "near-normal," etc., have become increasingly common. In particular, moderate autistics often resemble the typical child with a severe case of "minimal brain damage."

Researchers sometimes wonder if these "high-functioning" autistic children are really "autistic" or rather constitute a different defineable disease:

> I've seen a number of children who share specific problems and symptoms with [autistic] chidren, but they cannot, even with a broadened definition, by any stretch of the imagination be called autistic. I've seen two children who are the most rigid children I've ever seen, as rigid as any autistic child in their insistence on sameness and their violent responses to minor shifts. But they are social . . . have good language relationships, and they are not autistic unless you want to call everyone who has any symptom an autistic child. . . . Now where do these children belong? . . . I have other children who have stereotypies. They are not autistic, but they have regular stereotypic patterns, some rocking and some hand clapping—even very high level children. Not by history and not by definition are they clinically autistic. I don't know what to call them, frankly, but they are not autistic.[135]

There is no need for soul-searching. To quote Kanner again, "in medicine . . . any illness may appear in different degrees of severity, all the way from the so-called *forme fruste* to the most fulminant manifestation." This holds true for autism and, as we will see, for the gradation to minimal brain damage, conduct disorder, and sociopathic behavior. The near-normal are merely milder versions of the classic autistic syndrome. They are not entirely cut off from others but have intellectual and emotional difficulties which impair their capacity for human contact.[136]

The condition called "Rett Syndrome," a severe variety of autism which only affects females and which first came to attention in 1965, is very probably another aspect of the post-encephalitic syndrome and generated by the same factors, i.e., the childhood vaccination program.[137]

A milder variant of autism is "childhood-onset pervasive developmental disorder," which commences after the age of three.[138]

The condition known as "autistic psychopathy," or Asperger's syndrome, after the Viennese psychiatrist who described the first cases in 1944, is another mild version of Kanner's autism. This group is thought to exhibit higher than normal intelligence and unusual originality.

The symptoms were described in 1971 by Van Krevelen:

The patient has an abnormal personality with less sensitivity, more rationality. His approach is a merely cerebral one. What he lacks is understanding of, and interaction with, other people's feelings. He is, so to say, obliged to interpret everything in its literal sense, to analyze the meaning of the words heard, to study the significance of the facts experienced by him, to scrutinize facial expressions of his fellow men. Just as he does not immediately understand whether his companion speaks seriously or jokingly, he is unable to imagine that his own words might hurt others. Hence his sense of humor, if any, is peculiar. He does not realize that he may be a bore to others. . . . The manifestation age of autistic psychopathy is in the first years of elementary school, or earlier if the parents have not been able to adjust themselves to the individualistic behavior of their child. . . . The school community requires adjustment to rules and norms. Moreover, schoolmates soon observe everything out of the ordinary . . . the behavior of the autistic psychopath is very unusual; his vocabulary bears the mark of parliamentary or townhall language reserved more for written than spoken address. . . . The intellectual functioning of the autistic psychopath has three peculiarities.

To begin with . . . he is unable to learn from others. . . . The child follows his own methods because he cannot accept instruction from the teacher. His intelligence may enable him to find original solutions. Because of this he is an unsatisfactory student, although he has the capacity to think autochthonously. Second, he does not possess that ingredient of intelligence that might be called *sense*. . . . The third peculiarity concerns a tendency to foster rather unusual circumscribed interest patterns, such as genealogy or astronomy or "life" in the abstract. Such topics do not generally appeal to other children—another obstacle to adequate peer relationships.[139]

Van Krevelen called this "lack of intuition": "By intuition I mean a higher quality of intelligence, a short-circuited intelligence, by which one is able to skip associations." A typical case was the boy who, when asked to speak at a football rally, predicted that the team was going to lose; the ensuing round of boos led him finally to modify his initially correct prediction, but the experience bewildered him.

Marginal autistics may be incredibly boring:

Although some autistic children do not talk at all, mildly autistic children are often handicapped by a tendency to talk too much when they are exceedingly interested in a topic. It does not occur to them that listeners may not share their enthusiasm. So they talk on, concentrating on what they are trying to say, without any reaction to signs of boredom. Such a monologue is not easily interrupted or changed in its course by the comments of others; therefore, the to-and-fro of normal conversation is missing. At best the autistic person is a poor listener, and sometimes he seems to be completely unaware of the fact that somebody is trying to talk to him.[140]

Parents often report that the mildly autistic child needs several moments to process any remark he hears . . . he cannot understand somebody at a normal rate of speaking . . . socially [this] makes him a bore because he tries to steer the conversation to topics he has anticipated . . . the autistic person . . . can heed only one thing at a time and tends to be lost in his own thoughts.[141]

Van Krevelen noted the occurrence of true autism and Asperger's syndrome in two brothers.

What all of these milder cases share with the more serious ones is alienation:

> These three autistic adults all conveyed the deep, unquenchable loneliness, the conviction that they were somehow incapable of forming a relationship which could satisfy them.[142]

And in their case it may be more emotionally trying, because they have the intelligence to appreciate their plight. "Ronald" states: "I never could have a friend. I really don't know what to do with other people, really."[143]

Autism, however, also incorporates a streak of naked hostility, a rejection of contact with others. "Jerry Goldsmith" responded to psychological testing with stories centering on "aggression toward the father and on characters dying," while "Tony W." stated about himself:

> I liked hellish environments, such as the spook-house at the carnival, Halloween, and horror movies. I daydreamed a lot and tried to actively communicate and get into that world. . . . I was very cold-hearted too. It was impossible for me to give or receive love from anybody. I often repulse it by turning people off. That's a problem today, relating to other people. I liked things over people and didn't care about people at all.[144]

The higher-IQ autistic will use verbal aggression, finding out the opponent's weak points and taunting him.

If autism is a manifestation of vaccine-induced encephalitis, the implications are very disturbing. The symptoms manifested with pathological intensity in a small group will of necessity appear in milder form in a much larger proportion of the population. For every "autistic" who is shut away in an institution there will be a thousand alienated individuals functioning as normal taxpaying citizens.

The parallel with the alienation and anomie of twentieth-century industrial society is striking. How much of this loneliness are we inflicting upon ourselves?

Compensating for Ego Weakness: Resisting Change

Because the autistic suffers from "inability to learn from and cope with new stimuli," loss of control is an ever-present threat.[145]

But control is threatened by change, so change is what the autistic fears and hates the most. "Small changes in ["Ronald's"] feeding, either in the schedule or the way in which he was nursed, led to anxious disorganization. . . . As a toddler, any change in his routine could lead to catastrophe. One time, when drinking from a glass, milk went up his nose. Following this, he refused to drink from a glass for over two years, using a spoon to eat liquids."[146]

Kanner noted their "anxiously obsessive desire for the maintenance of sameness":

> When John's parents were ready to move to a new home, the child was frantic when he saw the moving man roll up the rug in his room. He was acutely upset until the moment when in the new home he saw his furniture arranged in the same manner as before. He looked pleased, all anxiety was suddenly gone, and he went around affectionately patting each piece.[147]

When change does occur, it provokes a storm. "There may be resistance and even catastrophic reactions to minor changes in the environment, e.g., the child may scream when his or her place at the dinner table is changed."[148] Nothing can be changed in the daily routine; unpatterned situations are what the autistic fears the most.

A particular instance of incipient loss of control is the autistic's terror at separation from family and familiar surroundings. Harvey Jackson, Jr., is typical:

> *He always hated any disruption in his familiar routine, When he came home from vacation, for instance, when he was nine months old, and he saw that his father and sisters were not there, he put up a tremendous fuss. The familiar family was not there. Once the rest of the family got home that time, he calmed down. But until then he screamed loud enough to wake up the whole neighborhood. Even today [age fifteen] he is much better, but he will ask, "Is anybody home?" He likes that reassurance.*
>
> *Once his sister missed her bus, and I had to rush out and leave him. He went to the neighbors crying and screaming and com-*

*plained that I had left him. I never could leave him at all. Now he
is a little that way with his younger brother. He is afraid of something happening with him.*

Another manifestation of the autistic preoccupation with sameness is a fascination with objects: they may play for hours, days, and weeks, with the same toy—spinning a top, bouncing a ball, twirling a piece of string, arranging blocks into identical patterns, and the like.

Only objects can be really trusted not to change or behave unpredictably. They stay the way you leave them. This contrasts with animals, such as dogs, which are always doing the unexpected.

Kanner called attention to this loving and absorbing relationship with objects: "So intense was this relationship that minor alterations in objects, or their arrangement, not ordinarily perceived by the average observer, were at once apparent to these children, who might then fly into a rage until the change had been undone."[149]

In the severely autistic child the environment is controlled, and sameness maintained, by unendingly repeated motions and actions, described as "ritualistic and compulsive behavior," "stereotyped movements," etc. These take the form of whirling around and around, shaking their heads from side to side, banging their heads against some object, hand-flapping, hand-waving, hand-twisting (choreoathetoid movements), opening and shutting the hands continuously, knocking on objects in a stereotyped way, and the like.

Of all these movements, "body rocking," meaning rocking back and forth in a rhythmic way, is the most common:

Hour after hour he rocks there, this beautiful little three-year-old stranger who is our son. . . . Brothers and sisters run by, calling his name. He stares, riveted in his rhythmic rocking. . . . We mentioned Brian's constant rocking to friends who assured us that most of the children in their family rocked as babies. However, curtailing Brian's incessant rocking proved to be an impossible task for us. . . . On occasion he did enjoy being tickled, but the minute we stopped he was back in the chair, rocking again. His forcefulness and determination were most frightening as he constantly threw his whole upper torso against the back of the rocking chair, crashing it into the wall behind him.[150]

Rocking may involve banging the head against the headboard of the crib, possibly to relieve the pain of a headache. The principal function of this and other repetitive movements, however, is to provide the child's life with structure. They are a way of organizing the outside world.

As they grow older autistics develop new types of obsessions, rituals, and procedures:

> A persistent problem is use of rituals that have replaced his need for sameness. For example, it takes him up to two hours to take a shower because he has to place the nozzle, bath mat, curtain, etc., in an exact relationships and then wash in a prescribed manner. Other rituals involve dressing, going out of the house, and going to bed.[151]

> Ruth, a charming preadolescent, went through a period marked by ritualistic involvement with every door which she had to touch and "test" prior to opening or closing. She kept excusing herself, each time, seeking forgiveness for this rather innocent indulgence.[152]

Compensating for Ego Weakness: Aggression

Loss of control, or incipient loss, can provoke more or less hostile and violent reactions. The autistic becomes uncooperative, stubborn, obstinate, negative, etc.

This is seen in small things—the child whose first three words were "Mama," "Papa," and "No," or the one whose first sentence was: "I don't want to. . . ."[153] Negativeness is also manifested in "avoidance of a requested response by substituting an alternative." The high-IQ autistic will go to extreme lengths and adopt complicated strategies to avoid answering questions or complying with requests.

But the reaction can be more violent, commencing with temper tantrums, screaming, shouting, and crying, and proceeding to the full-scale rages for which these children are famous.

The autistic is often furious with the outside world, which is unpredictable and incomprehensible and seems always to be acting against his interests. "Rages at alterations in his routine, or at the failure of others to provide him with relief from his constant feeling that something was wrong, left him no peace, only increased anger, blunted, after a while by withdrawal inside."[154]

Even the near-normal autistic has profound difficulty seeing any point of view but his own.[155] Those with a low IQ will be even more self-centered and self-assertive.

One of Leon Eisenberg's original cases, four years old, "'related' to the examiners only insofar as he made demands or became enraged at interference from without . . . [with] outbursts of aggressive behavior"; at age fifteen he was "destructive."[156] Jerry Goldsmith is described at age four: "screams when frustrated"; at age eighteen: "surly or withdrawn attitude toward examiner . . . angry, withdrawn attitudes toward relationships."[157]

The frustration threshold is very low in autistics, reflecting the immature or nonexistent ego:

> *The other night he wanted fried chicken before it was even cooked, and he took a cup of orange juice and threw it at me, because the fried chicken wasn't ready.*

The desire for control and the low level of frustration tolerance easily lead to "bossiness" or "bullying," "demanding his own way with peers," and even to naked aggression against persons or objects perceived as standing in the way:

> *Once she would even attack a stranger in the street. She would go up to him and say, 'Take your hat off!' She would tell you that you are old, because you have gray hair. And even when she is being affectionate with us, she has trouble sustaining it, aggressively exploring my face, my hair, etc.*

Harry, who is twenty-four years old:

> . . . had learned to intimidate people by staring them down when he wished to escape an educational activity. He had no trouble doing so because of his size—six feet, six inches. Thus . . . Harry used physical intimidation as an effective way of maintaining his noncompliance when demands were placed on him.[158]

Few restraints are imposed by morality or decency, for the autistic lacks any empathetic relation with others which might moderate incipient aggressive tendencies:

Most frustrating to the family was Brian's seemingly non-caring attitude toward others. He did not want to join in family activities, he did not respond to outreaches of his siblings, and he did not develop a respect for others' property.[159]

The underlying theme beneath his rationalizations was his inability to deal adequately with what he perceived as the unpredictability of other people. He simply could not empathize with others and so could not predict what they would do, which left him confused and frightened.[160]

Alienation and cold-heartedness can lead to fantasies of violence as well as actual violence against people and animals. For a six-year old in school:

Interactions with peers were associated with bizarre stories and play about themes of murder and blood. He became increasingly preoccupied with such verbalizations, aggressive acts, and destructive themes. At school he repeatedly took a plastic toy knife and was "found sawing on a peer's neck or arm." His comment, with delight, was "You could kill someone with this knife." On one occasion he tried to choke a child with a rope. He showed decreasing tolerance to stress and increasing disruptive behavior, e.g., tantrums. . . . He threatened physical harm to his younger brother.[161]

Tony W. wrote about himself as a child:

I remember the Yale Child Study Center. I ignored the doctors and did my own thing. . . . I was also very hateful and sneaky. I struggled and breathed hard because I wanted to kill the guinea pig; as soon as the examiner turned her back, I killed it. I hated my mother because she tried to stop me from being in my world and doing what I liked; so I stopped and as soon as she turned her back, I went at it again. I was very rebellious and sneaky and destructive. I would plot to kill my mother and destroy the world. Evil things astonished me such as an H. bomb. . . . I also had a very warped sense of humor and learned perverted things very quickly. I used to lash out of control and repeat sick, perverted phrases as well as telling people violent, wild, untrue things to impress them.[162]

Billy McCoy:

. . . has spent the past fifteen years in and out of institutions. He was considered uncontrollable by all of them because of his fits of rage. Julia McCoy says that the only thing her son learned in the institutions is that he is stronger than six or seven full-grown men. The family has learned to live with his fits, during which a boy who can hardly articulate the sounds necessary to pronounce his own name screams loud and clear, "You son of a bitch, I'm going to kill you."[163]

The mother of an autistic youngster describes driving him in the car:

Suddenly I felt like somebody dipped ten razor blades in tabasco sauce before throwing them into my neck and shoulders. Jeff without warning had plowed his claws into me. . . . He grabbed a handful of my hair and started slicing away at me with the ten switchblades Larry thought he had just clipped and filed down. It was hard to duck, dodge, and capture him at the same time, especially hemmed up in the car. . . . Jeff is five years old and still in diapers. [164]

The immediate family, of course, bears the greatest burden—especially the mother who must often stay home with the child. Many live in a state of near exhaustion. One, who had just undergone an operation, described having to carry a pillow at all times to protect herself. Another sought refuge from her adolescent son's rages by locking herself in the family car. "We kept the outside doors locked with a two-way lock day and night because he would run away. I would leave the patio door unlocked for him to play in the daytime in our backyard, where we had a five-foot fence with a padlock on the gate. . . . I was virtually a prisoner in my home, with a tiger loose and no respite, not even for a night or a weekend or a week."[165]

One family interviewed for this book had to keep their twenty-year-old son in a locked room with barred windows—a real prisoner in his own home.

An autistic adolescent's weekend at home is described by his younger brother:

The first event occurred about two years ago when I was sixteen. Eddie had just come home from Western State for an overnight on Friday. We were going to take him back Saturday after lunch. . . . Friday evening was fairly uneventful, none of the usual tension in the air that is so characteristic of the times when Eddie comes home. Part of this tension is due to our own anxiety caused by the memory of previous overnights with him that have ended in disaster, when we had literally to drag him back to Western State, screaming and crying.

Saturday morning started off badly. I came down from my bedroom early and was sitting in our living room trying to wake up when the house's tranquillity was shattered by some choice words that I do not care to mention. . . . Oh, great, I thought, he's starting early. If he was acting this way now, in no time he would blow up and create an unpleasant situation for the family. . . .

Throughout the rest of the morning, Eddie seemed very keyed up, and I was starting to get worried that he would suddenly lose his control and run out of the house to Lord-knows-where, and we would spend another Saturday trying to find him. My parents sensed this too, so as soon as we could, we got him in the car and on his way. . . .

That's when the fun started. . . . Eddie didn't think that was a good idea, so he ran out. . . . My father and I spent the next thirty-five minutes chasing him all over the scenic routes of Brentwood.

We finally caught him with the help of the local police and had him in the back seat of our station wagon. I sat with him so that he would not hit my dad while he was driving. During the whole ride back he went through a series of emotional states— first violently upset, then sobbing, then screaming and swinging at dad, then crying again. . . .[166]

The tendency to violence can be combined with sleeping difficulties:

When he reached puberty, all hell broke loose. . . . Nights were as bad as days. We slept with our bedroom door locked because of the violent rages he would have during the night.[167]

The violence of autistics is thus a mixture of ungovernable impulses and—depending upon the level of intelligence—justifications and rationalizations of these impulses in terms of need to protect the vulnerable ego and to assert one's own point of view in life.

The uncontrollable impulsive component is seen, above all, in violence directed at the self.

Harry has spent a good part of the first twenty-four years of his life in institutions because of his serious self-abusive behavior. As early as age 3½ he wore arm restraints and a football helmet to prevent him from self-abusing. Between the ages of 5½ and fifteen he was in and out of various schools and centers for the retarded. At age 15½ he was placed in an institution where he began to receive massive dosages of drugs as an attempt to control his extreme outbursts of self-abuse. However, Harry's self-abuse continued in the form of (1) head- and nose-banging with his fists, (2) thigh-hitting with his fists, (3) ankle-kicking, and (4) arm-biting. Harry's repeated blows to his face resulted in a permanent disfigurement of his nose as well as a number of hematomas to his face and body. His ankle kicks had caused his ankles to begin to calcify. Finally, biting had resulted in numerous scars and scabs on his arms.[168]

He used to bite his arm, bang his head on things, slap himself. He is very aggressive with others. Slaps them on the head, the arms, flicks you (even on the eyeball), throws things at you. . . .

He used to pull my hair and his own hair out when he was angry. He also attacked the teacher in his new school, grabbing her hand and digging his nails in. When he was five he used to grab my hand and put it up to his mouth and bite; or he would dig his nails into my hand; or he would grab my hair. He would attack the girls in school. He attacks his bedroom and the furniture there. He bites his lips sometimes. They get so swollen that he can't chew on anything without them getting caught.

In very severe cases autistic children have bitten off their own lips and fingers, or chunks from their shoulders; they have suffered detached retinas from repeatedly hitting themselves in the face and eyes. The level of intelligence plays a role, with retarded autistics having a greater tendency to self-mutilation, while those with a higher IQ might simply hate themselves.

One very hostile and violent sixteen-year-old, interviewed for this book, started biting himself at age fourteen months:

It is more mental abuse now. He says, "I hate the way I am. How long will I have to be this way? Is it forever?" This is very hard on all of us. He is looking for a cure. He likes to go to the doctor because he thinks the doctor will cure him.

Psychologists and psychiatrists have attributed self-destructive-ness to feelings of sexual frustration. But how can sexual frustration cause a two-year old to start pulling his hair out, or hit himself on the head until it is black and blue? While self-hatred undoubtedly plays a role in some cases, a purely neurologic impulse seems also to be at work. Some hit and pinch themselves only when they are excited, others when angry. The mother of one nine-year-old was asked why he did it:

Q. Does he touch people?
A. Yes, he will touch your hair, or hit you. He is quite unpredictable.
Q. What does he say if you tell him not to hit people?
A. He will hit you and then say, "You need to face down," meaning "I need to lie face down on the floor."
Q. Do you think it is deliberate?
A. Sometimes he just can't help himself. Sometimes he does it delib-erately, because he wants to.

The self-destructive neurologic impulse is seen most especially in a condition peculiar to boys known as the Lesch-Nyhans Syn-drome (a combination of mental retardation, with autistic features, inability to speak, and violent aggressiveness directed at the self and at any others within reach). These boys must be kept permanently in strait-jackets to prevent them from destroying themselves physi-cally. They are aware of their state and terrified of it, so that when their strait-jackets shake loose, they gesture to the nurses to come quickly and tie them in again.[169]

Undirected, unfocussed, impulsive violence is, of course, a serious problem of late twentieth-century American society. In Chapter V we discuss the possibility that it is related to a high prev-alence of post-encephalitic neurologic damage. The very common association of impulsive damage with autism and, as we will see, with minimal brain damage, makes it very probable that social vio-lence springs in part from the same causes.

Compensating for Ego Weakness: Hypersexuality

An important way to compensate for one's own perceived inade-quacies is through intensified sexuality, and this is found quite often in autistics.

In some the sexual function is underdeveloped. Sybil Elgar, a specialist in the care and training of autistics who heads a residential working community for forty autistic men and women in England, notes that "interest in sexual experience is not usual" among autistics. Only a minority of "more able and adjusted autistic people" can become involved with others. The majority "lack any capacity for affection, tenderness, and solicitous care of a sexual partner." They "remain self-absorbed and lack the capacity to form relationships because their level of social and emotional development is obstructed by the characteristics of autism."[170]

The wives of some marginal autistics leading normal sexual lives describe them as "never very interested, mechanical, never with feelings." "I have to tell him what to do." "Sex drive normal but performed with no feelings. He uses me like an object."[171]

But many parents describe their autistic children as "hypersexed," and Soviet researchers have found "precocious puberty" in autistics.[172] The sexually aroused autistic, moreover, pursues this gratification for its own sake and not as part of a relationship with someone else.

Sexual drives tend to be satisfied through masturbation. One of Kanner's first cases, at age five, "often masturbated with complete abandon."[173] The same has been reported by others: "noisy, incontinent, and destructive, and masturbated excessively during his first weeks on the pediatric ward, taxing the patience of ward personnel"; "hypersexuality, expressed in excessive masturbation and sadomasochistic actions"; "public masturbation occasionally noticed at about eight years" (in a girl).[174]

> *For about the past year, starting at age four, he has been masturbating. I couldn't believe it. Once I found him under the covers, completely naked, and he had a huge erection. This has been a real problem for us. With him it has been a constant thing. Coming home from school he would take his clothes off and go into the bedroom and spend as long there as I would let him, and then he would come out naked. It has diminished a little since. For a while it was almost constant.*

Seeking Structure: Music

Mention has already been made of the extraordinary musical talents of many autistics and their ability to remember and repeat arias, symphonies, and whole scenes from operas.

According to Rimland, "Astonishing musical ability is found in these children quite frequently."[175] And it is manifested at an early age. Kanner describes a one-year-old [!!] who "could hum and sing many tunes accurately." Another could discriminate among eighteen symphonies at age eighteen months; at age four, in kindergarten, "if there is music, he will go to the front row and sing." Another four-year-old "can tell victrola records by their color, and if one side of the record is identified, he remembers what is on the other side."[176]

He loves music. As soon as he comes home he wants to turn on the stereo. He was raised with a lot of music around him. It calms him down.

He likes music very much. He sings very well, on pitch, and knows all the words. He used to be very into commercials. He would have rather died than miss a commercial.

At age three or four he had a prodigious memory. He could memorize music and repeat it from memory. He could sing and hum all kinds of musical things after hearing them just once. He would even correct people. The most complicated things he knew were themes from television shows—background music and the like, which is not very memorable. Or a theme from a Beethoven symphony. His teacher said he had a three-octave range and perfect pitch.

Leonard, a moderately severe autistic,

. . . by age eleven . . . composed his own songs. His piano playing developed with virtuoso skills, although it was not until his late adolescence that he could play his songs with any feeling, distinguishing a slow, serious classical piece from a lively dance.[177]

Love of music is not surprising. These children suffer from, among other things, inability to organize their perceptions and their thoughts. Music, especially when there is a pronounced beat, will

48

provide structure for them. "They rock. They hum, and they love to dance."[178]

The only time he will rock is when he hears music.

The beat of music for them fulfills the same function as cradle-rocking. Was it pure coincidence that "rock music" burst on the world in the late 1950s, just when the first vaccinated generation was reaching adolescence?

Chronological Parallels

After Kanner's first articles on autism, researchers combed the literature to find if the condition really was unprecedented. Indeed, it seemed to be novel, as only a handful of cases could be found before 1943.

By 1958 Kanner had almost 150 in his files, but the 1960s saw a tremendous upsurge. The Goodwins, prominent child psychiatrists, commented: "Childhood autism had been a rare entity in the pediatric clinic before 1964. We had seen six autistic children during the preceding twelve years. They had prepared us for complexities in management and uncertain prognosis. They had not prepared us for the events that followed, as sixty-five children came, in turn, to the center."[179]

In the 1960s a rising tide of parents with autistic children flooded the offices of child psychiatrists and psychologists, begging for help they could not give.

The increased prevalence of autism in the 1950s and 1960s precisely reflected the expansion of mandated vaccination programs during these same decades.

Today autism is a growth industry. The eleven cases singled out by Kanner in 1943 because they differed "so markedly and uniquely from anything reported so far" have expanded to 200,000 or more in the United States alone. While the precise total is not known and depends upon the definition of autism accepted, the incidence is estimated by the National Society for Children and Adults with Autism at 15/10,000 live births. Since there are three million live births each year in the United States, this comes to over 4500 new cases of autism each year.[180]

Total deaths in the United States during the 1980s from "acquired immune-deficiency syndrome" (AIDS) have been about 45,000. Thus the living death of autism has affected as many children, and their families, as have died from AIDS in the same period.

The first cases of Rett Syndrome were reported from Austria in 1966.[181]

The same chronological parallel between autism and childhood vaccination programs is found in other countries. In Japan, for example, the first autistic was a boy born in February 1945.[182] One of the first public health measures introduced by the United States Occupation was a compulsory pertussis vaccination program, and this case seems more than a coincidence.

Today the prevalence of autism in Japan—4.5/10,000 live births—is lower than in the United States but comparable.[183]

In France, Chile, Austria, Holland, and the Scandinavian countries the first cases of autism started appearing in the early 1950s—reflecting introduction of the pertussis vaccine in this same decade.

In England the pertussis vaccine was introduced on a broad scale only in the late 1950s, after a series of trials from 1946 to 1957. Prior to this time it had been used only sporadically by physicians. When a society of parents of autistic children was established in London in 1962, most of the children were found to have been born in the late 1950s, with a few from the early 1950s.[184]

In England the incidence of autism is the same as in Japan, 4.5/10,000 live births. Why these countries have less autism than the United States has never been explained, but it is probably because the pertussis vaccine is given later in these two countries than in the United States (at six months in England and at two years in Japan); coverage in England is optional and, depending on circumstances, ranges from eighty to as low as thirty percent; British physicians, finally, take more care to elicit contraindications and are less eager to vaccinate a child at risk than are physicians in the United States.[185]

A Puzzling Feature

An unexplained feature of autism on its initial apearance was its curious frequency in well-educated families—especially professionals such as physicians, lawyers, professors, and accountants.

Of Kanner's first 100 cases, 96 of the fathers were high-school graduates, 87 had attended college, 74 had graduated from college, and 38 had done graduate work.[186] Of the mothers, 92 were high-school graduates, 49 had graduated from college, and eleven had done graduate work. This was an astonishingly high level of educational attainment, especially for women and especially for the 1930s. Also unexpected was the finding that 70 of the women had taken jobs, while many had continued working even after marriage! "To this day," Kanner observed in 1954, "we have not encountered any one autistic child who came of unintelligent parents."

In 1964 Rimland concluded that "the parents of autistic children form a unique and highly homogeneous group in terms of intellect and personality."[187]

In 1967 a systematic study was done proving that Kanner's observations were correct.[188] A 1970 study made a similar finding—that 47 percent of the parents of autistic children had completed college, while a number had done advanced study for the M.A. or Ph.D. This contrasted sharply with the parents of other categories of mentally disturbed children, where as few as nineteen percent of the parents were college graduates.[189]

Attempts have been made, but without success, to link this skewed distribution of cases to genetic factors in the middle-class or upper-class population of parents.

One point insufficiently stressed in the early surveys was the high incidence of parents working in medicine or connected with it. Kanner's first 100 cases included eleven physicians (five psychiatrists), three Ph.D.'s in the sciences, one psychologist, and one dentist; of the mothers one was a physician, three were nurses, two were psychologists, one a physiotherapist, and one a laboratory technician.[190]

But there were other medical connections which did not necessarily appear in the statistical breakdown. One mother told Kanner:

> I majored in zoology. . . . I wanted to be a doctor, but my family
> didn't have the stamina. I have often regretted it. I taught school
> for two years, then worked in an endocrinology laboratory.[191]

In another case the father was a clothing merchant, the mother had "a successful business record, a theatrical booking office in New York." But her uncle, a psychiatrist, came to the physician's office instead of the father and clearly had much influence over the family's medical decisions. One New England mother had studied child psychology in college. In a fourth case the father was a psychiatrist, while the mother, a high-school graduate, "worked as a secretary in a pathology laboratory before marriage—a 'hypomanic' type of person; sees everything as a pathological specimen rather than well; throughout the pregnancy she was very apprehensive, afraid she would not live through the labor."[192]

Kanner noted: "Many of the fathers and most of the mothers are perfectionists. . . . The mothers felt duty-bound to carry out to the letter the rules and regulations which they were given by their obstetricians and pediatricians."[193]

But these early data showing a preponderance of educated parents have now been superseded; since the 1970s the skewed distribution no longer obtains. In the United States autism is now evenly distributed, with no social class or ethnic group being particularly favored.[194]

Hence the conclusion is now reached that the earlier data were mistaken, "based on outdated research. . . . No social or psychological characteristics of parents or families have proven to be associated with autism."[195] But is this correct? Was the earlier research done badly, or did the source population for autistic children change between 1940-1950 and the 1970s? This latter possibility has not been investigated.

A real shift in the socio-economic distribution pattern of autism can readily be explained in terms of childhood vaccination. When the pertussis vaccine was first introduced, being offered by the occasional forward-looking pediatrician to parents anxious to do "everything possible" for their children and avid for the latest wonders off the medical assembly-line, who were the first takers? Not the blue-collar workers, who could not afford these frills and are, in any case, often suspicious of doctors. Free vaccination at public health clinics (where today the vast bulk of lower-class children get their shots) was still for the future. Only the prosperous—who could afford private physicians—were in a position to request this vaccine. And these same prosperous and educated parents, especially educated and ambitious mothers with some exposure to medicine, would have insisted on it.

This explains the skewed distribution of autistics in the early decades. Kanner, who was such an acute observer in all other respects, was no less so in this one.

As vaccination programs expanded and became obligatory in nearly every state, rich and poor alike could seek the benefits of the DPT shot. The incidence of autism evened out, and researchers assume that the earlier statistics were incorrect!

*   *   *

Today the more enlightened specialists realize that autism is not a discrete entity of psychological or "emotional" origin, but a many-faceted neurologic condition with close links to other recognizably neurologic disabilities such as mental retardation and epilepsy.

Although it occurs frequently enough to be classified as a true epidemic, no theory as to its cause has yet been accepted.

The next chapter brings out the parallels between autism and the much more widespread condition—minimal brain damage.

Chapter I Notes

1. Kanner, Leo, 1942/1943, 250.
2. Kanner, Leo, 1944.
3. Kanner, Leo, 1942/1943, 242.
4. Kanner, Leo, 1954, 379.
5. Kanner, Leo, 1942/1943, 236.
6. Eisenberg, Leon, 1956, 609–611.
7. Creak, E.M. *et al.*, 1961, 502.

8. Yates, Alayne, 1984, 396,397.
9. Bemporad, J.R., 1979, 195.
10. Creak, E.M. *et al.*, 1961, 502. Cohen, D.J., 1980, 396.
11. Cohen, Donald J., 1980, 388.
12. *Ibid.*, 387.
13. Katz, Donald R., 1979.
14. Kanner, Leo, 1944, 215.
15. Kanner, Leo, 1942/1943, 236.
16. Katz, Donald R., 1979.
17. Katz, Donald R., 1979.
18. Pingree, Carmen, 1984, 331.
19. Kanner, Leo, 1944, 217.
20. Volkmar, Fred R. and Cohen, Donald J., 1985, 49–50.
21. Bemporad, Jules R., 1979, 192.
22. Cohen, Donald J., 1980, 389.
23. Kanner, Leo, 1944, 217.
24. Kanner, Leo, 1949, 422.
25. Kanner, Leo, 1954, 384.
26. Kanner, Leo and Eisenberg, Leon, 1957, 62.
27. Kanner, Leo, 1944, 217.
28. Kanner, Leo, 1949, 426.
29. Kanner, Leo, 1954, 384. Kanner, L. and Eisenberg, L., 1957, 62.
30. Kanner, Leo, and Eisenberg, Leon, 1957, 60.
31. Schopler, Eric. *et al.*, 1981, 258.
32. Despert, J.L., 1951, 347–350.
33. Bergman, P. and Escalona, S., 1949, 349–351.
34. Cappon, Daniel, 1953, 45.
35. *Loc. cit.*
36. Betz, Barbara, 1947, 267.
37. Despert, J.L., 1951, 345–346.
38. Bettelheim, Bruno, 1974, 12, 35, 425.
39. Akerley, Mary, 1975, 378.
40. Torisky, Constance V., 1978, 235.
41. Katz, Donald R., 1979.
42. Despert, J.Louise, 1951, 344.
43. Rimland, Bernard, 1964, 47.
44. Chess, Stella, 1971, 44.
45. Despert, J.Louise, 1951, 345.
46. Quoted in B. Rimland, 1964, 17, 49.
47. DeMyer, W. and M., 1984, 151.
48. Ritvo, Edward and Freeman, B.J., 1984, 299.

49. Rimland, B. 1964, 65.
50. Tinbergen, N., 1974, 23.
51. Sholevar, G.P. *et al.*, 437.
52. Pingree, Carmen B., 1984, 336.
53. Lewis, Dorothy O., 1981, Forward.
54. Kanner, Leo, 1942/1943, 250.
55. American Psychiatric Association, 1980, 88.
56. *Ibid.*, 89.
57. DeMyer, W. and M., 1984, 147.
58. Coleman, Mary, 1976, 28.
59. American Psychiatric Association, 1980, 37.
60. Kanner, 1942/1943, 248.
61. Schain, R. and Yannet, H., 1960, 563, 564.
62. Wolf, L. and Goldberg, B., 1986.
63. American Psychiatric Association, 1980, 89. Bartak, L. and Rutter, M., 1976, 119.
64. New York: Harper and Row, 1974.
65. Ornitz, E.M. and Ritvo, E.R., 1976, 616.
66. Katz, Donald R., 1979.
67. Goodwin, Mary S. and T. Campbell, 1969, 559.
68. Katz, Donald R., 1979.
69. Ornitz, E.M., 1974, 199.
70. Tsai, L., 1982, 1983, 1984. Sarz, Paul *et al.*, 1985. Yates, A., 1984.
71. Yamazaki, Kosuke *et al.*, 1975, 330.
72. Sullivan, Ruth Christ, 1979, 113.
73. Kanner, Leo, 1942/1943, 237.
74. *Ibid.*, 239.
75. Whitehouse, D. *et al.*, 1984.
76. Kanner, Leo, 1942/1943, 237. Smith, Donald E.P. *et al.*, 1988. Konstantareas, M. Mary *et al.*, 1987.
77. Karlin, Isaac W., 1951, 60.
78. Rutter, M., 1972, 330.
79. Sherwin, Albert. C., 1953, 825.
80. Cohen, Donald J., 1980, 389.
81. *Loc. cit.*
82. Goodwin, Mary S. and T. Campbell, 1969, 560.
83. Kanner, Leo, and Eisenberg, Leon, 1957, 56.
84. Katz, Donald R., 1979.
85. Realmuto, George M. and Main, Bart, 1982, 368. Bemporad, Jules R., 1979, 182.
86. Bemporad, Jules R., 1979, 192. Komoto, Junko *et al.*, 1984, 82. Coleman, Mary, 1980, 17.

87. Gastaut, H. *et al.*, 1987.
88. Chess, S., 1971, 39, 44. Myklebust, H.R. *et al.*, 1972, 158.
89. Cohen, Donald J., 1980, 396.
90. Eisenberg, Leon, 1956, 611.
91. Rimland, B., 1964, 79.
92. Student, M. and Sohmer, H., 1978, 18.
93. *Ibid.*, 18.
94. Rosenblum, S.M. *et al.*, 1980, 222.
95. Tanguay, P.E. and Edwards, R.M., 1982, 181–182.
96. Freeman, B.J. and Ritvo, E.R., 1984, 287. Bartak, L. and Rutter, M., in Neal O'Connor, ed., 1975, 199.
97. American Psychiatric Association, 1980, 88.
98. Cohen, Donald J., 1980, 387.
99. Kanner, Leo, 1942/1943, 239.
100. Petty, L.K. *et al.*, 1984, 130. Van Bourgondien, Mary E. and Mesibov, Gary B., 1987.
101. Petty, L.K. *et al.*, 1984, 130.
102. Kanner, Leo, 1942/1943, 238.
103. Kanner, Leo, 1944, 215.
104. Komoto, Junko *et al.*, 1984, 82–83. Eisenberg, Leon, 1956, 609.
105. Cohen, Donald J., 1980, 387.
106. Petty, L.K. *et al.*, 1984, 132.
107. Bemporad, Jules R., 1979, 186.
108. Sullivan, Ruth Christ, 1975, 177, 181.
109. Kanner, Leo, 1942/1943, 237. Pasamanick, B. and Knobloch, H., 1963.
110. Markowitz, Philip. I., 1983, 250. Betz, Barbara, 1947, 269. Sherwin, Albert C., 1953, 825.
111. Petty, L.K., 1984, 130.
112. Stiver, Richard and Dobbins, John P., 1980, 70–71.
113. Goodwin Mary S. and T. Campbell, 1969, 560. Lotter, V., 1966/1967, 136.
114. Gillberg, C., 1983a. Gillberg, C., 1985a.
115. Sauvage, D. *et al.*, 1985, 197.
116. Mnukhin, S.S. and Isaev, D.N., 1975, 106. Gillberg, C. *et al.*, 1987, 282.
117. Sullivan, Ruth Christ, 1975, 180. Goodwin, Mary S. *et al.*, 1971, 61. Coleman, Mary, 1976. 19, 221.
118. Kanner, Leo, 1942/1943, 236.
119. Sullivan, Ruth Christ, 1975, 177, 181.
120. Personal communication from Bernard Rimland, Ph.D.
121. Volkmar, Fred R. and Cohen, Donald J., 1985, 51.

122. Geschwind, N. and P. Behan, 1982. Kolata, Gina, 1983, 1312.
123. Kanner, Leo, 1971, 144–145.
124. Cited in Tinbergen, N., 1974, 20.
125. Coleman, Mary, 1976, 1.
126. Schopler, Eric *et al.*, 1979, 4.
127. Hetzler, Bruce and Griffin, Judith, 1981, 317.
128. Fejn, Deborah *et al.*, 1981, 312.
129. DeMyer, W. and M., 1984, 145.
130. Reichler, Richard, 1980, 95–96, 126.
131. American Psychiatric Association, 1987, 38.
132. Rutter, M. and Schopler, Eric, 1987, 172.
133. Kanner, Leo and Lesser, L.I., 1958, 711. Rimland, B., 1964, 21.
134. DeMyer, W. and M., 1984, 146.
135. Reichler, Richard, 1980, 96.
136. Ritvo, E. *et al.*, 1988.
137. Nomura, Y. Segawa, M. and Hasegawa, M., 1984.
138. American Psychiatric Association, 1980, 90; 1987, 39.
139. Van Krevelen, D.A., 1971, 83–84. See, also, Wing, L., 1981. Wing, L., 1986.
140. Dewey, M. and Everard,M., 1974, 348–349.
141. *Loc. cit.*
142. Cohen, Donald J., 1980, 389.
143. *Ibid.*, 388.
144. Volkmar, Fred R. and Cohen, Donald J., 1985, 50.
145. DeMyer, W. and M., 1984, 142. Bemporad, J., 1979, 185.
146. Cohen Donald J., 1980, 387.
147. Kanner, Leo, 1942/1943, 245. Kanner, Leo, 1944, 215–216.
148. American Psychiatric Association, 1980, 87–88.
149. Kanner, Leo and Eisenberg, Leon, 1957, 56.
150. Pingree, Carmen, 1984, 330, 331.
151. Bemporad, J. R., 1979, 190.
152. Simons, Jeanne M., 1974, 7.
153. Sherwin, Albert C., 1953, 824. Clark, P. and Rutter, M., 1977.
154. Cohen, Donald J., 1980, 388.
155. Everard, Margaret P., 1976.
156. Eisenberg, Leon, 1956, 609.
157. Bemporad, J.R., 1979, 181, 185.
158. Foxx, Richard, 1980, 51.
159. Pingree, Carmen, 1984, 331.
160. Bemporad, Jules, R., 1979, 191.
161. Petty, L.K. *et al.*, 1984, 132.
162. Volkmar, Fred R. and Cohen, Donald J., 1985, 50.

163. Katz, Donald R., 1979.
164. From Carolyn Betts, *A Special Kind of Normal* (1979). Quoted in: Park, Clara Claiborne, 1985, 115.
165. Park, Clara Claiborne, 1985, 115. Sullivan, Ruth, Christ, 1979, 113, 114.
166. Torisky, Jesse A., 1979, 288–289.
167. Sullivan, Ruth Christ, 1979, 118.
168. Foxx, Richard, 1980, 50–51.
169. Nyhan, William L., 1972. Nyhan, William L., 1976.
170. Torisky, D. and C., 1985, 214–216, 224–227. Deslauriers, A., 1978.
171. Ritvo, E. *et al.*, 1988.
172. Mnukhin, S.S. and Isaev, D.N., 1975, 106.
173. Kanner, Leo, 1944, 213.
174. Goodwin, Mary S. and T. Campbell, 1969, 561. Verhees, B., 1976, 58. Stiver, R.L. and Dobbins, John P., 1980, 69. Lotter, V., 1966/ 1967, 136.
175. Rimland, B., 1964, 12.
176. Kanner, Leo, 1942/1943, 217, 236, 238.
177. Cohen, Donald J., 1980, 389.
178. Katz, Donald R., 1979.
179. Goodwin, M.S. and T.C., 1969, 558.
180. American Psychiatric Association, 1987, 36–37. Figures also supplied by National Society of Autistic Children and Adults.
181. Nomura, Y. *et al.*, 1984.
182. Wakabayashi, S. *et al.*, 1984.
183. Information supplied by the Higashi School, Boston, Mass.
184. Everard, M.P., 1973, 278.
185. Coulter, H. and Fisher, B., 1985, 200–204, 235.
186. Kanner, Leo, 1954, 382.
187. Rimland, B., 1964, 38.
188. Rutter, M., 1972, 328.
189. Coleman, Mary, ed., 1976, 12.
190. Kanner, Leo, 1954, 382.
191. Kanner, Leo, 1949, 421.
192. *Ibid.*, 424. Kanner, Leo, 1944, 214. Kanner, Leo, 1942/1943, 238.
193. Kanner, Leo, 1949, 422, 424.
194. Gillberg, C. and Schaumann, H., 1982, 223. Tsai, Luke *et al.*, 1982, 211.
195. Freeman, B.J. and Ritvo, E.R., 1984, 286.

II

Minimal Brain Damage

In the mid-1950s, a decade after the emergence of autism, medical science and the public became aware of a spreading disorder among schoolchildren called "hyperactivity":

> The children show involuntary and constant overactivity which greatly surpasses the normal. This may already be present during early infancy. Motor development is often advanced, and histories frequently indicate that the child climbed out of the crib well before a year of age. Parents often say that he walked early and there was "no holding him" after that, or that he could not be kept in a play pen and was into everything, having to be tied to keep him in the yard.[1]

The U.S. Public Health Service in 1963 listed nearly 100 signs and symptoms associated with hyperactivity and altered the name to "minimal brain dysfunction."

However, the expression "minimal brain damage" is preferable, since the "dysfunction" is the consequence of actual brain damage.

Within a decade minimal brain damage was presenting a major challenge to the American school system, and to child psychiatry generally. Paul Wender, a leading authority, wrote in 1971 that the disorder "occurs in conjunction with—and *possibly* as the basis of—*virtually* all . . . categories of childhood behavior disturbances . . . embarrassing but true," and that it is "probably the most common single diagnostic entity seen in Child Guidance Clinics."[2]

The Shaywitzes, professors of pediatrics at Yale Medical School, wrote in 1984 that minimal brain damage is "perhaps the most common, and certainly one of the most time-consuming problems in current pediatric practice."[3]

And the *Journal of the American Medical Association* in 1988 called minimal brain damage "the single most prevalent disability reported by elementary schools and one of the most common referral problems to child psychiatry outpatient clinics . . . probably the most researched problem in child psychiatry."[4]

Boys manifest it five or ten times as frequently as girls, and it was once thought to be an exclusively male disorder.

The American Psychiatric Association estimates that three percent of U.S. prepubertal children suffer from one or another manifestation of minimal brain damage (from thirty to seventy-five percent of these are also hyperactive, depending upon whose opinion one accepts).[5]

But the APA's figures are certainly understated. If the figure was only three percent, this disorder would not be "the most common single diagnostic entity seen in Child Guidance Clinics." Those who have estimated the prevalence level at fifteen to twenty percent of school children are closer to the mark.[6]

But even this may be an understatement. Kathleen Long and David McQueen, studying the Maryland and District of Columbia school systems in 1984 (where thirteen percent of children are already in "special education classes"), concluded that "[minimally brain damaged] children are significantly underdetected . . . nationally in public school systems."[7]

In any case, the prevalence of minimal brain damage with hyperactivity is steadily rising.

Defining the Syndrome

A 1984 U.S government pamphlet described three typical cases:

> My son Johnny is two years old and has totally disrupted our household since he was an infant. He has few friends because he kicks, pushes, shoves, and screams at other kids. He opens the refrigerator and tries to sit in it. He climbs onto kitchen counters, turns off the water heater and unscrews almost anything, even the storm door. Nothing seems to please him. . . .

Tommy can't sit still. He is disruptive at school with his constant talking and clowning around. He leaves the classroom without the teacher's permission. Although he has above-average intelligence, Tommy has trouble reading and writing. When he talks, the words come out so fast no one understands him.

Joe won't go to school. Instead, he explores the house. When he grew tall enough to unlock the screen door, those explorations shifted to the neighborhood. He was the neighborhood terror. Once we found Joe wandering down the middle of the street! He looks like an abused child. He has a mass of bruises from bumping into anything that gets in his way.[8]

As with autism, when the attempt was made to define minimal brain damage, it was seen to ramify and become associated with other disabilities.

*Hypo*activity (sluggishness) is found in this population, although less common; the child is lethargic during the day and requires an unusual amount of sleep.[9]

Minimally brain-damaged children usually have a limited attention span; even when of normal or superior IQ, they do poorly in school because of easy distractibility and failure to complete work within the allotted time. Such a child may be called "absent-minded."[10]

The opposite occurs also: an excessively long attention span: "If he's interested," says the mother, "he's there until its completely done." The five-year old can spend four or five hours on a building-block project; he seems unable to withdraw his attention from the task at hand.[11]

While children were formerly thought to "grow out" of minimal brain damage, this is now known to occur only in a few of the milder cases. Hyperactivity in particular often slackens with age. But other symptoms, especially attention-span difficulties, continue into adult life.

There is no cure.

Once minimal brain damage had been identified as a syndrome, psychologists and psychiatrists came forward to explain why children were acting in these bizarre ways. But then, just as with autism, investigators found to their surprise that the MBD syndrome was associated with mental retardation, seizures, cerebral palsy, "hard" and "soft" neurologic signs, and other disabilities which did not readily fit into "behavioral" or "emotional" categories.

The *Diagnostic and Statistical Manual* estimates that five percent of children with minimal brain damage suffer from one or another of these more serious conditions.[12] But this statistic is likely to be severely understated, being distorted by the aversion of mental hospitals and insurance programs to multiple diagnoses. When a child is diagnosed with two or more disorders—such as, for instance, epilepsy and minimal brain damage—the more serious neurologic defect will overshadow the less serious. The diagnosis written down on the chart will be "epilepsy," and the minimal brain damage aspect of his condition will be forever lost to medical statistics-gathering.[13]

Nonetheless, there is indeed a high association between minimal brain damage and these other neurological defects—which are, of course, the same disabilities already noted in connection with autism.

Mental retardation, for example: while many children with minimal brain damage are of average or even above-average intelligence, on the whole they have a lower IQ than normal children.

By the same token, minimal brain damage is three to four times more common in the mentally retarded than in those with a normal IQ.[14]

MBD children also have a high incidence of seizure disorders: epilepsy, tics, tremors, choreiform (twisting) movements, facial grimaces, infantile spasms, and others. And, conversely, children diagnosed as "epileptic" have a very high incidence of severe learning disabilities and attention-span difficulties.[15]

If the MBD child does not have a seizure disorder per se, he may still show one or more of the "hard" or "soft" signs indicating a "subclinical" neurologic disorder. Half of these children manifest such typical "hard" signs as EEG abnormalities and muscle hypertony or hypotony. Typical "soft" signs are motor impairments, extremely poor handwriting, inability to balance, poor visual-motor coordination, clumsiness, awkward gait, impaired hopping ability, and a tendency to walk on the toes.[16]

"Clumsiness" in its most severe form becomes cerebral palsy. In one study a quarter of the children with cerebral palsy were also hyperactive.[17]

Children with minimal brain damage are disproportionately left-handed or ambidexterous (described technically as "left and mixed laterality" or "poorly defined unilateral dominance"). The child cannot readily distinguish right from left, up from down, beside from behind, etc. If asked to touch his left ear with his right hand, he becomes baffled.[18]

The 1982 article by Norman Geschwind and Peter Behan mentioned earlier showed a significant correlation between left-handedness and dyslexia.

A 1987 *Washington Post*-ABC News poll made a curious discovery—that sixteen percent of Americans under thirty are left-handed or ambidexterous, as against only twelve percent of those over sixty. Another recent survey found an even greater disparity: thirteen percent of twenty-year olds were lefties, compared to five percent of persons in their fifties. The accepted interpretation is that lefties in the past were forced to switch to right-handed writing while in school, and this may, indeed, be one factor, but is not necessarily the only one. There is a strong possibility that the epidemic of vaccine-induced sub-clinical encephalitis since 1945 has generated a disproportionate incidence of left-handedness and ambidexterity in the under-forty or under-thirty age groups.[19]

Sleep disturbances are very common in this population.[20] In the mid-1950s, concomitant with the emergence of minimal brain damage on the medical scene, psychiatrists were inundated with children who could not sleep at night. Two authorities wrote in 1957: "It has frequently been observed that, in the present permissive era of child management, the previously common feeding problems have been replaced to a large extent by sleeping problems."[21]

The MBD child turns day into night. Hyperactivity increases at bedtime, with difficulty in falling asleep. Or the child falls asleep at the proper time but wakens after a few hours. A variety of misdemeanors may follow, from talking or singing in bed to turning on the lights and rampaging through the house in noisy and sleep-disturbing play.[22]

In other MBD children sleep is fitful and without established patterns; they catnap both day and night. Or they have trouble falling asleep but are then almost impossible to arouse.[23] The minimally brain damaged child who is "hypoactive" is particularly prone to this "sleep drunkenness."

Physicians since 1970 have discovered a new condition in adults labelled "delayed sleep phase syndrome"—meaning inability to fall asleep before three or four in the morning. Although data on the origins of this syndrome are lacking, certainly these could be the MBD children now grown up.[24]

In children sleep may be accompanied by teeth-grinding, night sweats, nightmares, and night terrors.

Darnell has very bad night terrors. He had a stage at age two, and now he has another one. Recently he was sure there was a cereal box and out of it came green men with long legs and long tongues; they jumped on him, and he screamed bloody murder. They were in his hair, etc.

Enuresis (bedwetting) and "unreliable sphincters" often accompany the sleep disorder. The child sleeps very deeply and wets his bed until early or late adolescence.[25]

Eleven million adult Americans are thought to have a problem with urinary control, and the causes are unknown.[26]

Encopresis (lack of control over the anal sphincter, with bowel movements at inappropriate times and places) is also seen (in adults as well as children).

MBD children often have appetite disorders, refusing to eat even when hungry. As babies they may have a weak or nonexistent sucking reflex, along with gagging and drooling and difficulty swallowing.[27]

Refusal or reluctance to eat (*anorexia nervosa*) may continue into childhood, adolescence, and adulthood.

Anorexia can also be caused by the amphetamines given to these children to control hyperactivity.*

Or these MBD children may eat too much and indiscriminately

*See discussion in Chapter V

(bulimia), a condition which, like anorexia, came into prominence in the 1960s.[28]

Anorexia is thought to occur in up to one percent of adolescent females (ages twelve to eighteen). Bulimia is even more common, as college student surveys detect it in 4.5 to thirteen percent of females and 0.4 to five percent of males.

The rule of thumb is that fifteen percent of adolescent girls in the United States experience serious problems with anorexia and/or bulimia.[29]

Thus the post-encephalitic syndrome seems to be manifested in males predominantly as hyperactivity and in females predominantly as appetite disorder.

Even if the child does eat, he may still have severe colic as an infant, arching his back from the pain in his stomach. He may have suffered inordinately from stomach aches in childhood and adolescence.[30] Bad breath has also been noted.

The MBD child may have a high tolerance for pain and discomfort, especially temperature changes. He will wear his long-johns every day, even in the summer, when others are suffering from the heat. Or he may play outside in January in his tee-shirt.

Cranial Nerve Palsies

These neurological impairments are identical with those already found in conjunction with autism. Thus cranial nerve palsies also play a prominent role in the syndromes associated with minimal brain damage.

While the MBD child may have a defect in the sensory organ itself, more commonly the problem stems from a "processing defect" (also called "perceptual handicap," "cognitive disorder," "discriminatory sensory loss," etc.), meaning an interruption in the cranial nerves connecting the sensory organ with the brain.

Vision: the MBD child may suffer from oculomotor incoordinations and visual defects, disturbances in eye movements, or crossed eyes (strabismus).

These motor and other disturbances of the eyes, moreover, are often associated with chronic migraine headaches later in life. Four percent of U.S. school children have migraine headaches, and the minimally brain-damaged have a disproportionate share of them. Geschwind and Behan's article called attention to the connection between migraine headaches, left-handedness, and dyslexia. Alan Leviton concluded in 1986, from his experience at the Boston Children's Hospital, that "children who are brought to medical attention because of frequently recurring or disabling headaches appear to have an increased prevalence of learning disorders."[31]

Headaches are often associated with sleep disturbances: night terrors, somnambulism, head-banging before sleep, uneasy sleep, sleep apnea (waking up with a feeling of suffocation), etc.

Morning headaches and headaches that awaken patients in the middle of the night are often described as frontal or diffuse over the scalp. In general, they improve or dissipate after the patient awakens, but can persist for several hours. They were reported in 52 percent of 120 surveyed patients with obstructive sleep apnea syndrome. Long afternoon naps may also be followed by a headache.[32]

Even when the eyes are physiologically sound and capable of movement, the child may be unable to read—leading to dyslexia or learning disabilities. The individual so affected is commonly of good intelligence but has extreme difficulty associating the visual symbols of letters with the sounds they represent.[33]

Dyslexia is the reason why "Johnny Can't Read" today. Although solutions to the problem of galloping illiteracy in the United States are continually being proposed, no one really believes they will work. Our educational establishment is just conducting a holding action in the hope that they will wake up one day and find that Johnny can read after all.

This will never occur, however, as long as all the Johnnies in the country are being vaccinated with substances capable of making them dyslexic.

"Dyscalculia" is the name for inability to perform arithmetic. The child has trouble with numbers and cannot establish a relationship between the symbol and the concept. He cannot associate the concept of "sevenness" with the word "seven" or the symbol "7." In other words, he can count to seven by rote but will not recognize the word "seven" or the symbol "7" when used in a sentence.[34]

In "dysgraphia" the child can recognize words but has trouble spelling them, since he cannot remember the sequence of the letters; he may be unable to write cursively and have to print instead.

Hearing: minimal brain damage also involves disabilities of aural perception, including "audiomotor incoordination," "auditory imperceptions," "developmental receptive language disorder," "auditory perception deficits," "high-frequency hearing loss," and the like.

The opposite condition, "hyperacusis" or preternaturally sensitive hearing, is also found. It can cause the individual to be confused and distracted by multiple aural intakes.

Hearing disorders are frequently associated with a chronic otitis in childhood which may have damaged the eardrum.

Speech can be affected as well. Some children have "paucity of speech" or even "complete absence of speech." Most start talking later than normal and then have a variety of speech problems: "defects of articulation and language," "deficit in a language or symbol function," "disorders of speech and communication," "developmental articulation disorder," "infantile speech," "deficits in receptive, integrative, and/or expressive language," etc.

A common speech impediment of the MBD child is stuttering or stammering. Samuel Torrey Orton, whose work on dyslexia in the 1920s and 1930s was the basis for later developments in this field, pointed even then to the strong relationship between stuttering and dyslexia. This fact was later forgotten, and was resurrected only recently.[35]

A variation on stuttering is inability to complete a sentence because the right word cannot be found (called "anomia", "clear lapses in naming objects, places, or people").

At age four he would start a sentence, which might have been a complicated one. Or he might be reaching for a word. He would keep repeating the beginning of the sentence. He couldn't get to the word he wanted. So he would have to keep repeating the sentence. This went on all during age four.

Other disabilities are: speech usage below age, severely limited vocabulary, oddities of articulation or intonation ("slow, monotone,

68 Minimal Brain Damage

loud sing-song, incontrollable sounds, unmodulated, sharp, or peculiar syllabilization, and pressured speech"). The voice becomes monotonous and less resonant. The speaker is unable to modulate his tone of voice in response to the environment.[36]

Sometimes the child starts to speak and then loses this ability: "He spoke in sentences at about three years. . . . Having entered nursery school at age four, he refused to talk, and he began to talk again only when he was five."[37]

Sometimes the child can talk but refuses to—labelled "elective mutism":

> The essential feature is continuous refusal to speak in almost all social situations, including at school, despite ability to comprehend spoken language and to speak. These children may communicate via gestures, by nodding or shaking the head, or, in some cases, by monosyllabic or short, monotone utterances.[38]

But the opposite can occur, unnatural verbal ability, such as a talent for mimicry.

He constantly listens for animal sounds and then imitates them. In the Bronx Zoo the wolves even answered back.

The American Psychiatric Association's "conservative estimate" is that ten percent of children below age eight, and five percent aged eight years or older, have one or another of these speech defects![39]

Phil A. Silva and coworkers in 1987 found these various speech defects to have serious implications for the child's future: children with early language delay turn out to have lower intelligence, lower reading scores, and a higher incidence of behavioral problems.[40]

As in autism, the senses of smell and taste may be overdeveloped in MBD children and partly offset deficiencies in hearing, vision, and voice. The mother will say that her child is "very particular about foods" and complains about the smell of cooking.

Salivation is sometimes unpleasantly enhanced. The child spits a lot, especially when angry. There may be weakness of the facial muscles, causing a "mask-like" appearance.[41]

Breathing and Asthma

The reflex control of breathing is also mediated through the cranial nerves (IX and X—the glossopharyngeal and vagus nerves); thus the MBD child often experiences breathing difficulties.

Bonnie Kaplan of the University of Calgary noted in 1987 the "commonly held clinical impression that children with attention-deficit disorder with hyperactivity show an unusual number of physical ailments, such as upper respiratory infections and ear infections." Her own study, relying on parent interviews, found a "consistently greater frequency" of respiratory symptoms in these children.[42]

Thus it is no concidence that asthma is on the increase among children in the United States, the United Kingdom, and several other industrialized countries.

Surveys find that eleven to fourteen percent of infants have "wheezing," while half continue these episodes into childhood and adolescence.[43] The condition then develops into asthma, which has been increasing in the United States since at least the early 1970s. It is now at the level of seven percent of the population: ten million Americans in all, with three million under the age of eighteen. It accounts for nearly a quarter of all days of school absence, and is third among all chronic diseases as a cause of physician visits.[44]

Twice as many boys suffer from it as girls, with the male excess being greatest in the more severe cases.[45]

Asthma mortality in this country has also been rising since the late 1970s.[46] Most disturbing are the deaths of very young children. Medical folk-wisdom used to hold that "No child ever dies of asthma," but since the 1960s there has been an "epidemic" of asthma deaths among young persons in the United Kingdom, New Zealand, Australia, and the United States.[47]

In 1985 there were 125 deaths in the United States from asthma in children under age fifteen, with another 156 deaths between the ages of fifteen and twenty-four.[48]

Many asthmatics overlap with the minimally brain damaged and reveal the same combination of symptoms—like Josh Cohen in Thomas Plaut's *Children with Asthma*, who was unable to keep

69

up with his class even in kindergarten:

> He was nowhere ready to deal even with the prereading. . . . The
> constant runny nose made him seem a bit sickly. . . . In the first
> grade he had a beginning, inexperienced teacher. She seemed not
> to worry about Josh's continuing inability to deal with reading and
> writing. She said he often appeared tired and would nap under
> her desk during the afternoon. Perhaps his constant runny nose
> wasn't helping things either? . . . What I saw was a child who
> wished he didn't have to go to school. . . . [by the second grade]
> He had learned virtually nothing in a year and a half of school.[49]

The connection between sudden infant death, asthma, and
other breathing difficulties—all due to impairment of the cranial
nerves governing respiration—should be investigated further, with
particular reference to childhood vaccinations.

The parallels between the various cranial-nerve palsies in
autism and minimal brain damage suggest a common origin of these
two conditions and even an overall identity, differing from one
another only in degree. Both are specific manifestations of a larger
phenomenon, the post-encephalitic syndrome (discussed in the following chapter) which is in most cases the consequence of childhood vaccinations.

Psychological or Neurologic?

Researchers such as Samuel Torrey Orton in the 1920s realized that
"emotional disturbances" originate in neurologic reality.[50] But this
insight was lost after World War II when psychology, psychiatry, and
especially Freudian psychoanalysis became overwhelmingly popular medical disciplines, while the link between mental illness and
neurology was largely broken.

Emotions were the stock in trade of these doctors of the soul:
sexual maladjustments, the Oedipus complex, the "nightmare" of
life in the nuclear family, and the like. The multiplying hordes of
minimally brain-damaged children were ideal grist for these mills.

Furthermore, in recent decades a neurologic interpretation of
mental illness has been seen to reflect a conservative political
stance—unwillingness to help the low-income social groups whose

inferior economic status gives rise to "emotional" disabilities.

Psychologists and psychiatrists, being professional intellectuals and thus usually left-of-center politically, prefer diagnoses which allow for the possibility of politico-medical intervention. A finding of neurologic damage is inherently distasteful to them (and it was rarely considered), since such a condition is nearly always irremediable, and no great hope of improvement through public health programs can be extended.

The idea of preventing future cases by *curtailing* one major public health program seems not to have occurred to anyone.

Bruno Bettelheim took the lead in generating soothing non-neurologic explanations of minimal brain damage:

> I am convinced, on the basis of my many years of work with severely emotionally disturbed children, that a child of normal intelligence will develop a reading block only if he has severe emotional problems. There is . . . a good inner reason which a normally intelligent child expresses in outward "inability" to learn . . . a child can have positive reasons for not learning (that is, reasons that fulfill an emotional need) as well as negative ones.[51]

What were these positive reasons, these unfulfilled emotional needs?

> Emotionally a child often equates learning with renouncing closeness to a beloved mother . . . to many children, learning signifies giving up, if not mother, certainly being mothered. This they are unwilling to do.

Other children refused to read—to maintain their self-respect!

> Does this sound contradictory and unbelievable? . . . Some children, who are behind the learning ball to begin with, come to the conclusion that it is better to be first among the lowliest than to be one of the mob of average learners.

If the child was poor or black, staying illiterate was a way to reject dominant white values and a white-dominated society:

> Sometimes teachers, wanting a child to accept middle-class standards, ask him to behave according to principles above and beyond those of his parents. Such a child may then express his

deep loyalty to his parents by rejecting all the school—and with it learning—stands for. . . . When a child from a crowded slum encounters images of "nice" family life that arouse his jealousy and envy . . . his envy may turn into fury.

This envy can be reinforced by peer pressure from other equally "disadvantaged" children in the class.

But Bettelheim and other knowers of the human heart could play both sides of the street. While some children refused to read out of deep loyalty to their parents, others did the same in order to punish them—especially the mother:

Some children are so overwhelmed at home . . . by being nagged to desperation or by being driven to achieve beyond their ability —that their need to defy is great. They will defy adult authority wherever they see a chance to without dire consequences . . . a child who doesn't dare oppose an overpowering parent defies the teacher instead by refusing to learn . . . [also] by not learning, he effectively punishes his parents to whom he is otherwise subservient.

Bettelheim recounted the story of the supposedly feeble-minded boy from an unhappy family who could not read until one day the teacher blacked out the words "father" and "mother" on the page. "The boy, who up to then had steadfastly maintained that he couldn't read at all, did so, reading proudly and without error a seven-page story. This was the turning-point in his academic career."

Bettelheim even managed to bring sex into the picture:

The inhibition of curiosity is another potent source of learning blocks. Sometimes a child interprets a parent's order not to explore his own body [masturbation!!] or what goes on in his parents' bedroom as meaning that all curiosity is wrong. But one cannot learn without curiosity.

He had only one song to sing, but he never wearied of it.

A legion of other reasons "Why Johnny Can't Read" were thrust by Bettelheim and others upon a gullible public, which was apparently willing to believe anything provided it was "emotional." "Some children are afraid to compete, or don't want to, because they feel competition is wrong." Children read letters and words, but can't understand sentences and paragraphs, because they "develop the notion that while they're permitted to see, they aren't supposed to understand the meaning of what they see. Typically this happens when a child knows his parents do not want him to understand their actions or motives." If the parents are quarrelling, "a child's need to undo, to change too painful a situation, may result in reversals, that is, substituting one letter for another in reading. . . ."

Other aspects of minimal brain damage also came in for their share of psychologizing. Asthma could easily be attributed to the "smothering" "asthmatogenic" [!!] mother:[52]

> Everyone knew asthma was a psychosomatic disease caused, of course, by *mother*! Oh God, Sigmund Freud has my number. This is it. I thought I had been doing such a good job of faking parenting.[53]

Anorexia in young girls was treated psychiatrically by "maintaining the patient's disengagement from parental conflicts and encouraging her development of self-care, self-esteem, and interpersonal trust." And for the parents, "marital therapy . . . centered on the need of the couple to attend to themselves, their future, and their relationship."[54]

Enuresis, being a frequent concomitant of minimal brain damage, has spawned an enormous psychiatric output:

> The enuresis is seen as the child's retaliation against the parents or the sign of a persistently infantilized relationship. The symptom has also been described dynamically to represent a masturbatory equivalent [!!], an expression of bisexuality [!!], or a somatization of a defect in body image. [??][55]

Equally great powers of imagination were displayed by the psychological and psychoanalytical fraternity in interpreting the rising incidence of sleep disorders ("one of the major problems of present child-rearing") noted in American children in the late 1940s and after.[56]

A 1956 panel meeting of the American Psychoanalytical Association on "sleep disturbances in children" shows how this professional body responded to the various neurologic symptoms that were starting to emerge.[57]

Did the child have insomnia? "Anna Maenchen asked us to consider 'the unspecified maturational reluctance to retreat from all the activity and autonomy of waking life' [which] may express itself in a reluctance to go to sleep. One illustration was a patient who as a child was afraid that he 'might forget to breathe' while asleep. This quality of unlearning or feared loss of an ability was important."

That the child had apnea and was justifiably terrified of dying in his sleep did not occur to Anna Maenchen. Instead, she considered "presleep mechanisms of children":

> She mentioned the good-night kiss, the eternal drink of milk or water which for the child . . . serves by the very presence of the mother figure to remove guilt feelings arising from oral-sadistic impulses. She particularly emphasized fetishes such as soft clothes, a pillow, a blanket, a piece of wool, or a teddy bear which . . . might represent the mother's skin, and perhaps at the age of four, a phallic symbol. We should differentiate between prephallic and phallic situations. . . .

Marianne Kris commented on the "typical negativistic daytime behavior" of the toddler with a sleep disturbance—this being "only one aspect of the conflict between active and passive tendencies in this developmental period."

> The tendencies are perhaps almost equal and at this time when the mother demands an acceptance by the child of a passive, sleeping situation, sleep disturbances may be manifested because of poor internalization, and reliance on projective mechanisms is usual. Kris felt that this phenomenon possibly occurs a little bit earlier than the pinnacle of anal-sadistic conflict. She also felt that possibly because there are reduced demands by parents about feeding, stronger parental desires for regularized sleep occur.

Another small (thirty-two-month old) patient with an acute sleep disturbance had an obsession about people's eyes, interpreted by one participant as "a phobia of goggles and dark eye glasses."

> At the age of twenty-nine months he was acutely frightened by the sight of a truck driver who wore goggles. He became reluctant to meet people for fear that they wore dark glasses. . . . In addition, he had to "eye" things excessively. One of his defensive rituals was his particular edition of his nighttime prayer: "Now I lay me down to look. I pray the Lord my look to look. If I should look

before I look, I pray the Lord my look to look." When asked why
he insisted on this version of the prayer, he merely said, "I like
to say look."

One child presented with hypersomnia:

> At three months of age a prediction was made that this was a nar-
> cissistic child. The infant had no object relationships, and the
> infant's sleep was very satisfying to the mother. After feeding, the
> child went right back to sleep, and this pattern continued into the
> second year, although periods of wakefulness and activity became
> more prominent. . . . If a history had been obtained when this
> child was ten, most clinicians would have thought that this was
> an autistic child.

But the psychoanalyst herself concluded merely that the child had
a "high stimulus barrier."

Another participant discussed "parental anxieties accompanying sleep disturbances in young children," meaning the legitimate
concern of the parents that there might be something wrong with
the child who has breathing difficulties in the middle of the night.
To the psychoanalyst the real problem was the parents (of course!)
who sometimes viewed sleep disturbance as "an aggressive action."
*"Some mothers with hostile wishes [???] need to return after the
child is asleep to reassure themselves that the child is not dead."*

Or, alternately, in the case of small infants "there appeared to
be unconscious competition through helplessness and dependency
on the part of the mother . . . there were many suggestions of strong
oral-sadistic impulses in the mother preserved as unconscious threats
of disintegration of themselves."

Some noted correctly the correlation between sleep disturbances,
or "head-banging or body biting before falling asleep," and separation anxieties, nightmares, speech difficulties, "aggressive defiant"
behavior, anxieties, and "repressed rage." Several of the participants
mentioned hyperactivity, "discharge of motor impulses," etc.

But clinical insight into these neurologic manifestations was,
alas, sublimated in unintelligible digressions and speculations about
"qualitative differences of differing ego functions," "splitting of the
superego," " 'desomatization of reactions to excitations,' using Max

Schur's terminology," "acceptance of punishment for oral-sadistic wishes," and the like.

Ultimately, of course, the mom was blamed for everything: "The vast majority of sleep disturbances during the first year of life can be attributed to parental handling which varies from insufficient mothering to overstimulation"—in a precise parallel to the mothers of autistics who either overstimulated or understimulated the child's ego formation!

A mother who believed in these "psychogenic interpretations," and whose third-grade daughter was failing in school due to night terrors, tells her story:

> The bad marks came as a surprise to us, since Pat had always been curious and eager to learn. But lately she had been having trouble getting to sleep. As soon as the lights were out, she would be taken over by wideawake nightmares. I say "taken over" because she seemed unable to control her thoughts. . . . Again and again, after half a night shaken by her "bad thoughts," as she called them, she would trail in for breakfast looking peaked and wan.[38]

The school psychologist was consulted, and he explained:

> Children show strain in many ways—sleeplessness, lying, irrational fears, learning disability, bed wetting are some of them. . . . Pat was troubled by something that she couldn't tell us about for she didn't recognize what it was herself. But . . . just because she had buried her fear or guilt out of sight didn't mean that in the light of day it would be too terrible to look at. . . .

He recommended a private psychiatrist who helped her a little with the waking nightmares. Then, however, he urged the parents to come in for treatment:

> I thought of myself as fairly knowledgeable by this time, but I was completely unprepared for the broad implications of our talk with Dr. Mann. Briefly, the root of Pat's trouble had been a secret, guilty conscience. She felt that she was wicked and bad because, sometimes, and passionately, she hated us all—Dave and Jill and me. . . . Her fantasies of making us pay—sometimes quite violently—frightened her, and she became convinced that she was

wicked. Then her guilty conscience would take over in the form
of her bad thoughts about getting hurt. . . .

While we know nothing about the medical history of "Pat,"
she has to be seen as representing the class of children suffering
from sleep disorders and "night terrors" which was becoming more
and more numerous in these years. These symptoms are common
sequelae of encephalitis, including encephalitis from vaccination,
and it is reasonable to assume that in many cases vaccination was
the cause of the sleep disturbances.

But this factor was never considered in the diagnosis.

Since the 1950s American parents and their children have been
continuously subjected to psychologizing and psychiatrizing on a
vast scale. Geschwind wrote in 1982 that this prejudice "makes it
extremely difficult to accept that there are instances in which
difficulties in emotional adjustment are the primary result of alterations in the brain."[59]

Neurologically oriented professionals later welcomed the new
term "minimal brain dysfunction" as representing a slight movement away from purely psychiatric interpretations. It "rescued children and their parents from the rigid track of psychogenic interpretations which were used to explain all deviant behavior, and from
the consequent dependence on long-term psychotherapy with its
expensive and irrelevant probing for theoretical and stereotyped
causal complexes."[60]

Bettelheim and the legions of mental health professionals who
espoused, and still do espouse, the "emotional" theory of minimal
brain damage ignore a truth which has long been known and was
recently restated by Frank Elliott, Emeritus Professor of Neurology
at the University of Pennsylvania, "Material adversity can aggravate
human weaknesses but does not cause them."[61]

Intellectual Fragmentation

This multitude of palsies and other neurologic disabilities prevents
the child from developing the intellectual apparatus (concepts,
linked together in the memory) which would enable him to get an
intellectual grip on the outside world, to "make sense" of reality.

This is sometimes called "developmental deficits in symbol functions." It is also known as "adolescent thought disorder." The adolescent will say: "I can't get my act together" or "I just can't think straight."[62] Michael Aman calls it "inability to direct attention within a complex environment, with the result that the child reacts globally to what appears to him or her as a string of disconnected events."[63] He cannot distinguish among the stimuli offered from the outside and will respond to all of them equally.

"Adolescent thought disorder" is identical in nature to the confused thought process of the autistic, being only a milder manifestation: the data of perception cannot readily be organized into coherent patterns, i.e., abstractions, symbols, and associations.

Ability to grasp the meaning of abstractions and associate them with one another usually comes with age, in the normal process of mental growth and maturation. Children focus on the concrete, while the adult comes to understand abstractions. But the MBD child never moves out of the literal and concrete. He understands that an apple can be eaten but cannot understand that an apple and a banana are both fruit. In school he has an easier time with precise factual subjects such as history or geography but serious trouble with literature, poetry, or mathematics.

Since thought is integrated through abstractions, this adolescent is not integrated intellectually ("integrative dysfunction").[64] Ideas are experienced, if at all, in a concrete, discrete, "one at a time" sequence. The outcome is "loose, rambling, illogical thought processes," "disorganized thinking," "difficulty in organizing thoughts coherently."

These children closely resemble the description of Asperger's Syndrome. They are present-oriented, matter-of-fact, narcissistically egocentric, rambling, circumstantial, unable to get to the point. They cannot joke, since a sense of humor presupposes a background of abstract knowledge against which the situation described in the joke is seen as funny.

Their attention span is short, and they are very distractible. "He cannot keep his attention from wandering to the vague stimuli he senses around him—to the soft sounds from the next room, to the sharp edge of the chair or the gentle breeze on the back of his neck."[65]

They become overwhelmed by pure sensation:

> The teenager stops talking and is lost in fascination as he watches his cigarette smoke drift away. The adolescent forgets about her meal as she becomes preoccupied with the feel of the liquid in her coffee cup. The teenager who began to sweep the leaves from the stairs may suddenly become engrossed with the swing of the broom and spend the next twenty minutes just watching the broom swing . . . then he has to confess, "I'm sorry I got caught up with my thoughts."[66]

The memory, both short-term and long-term, is a leaky bucket. The adolescent knows something one day and has forgotten it the next. He complains that his memory does not work right: "I read it over and over again, but it will not stick."[67]

As the thought process and thought content break down more and more, the teenager finds it hard to think over a time span.[68] He can think only in the present, cannot recall the past or anticipate the future, and is unable to plan ahead or delay gratification.

The adolescent may seek intellectual structure, some integrating concept, in a religious, medical, or dietary fad.

This makes his already boring conversation even worse.

The continual effort to keep his thought processes integrated takes extra time and energy—one reason he is always so tired. School and homework are extraordinarily difficult and time-consuming. "Teenagers in this situation often become more obsessive in an increasingly frantic attempt to maintain control."[69]

Inability to Acquire Experience

The inability to conceptualize means inability to acquire experience or learn from experience.[70]

Experience is obtained through sense-perception and memory. But the minimally brain-damaged child is defective in both areas. His perceptions are fragmented, and his memory is weak. He can neither acquire experience properly nor store it in memory:

> He cannot transfer ideas or thoughts from one situation or context to another. He may be able to read a book with one kind of

print yet be unable to read the same material with a different kind of print. He may recognize a word or an object in one setting but not in another. He may understand and be able to apply a concept in one context, but be unable to apply it in another.[71]

Having no references from his own experience, he cannot assimilate the experience of others. Even when intelligent, he cannot understand directions or take guidance from outside, and has to deal with every new situation in his own way.

If there was a math problem which had to be solved in five steps, he wouldn't believe it. He tried to reinvent the wheel every time.

Lacking a counterweight in past experience, he behaves impulsively and without inhibition. "You never can tell which way the cat is going to jump!" "When things don't go his way, he just rushes out."[72] He gives up easily and, if pushed, finally collapses in tears, a regular crybaby. This is called "emotional lability," "acting on sudden inclination," "variability" and "unpredictability."

These problems usually persist into adulthood.[73]

Ego Weakness, Egocentricity

Sensing his own weakness and inadequacy, highly distractible, disorganized, and poorly integrated, the MBD adolescent knows he cannot deal with the world. He feels awkward, incompetent, ill at ease, friendless, unliked, and unskilled.

His ego is either non-existent or weak. He has low self-esteem. He is afraid of being rejected by others. He cannot accept punishment, because his sense of self-worth would be undermined; he also cannot accept praise, because he does not feel that he deserves it.[74]

When the ego has disintegrated completely, the diagnosis is "identity disorder":

The essential feature is severe subjective distress regarding inability to reconcile aspects of the self into a relatively coherent and acceptable sense of self. There is uncertainty about a variety of issues relating to identity. . . . The individual experiences these conflicts as irreconcilable aspects of his or her personality and, as a result, fails to perceive himself or herself as having a coherent identity. Frequently, the disturbance is epitomized by the individual's asking the question, "Who am I?"[75]

All this leads to a panicky anxiety. The individual is emotionally labile, sensitive, vulnerable, and desirous of approval from parents, contemporaries, and authority figures. At the same time, he cannot perform at a level which will garner this approval.[76]

Fourteen million Americans are thought to suffer from clinical anxiety—almost nine percent of the population. It is described by the American Psychiatric Association as "overanxious disorder":

> The essential feature is . . . excessive worrying and fearful behavior that is not focused on a specific situation or object. . . . The child worries about future events, such as examinations, the possibility of injury, or inclusion in peer group activities. . . . An inordinate amount of time may be spent asking about the discomforts or dangers of a variety of situations.[77]

The very young child wants to solve every problem at once. He will ask his parents: "How am I ever going to make a living when I grow up?"

The ultimate outcome may be "narcissism"—exclusive focus on the self, its desires and needs. This is an increasingly common psychiatric diagnosis, especially in those who suffer from depression and inability to sustain relationships.

Some psychoanalysts claim that the roots of narcissism can be traced to "difficulties during the period from eighteen months old to three years."[78]*

---

*Magazines with names such as *Self* or *Us* are directed at this narcissistic group. The definitive studies of American narcissism are Tom Wolfe, "The 'Me' Decade and the Third Great Awakening" (*New York*, August 23, 1976), and Christopher Lasch, *The Culture of Narcissism* (New York: Warner Books, 1979).

Alienation and Emotional Immaturity

Since emotional maturation is impossible without an intellectual basis, intellectual fragmentation means emotional immaturity.

This underdeveloped emotional side is called by various names and described in various ways: "immature personality disorder," emotional "blunting," "diminished capacity for positive and negative affect," "marked impairment in the capacity to sustain lasting, close, warm, and responsible relationships with family, friends, or sexual partners," "lack of capacity to form emotional relations," "diminished capacity to experience pleasure," "lack of empathy," "withdrawn behavior," "inability to sustain affection," "poor peer relations," "no steady friends."

In the relatively normal adolescent, the typical reaction is an egocentric seeking of the limelight, insistence on being the center of attention, "clinging" to adults and others whose approval is desired. This self-centered greedy behavior marks him as immature and undeveloped, "childish."[79]

The more seriously disturbed child will be diagnosed with "reactive attachment disorder of infancy":

> The essential features . . . are signs of poor emotional development. . . . Infants with this disorder present with poorly developed social responsivity. By two months of age visual tracking of eyes and faces may not be established; the smile response and gaze reciprocity may be absent. At four to five months the infant may fail to participate in playful, simple games . . . to reach out when he or she is to be picked up. . . . At seven to eight months the infant may not yet be crawling, establishing visual or vocal communication with the caretaker, beginning to imitate the caretaker, or displaying any of the usual more subtle facial expressions of coyness, attentiveness, etc.[80]

This is readily seen to resemble the early stage of autism. And as these children grow up the autistic alienation from human contact remains—expressed in the literature as "withdrawal," "loneliness," "a sense of psychological aloneness and isolation . . . social alienation from peers and family," or simply "social incompetence." "He just doesn't relate." "He is too way out."

The teacher said he stood on the periphery of things.

I noticed that when he was four he just wouldn't look you in the eye. His nursery school teacher would grab his head to make him look at her. He seemed to be in another universe. He would tune out. The most difficult thing with him has been to get him out of the stars onto earth.

This aspect of minimal brain damage is labelled "avoidant disorder of childhood or adolescence":

The essential feature . . . is a persistent and excessive shrinking from contact with strangers of sufficient severity so as to interfere with social functioning.[81]

Even when behaving "vivaciously," these individuals are never free of tension and anxiety. They have no real sense of humor, and their "smile" is a stereotyped and frozen grin. They are never happy, never satisfied, even when successful in life.[82] The parents will say, "He can't find any joy!"

Alienation from contact with strangers may be associated with overdependence upon the immediate family—labelled "separation anxiety disorder":

The essential feature is . . . excessive anxiety on separation from major attachment figures or from home or other familiar surroundings. When separation occurs, the child may experience anxiety to the point of panic.[83]

Depression and Suicide

These cumulative disabilities, and the individual's unsuccessful fight against them, lead to depression. Today between nine and twenty-six percent of American females and from five to twelve percent of American males are suffering or have suffered from "major depression." According to the American Psychiatric Association, "there is evidence that prevalence of the disorder has increased in age cohorts that came to maturity after the Second World War."[84]

Other signs of personal distress include inability to tolerate boredome, tension, and paranoia.

These may lead to suicide:

Dear Ann Landers:
I am a twenty-two-year-old male who graduated from college in June. I have been thinking about suicide since junior high. Here is why . . . I have never experienced joy or satisfaction in anything that I've ever done. I have no real interests, no desires, and no ambition. I consider myself a total failure.

Dear Ann Landers:
I believe that I am a typical high school student. I get good grades, teachers like me, I'm happy most of the time and have never thought about killing myself. We had an assembly today on suicide prevention, and I couldn't believe it, Ann. One out of four teen-agers will attempt suicide before he or she is sixteen. Every minute of every hour a teen-ager attempts suicide. Every day, thirty-three kids will succeed. Why? Nobody knows for sure. The speaker at the assembly gave us the following . . . warning signs. . . . Dramatic change in appetite. . . . Sleeping difficulties. Some people want to sleep all the time when they're depressed, others can't sleep at all. . . . Poor performance in school. . . . Trouble concentrating; agitation; inability to sit still. . . . Constant feeling of worthlessness or self-hatred. . . .[85]

The suicide rate among late adolescents in the United States doubled between the 1960s and the 1980s; even small children are found to have suicidal ideas—thirteen percent in one group studied.[86] This is usually explained by psychiatrists and psychologists as a reaction to increased family tensions, divorce, and the like. No one has thought to inquire into the possibility that cause and effect run the other way: having a hyperactive, learning-disabled, anorexic, and suicidal child in the family might quite well contribute to family tensions and thus to an increased divorce rate.

In any case, more attention should be directed to the connection between suicidal impulses in childhood and adolescence and the burden of encephalitis-induced minimal brain damage in infancy. And, in a broader sense, the medical profession should focus on vaccine damage as a possible cause of many of the typical mental illnesses and syndromes of today's children and adolescents.

Compensating for Ego Weakness: Resisting Change

Just as the autistic must compensate in some way for his numerous disadvantages, so must the child or adolescent with minimal brain damage.

For he perceives society as, at best, unintelligible—at worst, inimical and acting against his interests.

> His world is rather disjointed, quite frightening, and at times potentially destructive . . . there is little stability in his perception of the world around him. One senses an intense struggle in his frantic efforts to identify with an environment which remains essentially hostile to him.[87]

One way to cope is by refusing to change. He tends to repeat the same behavior over and over (perseveration):

> The child is unable to shift easily from one activity to another. . . . In spelling, he may repeat the word *moon* for each of five different spelling words. In math, he may put the same answer for several different problems . . . in art, the child will tend to draw the same figure over and over again. The repetitive behavior reflects an inability to shift mentally from one frame of reference to another. The security that the child receives from a standard behavior pattern is very appealing.[88]

> *He definitely has trouble with changes. He couldn't stand sitting in a different place at the table. He was three, in a day-care situation, one day he became very violent—hitting, kicking, screaming, etc. He became a little windmill. The reason was that they had cubbyholes for the kids' things, and they covered them over with a yellow-patterned cloth. So he went crazy.*

This can become quite obsessive and is then a milder form of the autistic's adamant hostility to change:

> His parents noticed a concern with orderliness and a tendency to become upset when the pattern of things was changed . . . from the very beginning his shirt had to be tucked in in a certain way . . . his shoelaces had to be of equal length. . . . If his shirt comes out in a fight he lets himself get beaten up while he attends to tucking it in. He would become upset if he did not have the

same lunch every day; not only did the sandwich have to be the
same but he would become upset if the bread or brand of potato
chips was changed. Hal insisted on wearing the very same clothes
every day and his mother complied, washing them every night.
When his clothes wore out and had to be thrown away, or when
his mother attempted to substitute another outfit, Hal would throw
a prolonged tantrum.[89]

Resistance to change takes the form of resisting direction—
whether from parents, teachers, or other authority figures. These
children can be incredibly strong-willed and obstinate. They argue
and argue until they get their way. Sometimes stubbornness is manifested as good-natured non-compliance, "evasiveness, withdrawal,
and denial."

What Kanner said about the marginal autistic applies to them:
"These children learn while they resist being taught."[90]

But resistance is easily transformed into ordinary disobedience
and opposition, "resisting discipline," negativism, etc.[91]

"Obstinacy," "stubbornness," "negativism," and "lack of response to discipline" are given in the *Diagnostic and Statistical Manual*
as "associated features" of attention deficit disorder.[92]

Carried to an extreme, this balkiness becomes "oppositional
disorder":

> The essential feature is a pattern of disobedient, negativistic, and
> provocative opposition to authority figures. . . . The oppositional
> attitude is toward family members, particularly the parents, and
> toward teachers . . . if there is a rule, it is usually violated; if a
> suggestion is made, the individual is against it; if asked to do
> something, the individual refuses or becomes argumentative; if
> asked to refrain from an act, the child or adolescent feels obliged
> to carry it out. . . . If the individual is thwarted, temper tantrums
> are likely. These children or adolescents use negativism, stubborn-
> ness, dawdling, procrastination, and passive resistance to external
> authority. Usually the individual does not regard himself or her-
> self as "oppositional," but sees the problem as arising from other
> people, who are making unreasonable demands.[93]

This can also emerge as "bossiness" or simply as naked aggression. If not seriously impaired neurologically, these children will
assert control over their environment by "taking charge," bullying

others, and ordering them around. Expressions such as "leader, bossy, unpopular with other kids," "very demanding," "aggressive," and so on, crop up repeatedly in the discussion of learning-disabled children:

> He attempts to overcome his own insecurity by acting in a very aggressive way . . . he is an extremely dependent child who desperately tries to conceal his fears and his dependency, which are overwhelming and anxiety-arousing.[94]

> He does not play well with the neighborhood children. . . . He always wants to fight, wrestle, and poke people. . . . He is always playing he is Superman, Zorro, etc.[95]

> He's never had any close friends. . . . He likes younger children he can boss around.[96]

> *He once said, "God has the whole world, and I have only my body." He would rather be in God's place.*

At a milder level this aggressiveness can take the form of irritability ("frustration tolerance is much lowered; fits of anger are easily provoked") or moodiness. The child is happy and cooperative one minute, sullen and aggressive the next; he is easily upset over little things, and the emotional discharge is out of proportion to the situation.[97]

But open violence is never far from the surface in these children and adolescents. "Temper tantrums" of infancy and childhood become the boiling rages of adolescence. Expressions such as "aggressive," "short-fused," "short-tempered," "low boiling point," "violent behaviors," "explosive personality," are often encountered. *"The reactions of these children are often almost volcanic in their intensity."*

> Dear Ann Landers:
> I have a ten-year old daughter who is driving me insane. Any attempt to discipline her ends in screams that can be heard by the neighbors. I am not talking about spankings. I mean being sent to her room.
> Last week "Debbie" became so upset she vomited. The child cried so hard she had bright red circles around her eyes, and her hair was wringing wet. . . . Please help me before I do something terrible to this child.[98]

He keeps more to himself than ever before . . . he is not violent,
but when he is it is like a volcano exploding. He feels unloved,
angry at the doctor for giving him medicine . . . blames us, won't
do his chores.[99]

Dear Ann Landers:
    I heard something today that made my hair stand on end . . .
it is a symptom of a problem that warrants deep concern.
    Last October, the teacher of a fourth-grade class asked her stu-
dents to write a short essay on what they would like to do most
to celebrate Halloween. Eighty percent of her nine-year-olds
expressed the wish to "kill somebody."
    Where do children get such ideas? . . . What are we going to
do about this love of violence among the young? Frankly, it scares
me to death. . . .[100]

Violence may be manifested as "destructiveness or mutilation,
especially of others (persons or property)," arson, or cruelty to
animals.[101]

Most recently he has shown a fascination for knives and razor
blades, and "in jest" his parents reported he "playfully" held a
knife to his younger brother's throat, daring him to move.[102]

A favorite game involved building toy houses and then burning
them down. In addition, on a number of occasions he killed animals for pleasure. . . .[103]

The initial consultation was on an "emergency" basis. The boy
[age 7½] had twice set fire to the family's living-room furniture
within the previous week, and on both occasions the fire department had to be called . . . his mother stated that for two years
. . . he had been playing more or less compulsively with
matches. . . .[104]

*He had a little arson period, and we had the police here. He was
doing matches in the woods. He would go to town and buy aerosol
bottles and set them on fire. He did this once in the woods, and the
police came.*

The aggression engendered by frustration may be directed
against the very authority figures whose approval is being sought:

He appeared to resent authority and had to be supervised rather
closely. . . . He sought adult attention and preferred this on a one-
to-one basis.[105]

The most obvious finding on the psychological examination was the boiling hostility and undisguised rage Sean experiences, which is primarily directed toward his father.[106]

He was "almost kicked out of kindergarten" and had been maintaining a marginal adjustment to authority every since . . . as a brilliant adolescent he baited his teachers, thought circles around many of them, and vented his proficient sarcasm on the slower ones; not surprisingly he was very unpopular with them.[107]

The aggression can also be self-directed:

The boy had a surprising amount of insight: he saw himself as going to prison if he didn't "straighten out" and was at a loss to understand what was causing him to behave in a self-injurious manner.[108]

Relationships tend to be sado-masochistic, and he is primarily concerned about being hurt.[109]

Awareness of this potential in the child increases his ever-present anxiety about losing control:

He is very fearful that his aggression will get him into trouble and that it will cause him to either hurt others or that his own aggression will even hurt himself. He generally feels that he has to be the one to try and control his own aggression because he cannot rely on his own parents. . . . However, he finds it difficult to be his own control at this time because he has not been able to master the environment and so he is quite unadult in knowing how to take care of himself . . . a reflection of his anxiety and his guilt about his lack of impulse control.[110]

Compensating for Ego Weakness: Hypersexuality

Precocious sexuality is another way of coping with ego weakness and feelings of inadequacy, and, in an exaggerated form, is commonly encountered among the minimally brain damaged.*

---

*The American Psychiatric Association adds precocious sexuality to its definition only when minimal brain damage has passed into "conduct disorder" (see Chapter V). But there is obviously no firm line of demarcation.

As with the predisposition to violence, hypersexuality represents both an inherent urge rooted in neurologic weakness and a set of reactions to compensate for this weakness.

The 1960s "sexual revolution" can be seen in part as the manifestation of premature sexuality in a whole vaccinated generation, with the minimally brain-damaged component pioneering this new voyage of discovery.

The emotional blunting of these individuals contributes in two ways to an exaggerated sex life. Lack of capacity for genuine emotion generates the need for overindulgence in a purely sexual form of relating. And the resulting hypersexuality is not limited by any emotional ties.

When hypersexuality is combined with the urge to violence, the result is sexual aggressiveness, rape, and other sexual crimes. One hyperactive adolescent who murdered his middle-aged cousin because she nagged him about his dirty shirt revealed under questioning

> . . . the presence of overpowering ruminations and impulses to destroy property and to kill, both present since the age of thirteen. For two years prior to the crime, he had prowled the streets with a concealed weapon, window-peeping and engaging in fantasies of murder and rape. He also revealed that twice he had been unable to control himself and had viciously attacked women. His experience of sexual and aggressive drives was raw and primitive. He was unable to conceptualize sexuality or experience sexual pleasure except in terms of his fantasies of rape, murder, and violence. He spoke of sexual curiosity about his cousin, and the fact that he had used the knife in the murder to attack her genitals. At times his fantasy would be so vivid as to cause perceptual disturbance to near hallucination.[11]

Another adolescent, who shot and killed his thirteen-year-old sister revealed the following:

> Several years earlier he had impulsively attempted to rape his sister after accidentally viewing her undressing in her room. . . . A diagnosis of schizoid personality was supported by psychological testing, and it was felt that the patient experienced transient psychotic episodes at moments of overwhelming anxiety, usually in response to the pressure of his sexual and aggressive impulses

. . . and anxiety over intense hostile, aggressive, and sexual fantasies. He was preoccupied with fantasies of rape and murder, usually directed toward his sister, who reminded him of his mother. He fantasized the murder of his mother and five sisters, explaining that he could then live alone and peacefully with his father.[112]

At a lesser level, this violence with sexual overtones spills over into normal boy-girl relations in the form of physical abuse (usually by the male). A 1986 study of seventeen- and eighteen-year-old California high-school students found that one in four had been physically slapped, beaten, or subjected to some other violence. One girl said of her boyfriend, "He was real insecure. I think that was part of the reason. It was like, 'If I can't have you, nobody else can.'"[113]

Dating violence among college students is also well documented. A 1982 study at Oregon State University, covering fifteen- to eighteen-year-olds found that one in eight had encountered violence while dating. And when the threat of violence was counted, the figure rose to one in three. Sociologists have called this "one of the hidden social issues of the 1980s."[114]

This confirms the statement made by a speaker at the 1978 World Congress on Biological Psychiatry: "Pathological aggression in children, because of its high incidence and chronicity, the lack of effective therapy, and its widespread adverse effects on society, remains probably the main problem in child psychiatry and is likely to increase."[115]

Now that the first post-encephalitic generation has grown to adulthood and started to raise families, the combination of hypersexuality, low frustration tolerance, and tendency to violence is bearing fruit in a radically higher incidence of physical and sexual abuse of children, even small babies.

However, as in the autistic, sexuality can also be underdeveloped. This is called "avoidant disorder" where "inhibition of normal psychosexual activity may be noted."[116]

The unintegrated sexuality of the minimally brain damaged can also take the form of "gender identity disorders," meaning confused sexual identity, homosexuality, and bisexuality:

> The essential features of this disorder are persistent and intense distress in a child about his or her assigned sex and the desire to be, or insistence that he or she is, of the other sex. . . . In addition, in a girl there is either persistent marked aversion to normative feminine clothing and insistence on wearing stereotypic masculine clothing, or persistent repudiation of her female anatomic characteristics. . . . Girls with this disorder regularly have male companions and an avid interest in sports and rough-and-tumble play; they show no interest in dolls or playing "house" (unless they play the father or another male role). . . . Boys with this disorder usually are preoccupied with female stereotypic activities.[117]

Of course, the sexual revolution of the past three decades has seen the emergence of homosexuality as a major social and political influence in American life.

Seeking Structure: Music

Less destructive ways of compensating for ego weakness are available to the MBD adolescent. A positive approach is to impose structure from the outside. Thus, an eight-year-old boy diagnosed with "moderately severe classic hyperactivity" benefited greatly when a precise program was designed for him:

> With the boy's unwilling assistance, eight major household activities were decided upon. . . . Each of these activities was rewarded with a certain number of "points" per performance per day. . . . The progression in points earned per week over a four-week period is indicative of the effectiveness of the scheme: 140, 190, 245, 350 [out of possible total of 390].[118]

The Northern Virginia Regional Juvenile Correction Home disciplines its young inmates in the same way. Each is assigned a "demeanor level," numbered from 1 to 3 and depicted on a gold paper card. Merits are awarded daily for good conduct, allowing the youth to progress from one "demeanor level" to the next. This confers the right to later bedtime curfews and more recreational freedom. By the same token, misbehavior results in merit loss, which can lead to room restriction for up to three days.[119]

Music is an important source of structure. Like the autistic, children with minimal brain damage have an inordinate fondness for music, especially music with a pronounced beat; it provides an organizational principle within which their diffuse and random sensory strivings can find a home.

> *He listens to the record-player continuously. And even when the music is not playing, he claps his hands constantly and rocks continuously. He actually does it more when there is no music.*

That the minimally brain-damaged generation has a particular passion for music is seen in the huge upsurge of musical activities and involvement that started in the late 1950s. As already mentioned in connection with autism, the post-encephalitic generation is organically linked to the rock group.

> Children are born anarchists. Babies reign in the solitary kingdom of ego, unable to distinguish the "I wanna" of whim from the "I gotta" of need. In an age of instant gratification and infant attention span, the popular arts have played to this childish impulse. Heavy-metal rock beats out its primal demands like a child pulling a high-chair tantrum.[120]

Minimal Brain Damage and Autism

The past few years have brought dawning recognition that autism and minimal brain damage are linked and reflect "subclinical damage" to the brain, giving rise to "psychological" symptoms.[121]

Rimland in 1964 called attention to the parallels between autism and the "brain-injured" children described by researchers in the 1930s and 1940s.[122]

Brain injury is known to be caused by such factors as fetal alcohol syndrome, head wounds, chronic lead poisoning, whooping cough, oxygen deprivation during birth, meningitis, and other conditions. The role of encephalitis due to vaccination, however, has not been mentioned.

Research projects in the late 1970s found similarity, and overlap in the biochemical markers of autism and hyperactivity.[123] In 1981 Deborah Fejn noted overlap in the symptoms of "autism and other severe developmental disabilities."[124] And a 1983 project found that retarded, autistic, hyperactive, and learning-disabled children shared a set of minor physical abnormalities (large head circumference, malformed ears, gaps between the toes, and some others).[125]

William and Marian DeMyer, of the University of Indiana Medical Center, stated in 1984 that autism "belongs to a continuum of developmental brain disorders variously classified as mental retardation, cerebral palsy, and learning disabilities, and would appear to share the same causes. . . . None of the EEGs, CT scans, or physical findings . . . for autism can reliably distinguish it from other developmental brain disorders."[126]

In 1985 Victoria Shea and Gary Mesibov of the University of North Carolina again called attention to the overlap between the two conditions:

> Little has been written about the relationship of autism to the developmental disorder labelled learning disability (LD). At first autism and LD may appear to have few characteristics in common. . . . We propose that these continua have a significant amount of overlap in the area of severe LD and higher-level autism. . . . It . . . appears to us that the continua of LD and autism overlap on the dimensions of intelligence level, unevenness of developmental rate, language difficulties, deviant social and interpersonal skills, and cognitive disorganization.[127]

But a lengthy 1987 review article on autism by Michael Rutter and Eric Schopler, two of the major authorities in the field, discussed its relationship to mental retardation, schizophrenia, "disintegrative psychosis," and "severe developmental disorders of receptive language" without mentioning minimal brain damage.[128]

In any case, recognition of the possible neurologic origins of autism and minimal brain damage merely raises new, and equally insoluble, questions. What can be the source of so much neurologic damage? What is preventing ten or fifteen percent of American schoolchildren from learning how to read? As Frank Elliott queried, "What bends the twig in the first place?"[129]

Chapter II Notes

1. Laufer, M.W. and Denhoff, E., 1957, 463.
2. Wender, Paul H., 1971, 31. Rutter, M., 1977, 1.
3. Shaywitz, Sally E. and Bennett A., 1984, 429.
4. Cowart, V.S., 1988(b), 2647.
5. American Psychiatric Association, 1980, 42; 1987, 51. Gillberg, C. et al., 1983, 245. Millichap, J.G., 1976, 61.
6. U.S. Dept. of Health and Human Services, 1984. Cowart, V.S., 1988(b), 2647.
7. Long, Kathleen et al., 1984, 378.
8. U.S. Department of Health and Human Services, 1984, 2.
9. Wender, Paul H., 1971, 212. Millichap, J.G., 1976, 61.
10. Clements, S.D. and Peters, J.D., 1981, 189.
11. Wender, P. H., 1971, 211. 11. Freeman, S. W., 1974, 11.
12. American Psychiatric Association, 1980, 42.
13. *J. Autism* 5:2 (1975), 185. Rutter, M. *et al.*, 1975, 11.
14. American Psychiatric Association, 1980, 37, 43.
15. Lewis, D.O., 1981, 45, 61. Green, J.B. and Mercille, R.A., 1984, 105. Stores, G. *et al.*, 1978.
16. Elliott, Frank A., 1982, 682.
17. Laufer, M.W. and Denhoff, E., 1957, 467.
18. Freeman, S.W., 1974, 12. Johnson, D. and L., 1978, 11.
19. *The Washington Post*, Health, June 16, 1987, 5; June 6, 1988, A-3.
20. Kaplan, Bonnie J. *et al.*, 1987(a).
21. Laufer, M.W. and Denhoff, E., 1957, 464.
22. *Loc. cit.* Kaplan, Bonnie J. *et al.*, 1987(a).
23. Freeman, Frank A., 1974, 5.
24. *The Washington Post*, Health, Sept. 23, 1986, 11. Thorpy, M.J. and Glovinsky, P.B., 1987, 623. Mitler, M.M. *et al.*, 1987, 593.
25. Wender, Paul H., 1971, 204–205. Elliott, E.A., 1982, 684. Fritz, G.K. *et al.*, 1982, 286.
26. *The Washington Post*, September 2, 1987: Ann Landers. Fritz, G.K. *et al.*, 1982, 283.
27. Freeman, S.W., 1974, 4–5. Witt, E.D., *et al.*, 1985.
28. Halmi, Katherine A., 1982, 371. Johnson, C. *et al.*, 1984, 247.
29. American Psychiatric Association, 1987, 66,68. Halmi, K., 1982, 372. *The New York Times*, April 25, 1986.
30. Kaplan, Bonnie *et al.*, 1987(b), 306.
31. Leviton, Alan, 1986, 372. Also Egger, J. *et al.*, 1985; Bille, Bo, 1962; Kandt, R.S., 1984; O'Brien, J., 1982.

32. Guilleminault, C., 1987, 613. Bille, Bo, 1962.
33. Clements, Sam D. and Peters, John E., 1981, 187.
34. Freeman, S.W., 1974, 10.
35. Geschwind, Norman, 1982, 16.
36. Easson, William M., 1979, 473.
37. Wender, Paul H. 1971, 211.
38. American Psychiatric Association, 1980, 62.
39. *Ibid.*, 1987, 45, 47.
40. Silva, Phil A. *et al.*, 1987, 638.
41. Elliott, Frank A. 1982, 683–684.
42. Kaplan, Bonnie *et al.*, 1987(b), 305.
43. Godfrey, S., 1985, 997.
44. Sadler, John E., 1982, 334. Unpublished data from National Center for Health Statistics and National Heart, Lung, and Blood Institute, Washington, D.C.
45. Tudor-Hart, Julian, 1986, 80.
46. Unpublished data from National Center for Health Statistics and National Heart, Lung, and Blood Institute, Washington, D.C.
47. Benatar, Solomon, 1986, 423ff.
48. Unpublished data from National Center for Health Statistics and National Heart, Lung, and Blood Institute, Washington, D.C.
49. Plaut, Thomas, 1984, 17.
50. Geschwind, N., 1982, 18.
51. Bettelheim, B., 1960.
52. Sadler, John E., 1982, 333, 337.
53. Plaut, T.F., 1984, 15.
54. Sargent, John *et al.*, 1984, 243.
55. Fritz, G.K., 1982, 286.
56. Friend, Maurice R., 1956, 518.
57. *Loc. cit.*
58. Robison, Caroline, 1960.
59. Geschwind, Norman, 1982, 18.
60. Clements, S.D. and Peters, J.E., 1981, 183.
61. Elliott, Frank, 1986, 227.
62. Easson, William M., 1979, 471.
63. Aman, Michael, 1984, 42.
64. Levine, Melvin D. *et al.*,, 1984, 353.
65. Easson, William M., 1979, 471.
66. *Ibid.*, 472.
67. *Ibid.*, 471. Clements, S.D. and Peters, J.E., 1981, 185.
68. Easson, William M., 1979, 472.

69. *Ibid.*, 473.
70. Wender, Paul H., 1971, 198.
71. Freeman, S.W., 1974, 14.
72. Wender, Paul H., 1971, 205.
73. Wood, David R. *et al.*, 1976, 1453, 1458.
74. Wender, Paul H., 1971, 221.
75. American Psychiatric Association, 1980, 65.
76. Wender, Paul A., 1971, 208.
77. American Psychiatric Association, 1980, 55.
78. *The New York Times*, November 1, 1988, C-16.
79. Easson, William M., 1979, 474. Freeman, S.W., 1974, 11.
80. American Psychiatric Association, 1980, 57.
81. *Ibid.*, 53–54.
82. Kahn, E. and Kohn, L.H., 1934, 753.
83. American Psychiatric Association, 1980, 50.
84. American Psychiatric Association, 1987, 229. Lewis, D.O., 1981, 22. Milman, Doris H., 1979, 377.
85. *The Washington Post*, September 17, 1988, C-9: Ann Landers; September 24, 1988, C-4: Ann Landers.
86. Levine, M.D. and Zallen, B.D., 1984, 366. Check, W.A., 1985, 727. 92.
87. Wender, Paul H., 1971, 222.
88. Freeman, S.W., 1974, 12–13.
89. Wender, Paul H., 1971, 221.
90. Kanner, Leo, 1951, 23.
91. Freeman, S.W., 1974, 5.
92. American Psychiatric Association, 1980, 42.
93. *Ibid.*, 63–64.
94. Wender, Paul H., 1971, 208.
95. *Ibid.*, 198.
96. *Ibid.*, 210.
97. Freeman, S.W., 1974, 12.
98. *The Washington Post*, August 3, 87: Ann Landers.
99. Wender, Paul H., 1971, 219.
100. *The Washington Post*, January 6, 1988: Ann Landers.
101. Fineman, Kenneth R., 1980, 483.
102. Wender, Paul H., 1971, 207.
103. Wood, David R. *et al.*, 1976, 1457.
104. Wender, Paul H., 1971, 204.
105. *Ibid.*, 208.
106. *Ibid.*, 207.

107. *Ibid.*, 214.
108. *Ibid.*, 208.
109. *Ibid.*, 223.
110. *Loc. cit.*
111. Woods, Sherwyn M., 1961, 1349.
112. *Ibid.*, 1350.
113. *The San Francisco Examiner*, January 14, 1986, 16.
114. *Loc. cit.*
115. Simeon, J., 1979, 1223.
116. American Psychiatric Association, 1980, 54.
117. *Ibid.*, 1987, 71.
118. Wender, Paul H., 1971, 219.
119. *The Washington Post*, September 5, 1988, B-11.
120. *Time*, August 1, 1988, 53.
121. Rutter, M., 1982, 31.
122. Rimland, B., 1964, 60.
123. Rutter, M., 1982, 30.
124. Fejn, Deborah *et al.*, 1981, 312.
125. Firestone, P. and Peters, S., 1983, 422.
126. DeMyer, W. and M., 1984, 139, 145.
127. Shea, V. and Mesibov, G.B., 1985, 425, 427.
128. Rutter, M. and Schopler, E., 1987.
129. Elliott, Frank, 1986, 231.

III

The Post-Encephalitic Syndrome

What bends the twig is an attack of encephalitis in infancy—caused in most cases by a routine vaccination.

The symptomatic and pathological parallels between autism and minimal brain damage reflect their common origin in an attack of clinical or subclinical encephalitis.

Although a few perspicacious researchers have noted the parallels between autism and minimal brain damage, no one has called attention to their common origin in encephalitis.

This is, at first glance, a startling omission, since encephalitis was no mystery to American physicians of the 1920s and 1930s. Many had treated it, and the post-encephalitic syndrome was often discussed in the literature.

Kanner was mistaken in thinking that autism differed "markedly and uniquely from anything reported so far. . . ." While it was much less common in 1943 than it would later become, cases could still have been found in the insane asylums and reform schools, where they were labelled "post-encephalitic syndrome."

He may be excused for his error. He was not a neurologist but a psychiatrist. And because the initial descriptions of autism were so one-sided, focusing exclusively on the disorder's supposedly "emotional" aspects, the medical profession in the 1940s started out on the wrong foot. Psychiatrists were not willing later to relinquish control of a condition yielding so many clockable hours of patient time.

The neurologic origins of autism remained in obscurity for

years, and the "refrigerator mother" theory has had a long run.

But the more comprehensive picture which subsequently emerged should have put the profession on notice that autism was merely a new manifestation of a familiar condition—the post-encephalitic syndrome.

And when the blatantly and transparently neurologic dimensions of autism and minimal brain damage came to professional attention in the 1960s and 1970s—the tendency to seizures, mental retardation, cerebral palsy, and the like—which even the most Freudian of psychoanalysts could not in good conscience attribute to "emotional" impairment, mental health professionals should immediately have appreciated the tie with encephalitis.

Furthermore, it had long been known that a variety of encephalitis was caused by vaccination. So, one would think, the causal connection was evident.

But this is precisely why physicians shied away from the topic! Any suggestion of encephalitis ineluctably implicated the burgeoning vaccination programs. Since no one wanted to impugn these programs, encephalitis was never discussed openly and fully. While some more audacious souls nibbled around the edges of this taboo subject, no one examined it systematically.

In this chapter we show that autism and minimal brain damage are manifestations of the post-encephalitic syndrome. And the most probable cause of a widespread epidemic of encephalitis is the childhood vaccination program.

Encephalitis in the Twentieth Century

Physicians have always known that encephalitis, or inflammation of the brain (also called "encephalopathy"), can be caused by traumatic injury to the head, a severe burn, infectious illnesses such as measles, mumps, German measles, chicken pox, or whooping cough, and—last but not least—the vaccines against these same diseases: "post-vaccinal encephalitis."[1]*

---

*Strictly speaking, "encephalitis" ("brain inflammation") is a subclass of the disease category, "encephalopathy" ("brain disease"). But

An infectious variety of encephalitis, marked by extreme lethargy and sleepiness in the acute phase, erupted in epidemic form during the last years of World War I. It appeared first in China and then spread to Rumania, France, Germany, and Austria where Constantine von Economo published a comprehensive description of it.[2] Thereafter the disease was called *encephalitis lethargica* or "Von Economo's encephalitis."

Outbreaks continued after the war, with cases being found in most countries of the world; more than 500,000 deaths, and a million cases of severe neurologic impairment, were attributed to epidemic encephalitis between 1919 and 1928. It affected males more often than females, by a ratio of three to two.

Recent research concludes that this epidemic was a late manifestation of the post-World War I influenza outbreaks, and that both were due to the "swine 'flu" virus.[3]

The overall magnitude of this epidemic in the United States may be judged by the fact between 1917 and 1934, 10,000 cases occurred in Massachusetts alone. The most newsworthy outbreaks were in St. Louis in the summers of 1933 and 1937.[4]

Sporadic cases of epidemic encephalitis continue to be reported in Western countries to this day.[5]

A remarkable feature of encephalitis—whether of epidemic origin or due to an infectious disease, traumatic injury, or vaccination—is the multifarious diversity of its physical, neurologic, mental, and emotional symptoms. "Since any portion of the nervous system may be affected," notes H.H. Merritt, emeritus professor of neurology at Columbia University, "variable clinical syndromes may occur . . . meningeal, encephalitic, brain-stem, spinal cord, and neuritic."[6]

This is true, in particular, of encephalitis following whooping cough. Josephine B. Neal, also a professor of neurology at Columbia University, wrote in 1942 that pertussis encephalitis in early *childhood was likely to leave "very crippling residuals with motor*

---

physicians do not make a systematic distinction between these concepts (see, for example, John H. Menkes, 1980, 395), and in the following pages they are used as synonyms.

as well as personality handicaps . . . often there have been small hem-
orrhages in the brain. . . . However . . . there are sometimes inflammatory processes instead . . . . In still other instances the pathology is
not clearly accounted for at all. . . . *It is, therefore, possible to get
almost every possible motor, intellectual, epiliptoid and personality
deviation and combinations of them"* [emphasis added].[7]

Anna Lisa Annell, a Swedish researcher who in 1953 wrote a
major work on whooping cough, also stressed the multiformity of
the pertussis encephalitis syndrome: "The important fact . . . is that
pertussis may be associated with the most varying kinds of cerebral
complications and that they do not appear to be confined to any particular region but may be cortical, subcortical, or peripheral."[8]

Encephalitis after vaccination was known to produce the same
range of disabilities and impairments. "Atypical" cases could "mimic"
meningitis, viral encephalitis, or poliomyelitis, indeed, according
to H.H. Merritt, "practically all of the acute diseases of the nervous
system."[9]

Of all the childhood vaccines in use today probably the one
against whooping cough (pertussis) is the most dangerous. It is a
"whole cell" vaccine, meaning that it is made from the same bac-
terium (*Bordetella pertussis*) that causes the disease.[10] And this
microbe has been qualified by Margaret Pittman, a prominent U.S.
pertussis vaccine researcher, as "unique among infectious bacteria
in its marked ability to modify biological responses."[11]

If whooping cough can "modify biological responses" in this
polyvalent way, the pertussis vaccine can do the same.

That pertussis vaccine reactions are indeed varied and numerous is borne out, for example, by the 1986 package insert for the
Connaught Laboratories product:

> Adverse reactions which may be local and include pain,
> erythema, heat, edema, and induration . . . are common. . . .
> Some data suggest that febrile reactions are more likely to occur
> in those who have experienced such responses after prior
> doses. . . . Sterile abscesses at the site of injection have been
> reported. . . . Mild systemic reactions, such as fever, drowsiness,
> fretfulness, and anorexia occur quite frequently. . . . Rash, aller-
> gic reactions, and respiratory difficulties, including apnea [breath
> holding], have been observed. Moderate to severe systemic

events, such as fever of 40.5 C. (105 F.) or higher, persistent, inconsolable crying lasting three hours or more, unusual high-pitched screaming, collapse, or convulsions occur relatively infrequently. More severe neurologic complications, such as a prolonged convulsion *or an encephalopathy, occasionally fatal*, have been reported. . . . Rarely, an anaphylactic reaction (i.e., hives, swelling of the mouth, difficulty breathing, hypotension, or shock) has been reported. . . . *Sudden infant death syndrome (SIDS) has occurred in infants following administration of DPT.* . . . Onset of infantile spasms has occurred in infants who have recently received DPT or DT. . . . [emphasis added][12]

Acute Reactions in Encephalitis and after Vaccination

DPT: A Shot in the Dark described the typical acute reactions to DPT vaccination: high fever, excessive sleepiness, otitis, diarrhea and other gastrointestinal symptoms, vomiting, cough, high-pitched screaming and persistent crying, collapse (fainting), shock, seizures, convulsions, infantile spasms, loss of muscle control, headaches, breathing difficulties, and allergies.[13]

These manifestations of a vaccination reaction are identical to the symptoms of acute encephalitis from any other cause.

A raging fever is typical of the vaccine reaction. Parents report temperatures as high as 105 or 106 degrees.[14]

Sleepiness following upon vaccination is described by the mother of a child who is now sixteen years old, hyperactive, and with severe attention span difficulties:

Within one hour of the shot she went to sleep for twenty-four hours, and I couldn't waken her at all. I was so inexperienced at that time that it's hard to remember. All I know is that she acted very strangely and had a strange cry. Then she passed out. That was the beginning of hundreds of times of passing out. When she would get white and pass out, she would come to in seconds, but often she would just pass out again. . . . When she passed out for twenty-four hours after the shot, we could not wake her no matter what we did. She would not wake when her diaper was changed. She would not wake when you flicked her feet or tried to feed her. We took her to the hospital, and they told us we were overanxious parents, and to take our well child home. She was coming out of a deep sleep at the time.

Later the vaccine-damaged child may have chronic sleep disturbances—sometimes accompanied by night terrors.[15]

*At four months what brought us into her room was her scream. It
sounded like something was attacking her. But we couldn't arouse
her from the scream. It was like she was fighting it. We kept calling
her name, and then she suddenly stopped and turned white and blue,
chalky looking. We thought she was in the throes of Sudden Infant
Death Syndrome.*

This child is now learning-disabled.

Excessive sleepiness was, of course, the hallmark of the aptly
named *encephalitis lethargica.*

In almost all cases there was disturbance of the normal sleep
rhythm. Some would fall asleep in the daytime, standing up, in
school or on the street; one would fall asleep even when a plate
of ice cream was set before him, and sleepiness in a boy can go
no further than that.[16]

After recovery, the encephalitic patient might have a disturbed
sleep pattern. "These boys wanted to turn night into day. . . ."[17]

F.B., a boy, aged eleven years, entered the clinic November 12,
1923, on account of weakness. In December, 1919, he had a mild
attack of encephalitis. About four days later his habits of sleep
were noticeably changed. For two years he did not sleep at night
but remained awake, very active, pulling the bed to pieces, noisy,
yelling, talking, and running about the room. Toward morning he
became quiet and slept during the day in two or three hour
periods, waking and crying between times.[18]

There is in the school record that "in kindergarten Eva spent most
of her time sleeping," that in the first grade "it was impossible to
keep her awake," and when the teacher made her stand by a win-
dow to keep awake, "Eva fell asleep in that position."[19]

Severe headache was a another prominent symptom of epidemic
encephalitis. It could appear and reappear sporadically throughout the
whole course of the disease, while a tendency to recurrent migraine
and other kinds of headache continued into later life.

Headache is not given in the medical literature as an adverse
reaction to vaccination, but the two-month or four-month-old baby,

after all, cannot communicate this to his parents. Two California pediatricians in 1979 reported on "a bulging fontanelle associated with increased intracranial pressure" within twenty-four hours of a DPT shot. The baby was "irritable."[20] One interviewed mother describes her baby's reaction to the second DPT shot:

> *She got limp, her pupils dilated, and she couldn't eat or respond. I called another doctor, and he said that Jeanne's mole, the mole in her head, was protruding. I hadn't noticed it, but the doctor said to take her to the hospital immediately.*

An inflammation which causes the brain to swell in this way must cause a headache. Furthermore, the "high-pitched screaming" and "persistent crying" which are so common with vaccine reactions, as well as the fact that babies often pick at their ears, clearly indicates a headache (as well as incipient otitis).[21]

> *Another thing he was doing was to pound his head on the wall or on the floor. He wouldn't tell me why he was doing it, but it looks like it might have been a headache. Sometimes he still bangs on his head with his hands. I ask him why he does it, and he says it feels funny. When he was four and doing this, either he didn't know why he was doing it, or he didn't have the words to describe it.*

Diarrhea, vomiting, flatulence, gastroenteritis, stomach aches, enuresis, constipation, loss of sphincter control, etc. are all found in encephalitis and are frequently reported after the DPT shot.[22]

> *After she came out of the sleep she became very ill with diarrhea and vomiting. She had rarely vomited, and I would call this projectile vomiting that she did after she came to.*

> *After the fifth shot Gary lost control of his bowels and urine. He had been totally trained since the age of three, but now he was urinating and having bowel movements in his pants, and his bowels were very loose. He was very upset and frustrated; he told me he couldn't tell when he had to go to the bathroom. He is six now and still can't control his bowels or urine very well—he just doesn't know when he has to go.*

The "opisthotonic posturing" (back-arching) often noted in babies reacting to the DPT shot is probably a reaction to stomach pain. Ashley Harris, for instance, who is now autistic, would "arch his back and scream for hours."

Alberto Garcia received the MMR shot at fifteen months and the next day had a temperature of 104 together with a profuse soapy yellow-green diarrhea seventeen times per day which was diagnosed as salmonella infection; within a month he had stopped speaking, and then symptoms of autism developed.

Melvin Ellis reacted to both the first and the fourth shots with a severe gastroenteritis; the second time (eighteen months) he had to be hospitalized; his diagnosis today is "autistic-like."

Rosanna Hammond was born in 1960 and is diagnosed today as "profoundly retarded." Her mother recalls that the most striking symptom after her vaccination was intractable constipation.

Ashley Harris "has never had a normal bowel movement; he has very small movements about every half hour (in his pants)."

A commonly recorded feature of the acute stage of epidemic encephalitis was involvement of the respiratory system: spasmodic cough, rapid breathing, slow breathing, labored breathing, failure to breathe, respiratory tics, etc.[23]

> Most frequently the patient begins to breathe more and more rapidly and deeply until after a few minutes respiration has become very violent, the mouth is widely opened, and all the accessory muscles are employed, so that the patient is the picture of distress. . . . After minutes or a few hours, the disturbance slowly subsides . . . prolonged apnea [breath holding] may follow the attack of such a degree as to cause cyanosis and even convulsions. Less commonly there are . . . alternating attacks of deep and shallow breathing, sighing, yawning, sniffing, coughing, spitting, breath-holding spells, and innumerable other variations. . . .[24]

DPT: a Shot in the Dark discussed breathing disorders (specifically apnea attacks) following vaccination, suggesting that they cause sudden infant death (SIDS). At the time this symptom was not included in accounts of adverse reactions. The case of Harvey Jackson, Jr., reported in Chapter I is evidence of this connection, and the accuracy of this insight is confirmed by the 1986 addition of "respiratory difficulties, including apnea" and "sudden infant death syndrome" to the Connaught Laboratories package insert for its DPT vaccine.[25]

This conclusion, however, while recognized by vaccine manufacturers, is still rejected by the organizations whose function is to soften the impact of sudden infant death and justify it to American mothers. They ignore the possibility of a connection between SIDS and encephalitis from vaccination:

> Dear Ann Landers:
> Eight weeks ago we gave our baby his last feeding for the night, kissed him tenderly and put him to bed.
> The next morning we found him lifeless in his cradle, a victim of sudden infant death syndrome.
> I'm writing this letter to heighten public awareness of a syndrome that tragically kills thousands of babies (one in 500) each year.
> SIDS victims are seemingly healthy, usually between one week and six months old. The death is completely unexpected and for the most part unexplained.
> After our son died we received tremendous support and important information from the American SIDS Institute. *We learned that our son's death was caused by a specific disease that is unpreventable because there are no symptoms.* [emphasis added]
> Knowing this relieved us of the guilt that so many SIDS parents suffer—the nagging feeling that we might have done something to prevent our son's death.
> The American SIDS Institute is dedicated to the prevention of sudden infant death syndrome through research, education, and health care. . . .
>
> One Who Lived Through It
>
> Dear One:
> Thanks for mentioning this fine organization.
> I've mentioned it before. It continues to provide help for those who suffer this tragic loss.[26]

If this fine organization would cut back on its public relations budget and use the funds to study the tie between vaccination and the DPT shot, it might come to realize that SIDS is not due to a "specific disease that is unpreventable." It just might uncover cases like that of Harvey Jackson, Jr., and others whose breathing was affected by the DPT shot.

Her temperature went up to 102 again. She would turn blue. She would get so still that you couldn't even tell she was breathing. I know at times she definitely stopped breathing because we couldn't get a pulse on her or a breath out of her. We would shake her, and she would start breathing again.

The breathing problems of epidemic encephalitis—disorders of respiratory rhythm, breath-holding, and others—also plagued the recovered patient and were labelled "postencephalitic respiratory syndrome."

Four months later she began to have a dry cough, which shortly became continuous, so that it interfered with eating and talking. Almost every expiration was replaced by a cough. A little later she began to have spells of breath-holding. Then attacks developed during which she would jump out of bed, cross her arms with her hands on her shoulders, bend forward, and breathe forcibly and whimper as if in distress, then straighten up and hold her breath for a while.[27]

This same chronic condition is sometimes found in vaccine-damaged children.

What he had starting at 6½ months for at least a year and a half is that he would hold his breath—at least once a day—turn blue, pass out, and have what looked like a convulsion. It was exactly at 6½ months.

As noted in Chapter II, breathing difficulties due to vaccination are likely to be at the root of the steadily increasing incidence of childhood asthma and childhood asthma deaths in the United States.

Anorexia and Bulimia

In the past, recovered encephalitis patients often manifested appetite disturbances. Sometimes they had anorexia. They stopped eating, and ultimately died of "cachexia."[28] More common, however, was bulimia (morbid hunger).

Great increases in weight, leading to obesity, were noted, indicating derangement of the pituitary gland, hypothalamus, endocrine system, or other mechanism regulating weight gain. This was called "postencephalitic obesity" or "pathological obesity."[29]

S.T. was quite healthy until an acute attack of encephalitis in April, 1911. She was somnolent for almost a month. . . . In the next few months she developed a large appetite and a consuming thirst. She gained almost thirty pounds within two months. The polydipsia and polyuria [excessive drinking and urination] lasted only about six weeks, but the obesity persisted.[30]

In Massachusetts a 1937 report on 266 patients with epidemic encephalitis found that thirty had increased appetite, with twenty-four becoming "obese," while twenty had "marked loss of weight."[31]

These patients were also accused of having "food fads"—particular attraction or aversion to one or another article of diet.

Appetite disturbances are also found after the DPT shot:

About his eating, before the second DPT shot he was eating well. After the shot he wouldn't eat anything. It was months before I could get him to eat anything except milk and juices.

After his fourth shot he didn't seem to want to eat much. He would drink a lot but was really picky about his food.

"Post-encephalitic obesity" is also seen after vaccine damage.

After all of Sharon's convulsions, she started gaining a lot of weight. The doctors have found that her thyroid gland is almost destroyed.

Millions of Americans today are overweight to the point of obesity. Often this has little to do with the volume of food intake. How much can be ascribed to a post-encephalitic state?

Dear Ann Landers:

I am sick and tired of my friends being fat and getting fatter.

Last night another pal called me all excited to say she is on a diet and has lost six pounds. Then later in the conversation, she said, "I've gained thirty pounds since I last saw you." I was speechless.

This stunning girl is only 5'1". She says she is fat because she had a hysterectomy and quit smoking. Another friend is fat because she got a divorce. Still another one gained forty pounds because she now has to cook for her husband, who is on a special diet. The most common excuse is, "I just had a baby."

These are nothing but alibis, and I'm sure you've heard them all. Incidentally, the first woman's hysterectomy was seven years ago.

The husband "Mary" cooks for is not fat, and the "baby" is now four years old.

One of my friends has gotten so heavy that her knees hurt, and she is using canes. The woman refuses to acknowledge that perhaps her knees can't carry the extra 100 pounds she's put on in the last 2½ years. She says they all went bad when she started to jog.

Ann, please tell these women that obesity is the death knell to good health and looks and that diets work only if you stick to them. . . . I miss my thin friends in—Longview, Texas.[32]

Hyperactivity

In past epidemics the most striking feature of the recovered encephalitis patient was hyperactivity—inability to sit still or remain in one place, a perpetual urge to move about, often accompanied by excessive talkativeness, at home or in school, a restiveness which immediately became intolerable to those in the vicinity.[33]

These children seem to be driven by a constant nervous stimulation or irritation, are constantly annoying those about them, fighting impulsively, and running wild about the house and in the street.[34]

The patient may be sluggish or drowsy during the daylight hours and usually spends much of his time in sleep, but as night approaches becomes more and more active and restless. About midnight or later the child may be wildly excited, laughing and screaming and in constant ill-directed activity. As day dawns this overactivity slowly diminishes, and the child finally falls asleep just at the time when under normal conditions it should be awakening.[35]

I would like to ask if Dr. Bond, or any other doctors who have had experience, will tell us specifically how they handle these intensely disturbing motor difficulties which we meet in some of these children. Some of them are almost unbearable to live with or to have around. I refer to constant motor activity, rapid shift of attention and interest, purposely meddling with objects, destructive tendencies, etc.[36]

In school she was extremely restless and desired constant attention from the teacher. She talked aloud, quarreled with the other children, argued with the teacher, and wandered about the room at will while the school was in session. . . . Her behavior was so disturbing to the teacher and pupils that she was excluded from school.[37]

In 1934 two physicians in Cincinnati called this "organic drivenness," epitomizing these children's obsessiveness and relentlessness.[38]

It had sometimes been seen in extreme form during an acute attack of encephalitis:

> One may recall the horrible and pitiful sight of some of the hyperkinetic patients who, in the acute state of Economo's disease, literally rolled themselves to death. . . . There was no way out of this torture. One could only stand by and helplessly watch a hopeless fight . . . the fight of the personality against something it cannot stop, something which is beyond the grasp of the individual because of its very nature.[39]

A smaller group were hypoactive rather than hyperactive. In them everything came to a standstill: movement, thought, speech.

Hyperactivity was usually associated with inability to concentrate—attention-span difficulties, attention deficit.

> Besides exhibiting a certain degree of irritability, the boy's behavior was otherwise exemplary. However it was noted that he had difficulty in concentration, a disability which lost him many jobs and which seriously jeopardized his ability to earn a living.[40]

> He was hyperactive and restless and concentrated poorly. . . . He was provocative, restless, and aggressive, had a short attention span, was undependable, destructive, and slovenly about his person.[41]

Hyperactivity and attention-span difficulties are, of course, among the most common sequelae of vaccine damage and are discussed at length in *DPT: A Shot in the Dark*.[42]

Cranial Nerve Palsies

The DPT vaccine is capable of causing all possible cranial nerve disorders: from blindness, deafness, and muteness to the less severe dyslexia, stuttering, or auditory processing deficit.[43]

Vision: sometimes these children have "gaze palsy," difficulty moving the eyeball from side to side or up and down.[44] Or they will be crosseyed:

Another thing that happened after the second shot is that her eyes started crossing. I took her to the doctor with that, and he said: "Oh, that's normal with babies, you know. Don't worry about it." To this day, her eyes still cross sometimes.

When a physician reports, for instance, "oculomotor nerve paresis" coming on suddenly in a five-month-old baby, or "unilateral ptosis" (drooping of the eyelid) combined with "dilatation of the right pupil and inability to rotate the right eye" in a seven-month-old—"for several days prior to admission he was irritable and slept poorly. In addition to this he began vomiting and had three to four loose stools per day"—these look like typical reactions to a vaccination and should be investigated as such.[45]

But the disability can be more serious. Harold Forman, who reacted with a 104-degree fever and high-pitched screaming to his second DPT shot, was later found to be totally blind; his mother is certain he was not blind at birth and that it was caused by the shot.

How much of the blindness discovered in six-month-old children and diagnosed as "congenital" is actually vaccine-induced? No one knows. By the time the blindness is diagnosed, the baby will have had two or three DPT shots—which are capable of causing blindness.

Or the child will have trouble processing information through the eyes—the typical disorder associated with dyslexia. Ralph Packard had persistent crying and a 104 degree fever after his first three shots; now eleven years old, he has a "visual perception problem" and cannot read or write properly.

He skips words and letters. He is going to a man who works with kids who have visual perception problems. With his writing he puts all the words together, there is no spacing between the words. We have trouble reading it. One teacher said that he had written a report, and she couldn't read a word of it. She had him read it out in class like all the rest of the kids did, and he read through it real fast and knew exactly what he had written.

Judy Glick went into a grand mal seizure seven days after her second DPT shot at seven months. She later had two more grand mal seizures and is now on seizure medication.

She can write but has a tendency to reverse her letters and write things backwards. . . . She has a very low attention span.

Wayne Esterbrook reacted violently to his fifth shot at age five, began screaming and rocking from side to side, had a headache and a fever of 104; that night he began hallucinating. Today he is dyslexic:

He had mirrored handwriting in the first grade. If you held his writing up to a mirror, it was perfect. He would make a calender with every number backwards.

Often the vaccine-damaged child cannot write at all ("developmental expressive writing disorder"):

We have a terrible time trying to get her to write. She knows all the letters and all the sounds, but her coordination is so bad she can't write. I'm trying to find her a typewriter or something so she doesn't have to do all this writing. You know how much writing they have to do in first grade—she'll never be able to do it.

He still has no motor skills. He only recently learned to feed himself, hold a pencil or scissors. He has no muscle tone and no reflexes. He can't write because the motor skills are not there.

This same visual palsy was and is among the most frequent sequelae of epidemic encephalitis. Impairment went as far as total blindness, and there were numerous lesser disabilities. The encephalitic patient could suffer from an "oculogyric crisis" (the eyes roll up into the head and remain fixed in that position for hours); or the eyes could assume a staring expression; or they could oscillate back and forth or up and down (nystagmus); or they could be crossed (strabismus), causing double vision.

Sometimes the post-encephalitic had fixations about other people's eyes. One woman with "oculogyric crisis" described her obsession:

"I cannot think of another person's eyes. When I look at other people's eyes, it gives me a sinking sensation."

The record continues as follows:

When the patient looks into a pair of eyes, she feels herself sinking and her eyes go up.
   "My eyes start to move upward and I go into a spell. I cannot
close my eyes. As soon as I do, I see my daughter's eyes (age
eleven) posted on the door of my room. . . . Then, I go into a
trance, my eyes turn up, and I see the ceiling in the room. My
spell comes on with a sinking-heart sensation. Then, everything
goes blank and, though I can see, my mind becomes dull. I have
to lie down. When I do, the first thoughts are of my children's
safety. When I try to shut my eyes, my children's eyes are always
before me . . . and I only think of people and their eyes. I see
nothing but eyes, eyes, eyes, especially the eyes of the last person
I saw" . . .
   Because of this obsession the patient consciously avoids
looking into mirrors.[46]

   This sort of visual obsession is reminiscent of the autistic's
"avoidance of eye contact."
   The visual problem could take the form of dyslexia, dysgraphia,
or some other learning disability. Byers and Rizzo described the
school experience of children who had whooping cough encephalopathy in infancy: "marked reading difficulty and inability to deal
with abstractions, such as digits. Her attention spans were short and
abstract reasoning was inadequate for her age . . . visuomotor function and abstract reasoning ability were well below her age expectancy, in school . . . she had difficulties with technical subjects,
especially reading, and repeated the second grade, though she did
not start school until she was 6½ years of age."[47]
   In another study, Annell found that children with a history of
pertussis in infancy had a higher incidence of dyslexia than a control
group.[48]

Muteness is another effect of the vaccine. Paul Galloway, who
reacted violently to each of the DPT shots, gradually lost the ability
to speak and became mute at the time of the fourth shot (age eighteen months); he is now diagnosed as autistic. Keith Miller was the
same: he cried as a baby but gradually lost the ability to speak and
now communicates only with sign language. Also Gary Keys:

He had been talking before his shot, and then he just quit talking altogether, quit doing any babbling or anything. And he never started talking again. He was just never the same again. He was a perfectly healthy baby with not even a cold up until that point.

Ripley Forbes, now diagnosed as autistic, who had grand mal seizures after the second shot and continues to have uncontrollable seizures up to the present (age ten), is unable to initiate speech. His mother states:

He can sing commercials and songs from tapes, but he can't speak unless you tell him what to say, and then he can repeat the words after you.

The voice could be affected also in epidemic encephalitis, with the child experiencing either severe stammering and stuttering, a slowing up of speech, or a total inability to get the words out:

It is especially in patients with involvement of the speech mechanism that we get the impression of a fairly active mind, but with every avenue of expression effectively blocked. In some of these patients there is not only a speech difficulty, but an actual stopping, the impulses do not come through. The patient gets out a word or two, but the others stick in his throat, and he smiles.[49]

Some were totally mute. Others talked volubly, despite having a speech impediment, but made no sense.

He talked incessantly much of the day and night. His talk consisted largely of reminiscences of earlier childhood and quotations from sermons and school lessons.[50]

Dysphagia (inability to swallow food) may be present, due to loss of the nerve power in the throat and neck. There can also be disturbances of taste. These both contribute to the "food fads" and appetite disorders noted earlier.

Otitis with consequent hearing loss is one of the most common effects of vaccination. Today the United States is experiencing a true plague of this condition. At least half of all U.S. children have had an episode of "glue ear" by their first birthday. By the age of six, 90 percent have had such an episode, and they account for thirty million visits to physicians each year. In addition, a million children have tubes inserted in their ears every year, at a cost of $2000 per operation—for a total of $2 billion annually.[51]

Disturbances of hearing as well as partial or total deafness, often associated with otitis, were also common in the post-encephalitic syndrome.

Also reported were cases in which the hearing became more acute after encephalitis: "patients apparently had an increased acuity of hearing and were greatly distressed by ordinary sounds."[52] This is reminiscent of the hyperacute hearing reported in some autistic children.

Facial palsy was a commonly reported after-effect of encephalitis. The individual could not move his facial muscles, and his face took on a "masklike" expression, often with a "fixed" or "frozen" smile.[53]

Since the salivary glands are controlled by the cranial nerves, another consequence of epidemic encephalitis was a tendency to hypersalivation:

> He has acquired a spitting tic; every few seconds he has an irresistible desire to spit, and does so accompanying the act with an explosive grunt. He states that he cannot control this desire for more than a few minutes at a time.[54]

The post-encephalitic syndrome sometimes involved changed sensitivity to pain—especially to changes in temperature:

> He got out of bed on a hot day and was found standing on the slate roof without any apparent discomfort.[55]

Von Economo noted that the "centers regulating body temperature" could be disturbed.[56] The child is either excessively sensitive or unusually insensitive.

The parents of vaccine-damaged children have noted the same. Unusual sensitivity to heat is very common, and the child insists on very lukewarm baths.

Mental Retardation, Seizures, Cerebral Palsy, Paralyses, Hypotonia

DPT: A Shot in the Dark describes mental retardation, infantile spasms, epilepsy, other kinds of seizures, hemiplegia (severe one-sided paralysis), hemiparesis (slight one-sided paralysis), paraplegia (paralysis of the lower part of the body), and quadriplegia (paralysis of all four limbs).[57]

Seizures are well-documented consequences of the DPT shot, as seen by the case of Paul Hamill:

> *The four-month checkup was May 21, and he got the second DPT shot. He had a low-grade fever that night but was doing OK until May 27. We were sitting at the dinner table, and he was sitting in his infant seat on the floor. He had been babbling and cooing, but all of a sudden he stopped. I looked over at him to see why he was so quiet. He was staring up at the ceiling. I put my hand in front of his eyes, and he didn't notice it at all. That lasted about thirty to forty seconds. On May 28 he had four or five of those episodes, each one thirty to forty seconds. On May 29, at seven A.M., he woke up and was very happy. I had him on the changing table, and he started a sudden violent scream, a blood-curdling scream. He got very restless, and then he became unresponsive. I called his name. I clapped my hands, but he had no response at all. Both his arms dropped down to his sides, and he became flaccid. This episode lasted about thirty seconds.*

A month later the physician gave him another DPT shot, and the epileptic seizures became more frequent, up to 100 per day, even though he was taking five different medications. Today Paul Hamill is developmentally delayed with autistic features, and still has seizures.

These same sequelae were the most tragic consequences of epidemic encephalitis. They could appear at the same time as the acute symptoms or could take months or years to become manifest; they showed that the disease had—as was always feared—caused permanent damage to the brain, spinal cord, or neurologic system.

Only one encephalitis patient in four completely escaped such long-term sequelae—which were more frequent and severe as the victim was younger.

Mental retardation, "intellectual defect," "amentia," and total idiocy were often noted, while a slight decline in intellectual potency was found to be almost universal, even if only a few points on the IQ test.[58]

The destructive impact on mind and intelligence was more visible in the young. Frank R. Ford, professor of neurology at Johns Hopkins, wrote in 1937: "in infants mental development is often completely arrested, and idiocy or imbecility may result."[59] Adolescents and adults could sometimes escape with little or no retardation.

Whooping cough encephalitis was particularly implicated. Annell's study of this disease found mental retardation to be one of the most frequent sequelae; and it was worse in the younger victims.[60]

Epilepsy and other seizure disorders were often found after epidemic encephalitis. Annell: "Many cases of 'idiopathic' epilepsy may be the result of simple diseases of childhood" (and, she could have added, of childhood vaccinations).[61] The epilepsy was often of the "psychomotor" variety.[62] Other kinds of seizures were grand mal, petit mal, tics, tremors, convulsions, grimaces, choreiform movements, and other stereotyped movements.

Karen Nelson and Jonas Ellenberg, of the National Institutes of Health, observed in a 1986 article that no cause can readily be found for the greater part of childhood epilepsies.[63] But no one looks into vaccinations as a cause—even though vaccination is known to cause seizures and epilepsies!

Whooping cough is known to be particularly dangerous in children with epilepsy.[64]

Another set of sequelae from encephalitis included paralyses, cerebral palsy, hemiplegias, paraplegias, quadriplegias, weaknesses (hypotonia) of the arms and legs, spasticities, and clumsiness.

Parkinson's Disease was a well-known after-effect, and a third of encephalitis cases developed this later in life (noted particularly after the 1918 epidemic).[65] Von Economo observed: "The Parkinsonian patient with a dripping half-opened mouth has become a well-known and typical picture of chronic encephalitis."[66]

The same set of sequelae are found after vaccination. Alan Dombrowski, who reacted violently to his first three shots, is an example of hypotonia:

> *When he falls, he cannot react by putting out his arms to catch himself. He just falls flat on his face.*

Winford Mills, born in 1982, fell ill with a severe gastrointestinal disturbance a month after his first DPT shot; this continued for six weeks and was followed by a series of earaches and respiratory infections. During this sickness he was observed to be regressing intellectually and physically, to the point where today he has the IQ of a newborn baby, is mute, and lacks muscular power, lying on the floor or in a chair like a rag doll wherever he is put.

Mothers have sometimes detected slight changes in muscle tone after vaccination. The mother of Eric Hart noted that his Moro Reflex became more pronounced after the first DPT shot.* A month later he developed infantile spasms.

Many post-encephalitic patients in past studies were left-handed or ambidexterous, and this is also found in vaccine-damaged children.[67] The mother of Keith Miller (now diagnosed as moderately autistic) remembers that at about the age of two he switched from holding the spoon in his right hand to his left hand (the possible relationship between severe vaccine reaction and left-handedness or ambidexterity would be a good topic for research).

Must There Be a Severe Acute Reaction?

Researchers in the epidemiology of vaccine damage invariably assume that long-term sequelae will not occur in the absence of a severe acute reaction. This assumption was accepted by us in writing *DPT: A Shot in the Dark*. Thus it was puzzling to find that about half of the new families interviewed for the present investigation could not remember any marked vaccine reaction, even though the child began to develop symptoms of autism or other severe neurology shortly after one of the shots.

---

*The Moro Reflex is the "startle reaction" manifested by contraction of the limbs and neck when an infant is dropped a short distance or startled by a sudden noise.

Two conclusions could be drawn. Either the neurology in these cases had nothing to do with a vaccine reaction (i.e., was "congenital," as medical authorities often maintain) or, alternatively, serious long-term sequelae can develop in the absence of an acute reaction.

This important point should eventually be resolved through appropriate research. In the meantime, however, the second alternative must be accepted, or at least considered, on historical and theoretical grounds.

In a word, encephalitis *from all other causes* is known to produce severe neurologic damage in the absence of an acute reaction. Why should encephalitis from vaccination be an exception?

Epidemic encephalitis was notorious for this:

> In six cases there was a history of a definite onset of neurological manifestations without a history of a previous acute febrile attack.[68]

> It is not unusual to observe the development of the symptoms of the chronic phase unheralded by any acute illness.[69]

> In the great majority of cases, there is no history of an attack of encephalitis. It is only when the medical history of the child, as well as his behavioral reactions, are carefully scrutinized and evaluated . . . that the condition becomes apparent.[70]

Baker in 1949 wrote about measles and whooping cough: "Actually there is no correlation between the severity of the infectious disease and the cerebral involvement. In many cases with only a mild illness severe postencephalitic complications may arise months or even years later."[71]

Anna Lisa Annell's exhaustive treatise on whooping cough and its complications keeps returning to this point. "The degree of severity of [whooping cough] and intensity of the clinical symptoms do not appear to be decisive for the occurrence of sequelae, a fact that has also been stressed with regard to other infectious diseases of childhood."[72] "Even apparently uncomplicated attacks of infectious diseases of childhood may result in brain damage, which may then be the primary cause of subsequent behavior disorders."[73]

> There is little correlation between the severity of the infectious disease and the cerebral involvement. The resulting cerebral dam-

age is not in proportion to the degree of severity of the primary disease, but sequelae may occur even in such cases in which the clinical symptoms of cerebral involvement have been slight and have subsided rapidly. For example, they may only have been manifested as marked drowsiness or brief, slight clouding of consciousness, transient headache, or vomiting on one or two occasions. *Or symptoms of cerebral involvement may have been lacking altogether.* [emphasis added] Thus there is reason to search for symptoms of brain damage even in such cases in which the child has not been known to have had any disease of the central nervous system or any cerebral complications associated with some infectious illness.[74]

Roger Bannister writes about "acute disseminated encephalomyelitis" that "there may be no preceding general symptoms, or the neurological disorder may follow by a few days an infection of the upper respiratory tract or an influenza-like illness."[75] About encephalomyelitis *after vaccination* H.H. Merritt writes: "Symptoms of involvement of the meninges—headaches, stiffness of the neck, and drowsiness—are common early in the course of all types. In a number of cases there are no further symptoms."[76]

This leads irresistibly to the conclusion that severe neurologic sequelae may occur after vaccination even in the absence of an acute reaction. When the baby reacts to a DPT shot with "a slight fever and fussiness" or "drowsiness" for a few days, this may be, and often is, a case of encephalitis which is capable of causing quite severe neurologic consequences.

Any researcher who ignores or rejects the possibility that vaccination can cause the most serious neurologic disorders in the absence of a marked acute reaction will have to find grounds for distinguishing post-vaccinal encephalitis from encephalitis due to other causes.

Serious reactions may simply be overlooked by the parents. The baby may lapse into unconsciousness for an hour or more ("shock," "collapse"), and the mother may decide that he has fallen asleep at an unexpected time—or slept somewhat longer than usual.[77] If he is hard to arouse, she may just be philosophical about it. Ten or fifteen years later, when questioned about a possible reaction to the

DPT shot, she cannot remember anything out of the ordinary, even though her baby may have had a six-hour fainting spell (described in the literature of pediatrics, for obscure reasons, as "hypotonic hyporesponsive episode").

Thus, a patient manifesting the typical long-term effects of vaccination is probably a victim of vaccination, even if no acute reaction was observed at the time.

This can be illustrated by the dramatic case of Frank Maxwell (born: October 1978; diagnosis: delayed development with autistic features). His mother was contacted by telephone to arrange an interview but was not very forthcoming—having, like many mothers of autistics, already been overexposed to inquisitive physicians and researchers. She asked what was the purpose of the interview and, when told about a possible connection with the DPT shot, at once responded that she had never noticed a vaccine reaction and did not even remember when Frank had had the shots. When told that they are usually given at two, four, and six months, she replied that vaccination could not then have played a role, since Frank's autistic symptoms (emotional withdrawal and loss of eye contact) had definitely commenced at *six weeks*. She was certain of the date.

This was a startling piece of information, and she was asked to check Frank's Baby Book, just to be absolutely sure. She telephoned back an hour later in some distress with the news that, according to the Baby Book, Frank had had his first DPT shot at six weeks. "Do you think that's significant?" she asked.

Bill Follett (born January 1972; diagnosis: autistic) was a similar case. His father did not recall an acute reaction but stated that within a few days of the fourth DPT shot he became noticeably alienated, distant, and non-responsive. This gradually progressed to full-fledged autism.

David Montgomery (born: January 1975; diagnosis: autistic-like) had a change of personality precisely at the time of the MMR shot. He had earlier been making baby noises, but now lapsed into silence and developed an extreme fear of any changes in his routine. These would provoke him into screaming fits.

Herbert Irving (born: December 1981; diagnosis: autistic) also withdrew from contact after the third DPT shot:

The third shot was the turning-point. He should have had it earlier, but it was delayed because of his earaches. They gave it to him quickly when the earaches stopped momentarily. He had the shot on January 2, and we left on vacation about ten days later and were gone ten or fifteen days. While we were away there was a turn for the worse. When we got back he was just isolated in his crib and didn't want to see us or be picked up. Before that he had been interactive with the other children. He would watch them get ready for school and laugh at them. He would stand in the playpen and watch their antics.

Mary Dorfmann (born: March 1965; diagnosis: autistic) had the eighteen-month DPT booster when in the hospital to be operated on for crossed eyes (possibly caused by the earlier shots). At that time she "withdrew" from human contact, and the parents attributed it to the "emotional trauma" of the hospital stay.

Stephen Kennedy (born: March 1978; diagnosis: "atypical" with autistic tendencies) regressed in a number of ways at age 2½, shortly after the DPT booster shot. He stopped using words logically and became echolalic; he also started staring episodes (absence seizures).

Sometimes the only sign of a vaccine reaction is change in the baby's sleeping pattern. Mothers, of course, remember this very readily.

Margaret Atwood (born: September 1974: diagnosis: marginal autistic) did not react visibly to any of the shots, but her mother recalled a distinct change in her sleeping pattern at eighteen months (the time of the fourth shot). Before that she had taken daytime naps, but afterwards she became hyperactive, stopped taking naps, and slept very little at night.

Tammy Garrett (born December 1977; diagnosis: atypical development, autistic syndrome) "got her days and nights mixed up about her second month," i.e., starting at the time of the first shot.

This question deserves further research, if funds can be found for it somewhere in the multi-billion dollar budget of the National Institutes of Health. If vaccination was known to cause serious neurologic sequelae in the absence of an acute reaction, this would cast a different light on the whole U.S. program for tracking vaccine reactions.

The "Hot Lot"

Underlying much of the thinking about vaccine damage is the unspoken assumption that only an unusually virulent batch of vaccine, the so-called "hot lot" which somehow gets through the FDA's safety testing system, can cause serious neurologic damage. This assumption might be tenable if vaccine damage occurred only in one or two cases out of each million children vaccinated—as our official statistics have been insisting. But, if damage is occurring in fifteen to twenty percent of all cases (as estimated from the incidence of learning disabilities in the United States), it can hardly all be caused by defective batches of vaccine. Some inferior vaccine may be passed into the marketplace, but the neurologic damage described in these pages is too extensive to be blamed on "hot lots."*

It is not the vaccine which is at fault but rather the genetic or "constitutional" diversity of the population of babies vaccinated, which predisposes so many of them to react violently to a perfectly "safe" vaccine.

Laurence Steinman has noted, "The possibility that adverse reactions to routine immunization may be under genetic control seems novel," but it is confirmed by Charles M. Poser, M.D., of the Harvard Medical School Department of Neurology, writing about encephalitis:

> Neither the nature nor the severity of the pathological reaction depends on the type of specific antigenic stimulus (the previous viral infection or vaccine); rather, such reactions represent the idiosyncratic immune response of a particular patient. The same is true of the reaction's anatomic localization; it is likewise idiosyncratic and unpredictable . . . the response is determined by the host rather than by the stimulus.[78]

---

*See the discussion of "hot lots" in H. Coulter and B. Fisher, 1985, 216, 287–291, 298–300.

Completely "normal" babies can and do react disastrously to a completely "normal" batch of vaccine.

Developmental Delay

The common denominator of all these encephalitis-caused disabilities is "developmental delay." The individual is delayed, more or less severely, in all areas of physical, emotional, and intellectual development. The more serious cases remain children, or even infants, for their whole lives.

These children grow slowly. They are delayed walking and talking; they wet their beds until adolescence, and even beyond; teeth may come in very late: one boy had no teeth until age eleven.[79] Microcephaly (failure of the skull to grow) may occur, a dramatic case (from whooping cough) being described in 1869:

> While living in Ohio a few years ago I became acquainted with a boy twenty-two years of age who arrested my attention from several marked characteristics; his mind being apparently undeveloped, and incapable of becoming so in a great degree; and while his bodily stature was that of a man, his cranium was very small and seemed to have ceased growing in childhood, while the rest of the head, the face, etc. had grown, thus giving him an unseemly prominent appearance. Being quite interested in the youth, I made the acquaintance of his mother, and from her learned the following facts; at the age of six or seven years, he had an attack of severe uncomplicated whooping cough, which was very hard and persistent, continuing for several months without abatement . . . since that time his head has ceased to grow, and the little hat he then wore, his mother still keeps, and it fits him perfectly yet.[80]

Epidemic encephalitis had a delaying effect on personality development as well. T.R. Hill in 1928 commented on "the great exaggeration in these patients of primitive and instinctual tendencies and their consequent slavery to them."[81] Harry Bakwin wrote in 1949, "On the whole there appeared to be a retardation in personality development, the school age child behaving like a runabout and the runabout like an infant."[82] Annell wrote in 1953, "An arrest of personality development as a whole seems to occur, holding them at a lower level of behavior, perhaps because maturational mechanisms have been interfered with. . . . Primitive reactions usually outgrown in infancy continue through the runabout stage or longer."[83]

The pertussis vaccine causes identical developmental "delays" and "retardations," even "reversals."

At three years old he could read simple books and stories, and at five years he couldn't read at all, and still has reading difficulties. He has difficulty with math correlating where the numbers should go. He had an incredible memory. He could memorize long paragraphs and sentences before he was five years old, and can't do that anymore.

She just turned seven, and her coordination is very bad. She didn't walk until she was six. Everything was very delayed in her development . . . walking, talking.

At fifteen months of age he had been a wonderful happy compliant baby, gorgeous. Ate well, slept well, no problems of any kind. And also not too docile. Very interactive. Language skills, play skills. The first thing to go was his behavior. He became uncontrollably hyperactive [after MMR, oral polio, and DT shots]. *Within three days after that he began all of these symptoms: severely non-compliant, hyperactive, body was very limp, like a rag doll. He lost language and play skills.*

He had an ear infection when he was six months old. He was talking a little at that time. But by the time he was a year old he was deaf. He stopped talking and didn't start again until he was almost three.

Until that point Jeanne was the brighter one of the twins. After that she regressed. We knew she would be the first to talk because she was pulling herself up before the shot. But after the shot everything seemed to stop with Jeanne.

Worth considering is the idea (quite heretical in the context of late twentieth-century industrial medicine) that childhood diseases actually *benefit* the child. Physicians familiar with these diseases in the past often noted a spurt in growth and development after a bout of measles, mumps, or whooping cough. This wisdom has today been forgotten.

And how will the child's immune system be strengthened if he is never exposed to the stress of disease? "The most immunized child in history" grows up to be an immunologically incompetent adult.

Egotism, Ego Weakness, Alienation

The earlier chapters on autism and minimal brain damage outline the intellectual and personality traits typifying these conditions. The very same traits are described in the literature on epidemic encephalitis.

Children with the post-encephalitic syndrome suffered from egotism, narcissism, and solipsism which, after repeated rebuffs by the outside world, become ego-weakness, fearfulness, depression, and despair.[84]

The egotism is typically seen in disregard of physical danger and exhibitionism:

On the street she dashed heedlessly in front of motor cars, or jumped on the running boards. She would get into delivery wagons while the driver was absent, and drive around. On one occasion she caused a runaway by whipping the horses. She was finally rescued, unhurt and unfrightened.[85]

These girls . . . wanted the center of the stage, and one child at a Sunday-school entertainment ran on the platform and sang and danced until she was pulled off.[86]

When young, these children are oblivious of their disabilities. Pure surrender to instinctual drives leads to "euphoria."[87] But euphoria disappears when they grow up and realize that they are "different."

This undermines their self-confidence. The outcome is a weak ego, expressed in insecurity, anxiety, timidity, fear of the new, and unwillingness to take initiatives:

Case eleven, a boy who was scarcely 3½ years old when he was examined, appeared psychotic only at times, when his condition resembled a dreamy state. Even in the intervals between these attacks he was extremely anxious.[88]

Case twelve, a boy aged almost 5½ years, did not as a rule appear psychotic, but he had sudden attacks during which he seemed anxious, exhibited motor uneasiness, and lost contact with his surroundings.[89]

William proved to be a friendly boy who was liked by everyone because of his frankness and willingness to be of service. It was noted that he was emotionally unstable, socially immature, and showed a marked feeling of insecurity. . . . New experiences particularly frightened him . . . and he felt at times that he could not control himself. In one interview he said, "I'm afraid of the beginning of everything and afraid I can't do it. . . ."[90]

A personality review brought out considerable evidence of feelings of insecurity or inferiority. There are many indications of timidity. He says he is afraid to go out at night since his sickness. . . . He has a poor opinion of his own physical and mental ability and especially of his ability to learn at school. . . . He feels he is different from boys that haven't been sick.[91]

A great development during the summer was a feeling of fear. At home he was afraid to be left alone, and instead of going to bed he placed pillows on chairs to sleep on.[92]

These individuals become alienated from society and from themselves—hermits and loners. "A number stated that they had no desire to associate with anyone and preferred to be alone." "They were asocial and made very little effort to enter into group activities." "He was to some extent unsocial, was apt to wander away from the others, or be indifferent to them."[93]

Vaccine-damaged children have the same ego weakness: they are emotionally frail, anxious, fearful, on edge, and oversensitive to criticism:

One evening my daughter brought out a balloon to show him to cheer him up. She bounced it around, and when he saw it he started screaming really badly. He shook and screamed like he was terrified at the sight of it. Up until this time Clarence had been a happy adventuresome little boy. He was unusually brave and not afraid of much of anything. After this reaction he would scream in terror at the sight of balloons or chewing gum. He wouldn't even enter a room if someone was chewing gum. He wouldn't leave the doorstep when we went out—he would just stand there and scream and shake until we picked him up. He became a timid nervous little boy over-

night, and we couldn't figure out what had happened. This behavior lasted about three months.

They feel frustrated by their own inadequacies, their inability to be like others:

After the third shot he became much more difficult to relate to. He started whining a lot—not like he is in physical pain, but he is very frustrated. I can see it. He can understand what you are saying, but he can't translate it into speech. He can't get it out, you know, what he wants to say to you. It's the same with physical movement—he knows how to do something like tie his shoes, but his body won't cooperate with him all the time. He is very angry inside, very frustrated.

He doesn't like to feel that he is different. He whines and gets depressed.

All my life I have been frustrated with my disability—like I am imprisoned in a body that won't do what I want it to do.

She is very uncoordinated physically. She has a very low attention span and is emotional. She is very frustrated. If she can't do something and do it right, she doesn't even want to try. She cries in the classroom and cries at home. If she spills a glass of milk, she thinks the world has come to an end.

Jeanne has been frustrated a lot because of course she compares herself to Judy and doesn't think she measures up. Jeanne would stop and cry and say, "I'm stupid. I just don't know anything. I can't do anything right." She just seemed very frustrated for a long time.

In the children with epidemic encephalitis these traits led to anxiety, fearfulness, and paranoia:

The girl was very suspicious and felt that every one was talking about her. . . . The girl expressed many paranoid ideas and there were evidences of auditory and visual hallucinations.[94]

He felt that every one picked on him. . . . He bragged about his escapades and stated constantly that he had done nothing wrong and that every one else was to blame. . . . Although he had been in many serious difficulties, he minimized these and refused to admit that he had committed any wrong.[95]

Thus, wherever one looks—even in the finer points of personality development—the parallels between autism, minimal brain damage, the post-encephalitic syndrome, and vaccine damage are overwhelming.

A Moral and Emotional Vacuum

Children with post-encephalitic syndrome lack deep feelings. "Emotional poverty was an outstanding symptom." "He appeared indifferent to the rights of others and lacked affection." "Their emotions are dulled or even abolished."[96]

The same is seen in the vaccine-damaged child:

He used to be very affectionate, but now there is a very flat affect. He is passive and withdrawn. If anyone takes something from him, he will just walk away. Sometimes he has a mad look.

They lack a moral sense. As Frank Elliott comments, "even conscience has a physiologic substrate, it seems."[97] A researcher at Johns Hopkins Hospital in Baltimore wrote in 1922:

In school they were impudent, disrespectful, disobedient, or no longer amenable to discipline. At home they would curse their parents or even strike at them. They were indolent or indifferent. Several said they would do as they pleased. There has been frequent running away among them, and they would stay on the street at all hours. Some lost respect for personal and public property; they destroyed their own belongings or the house furnishings. . . . There was fabricating and lying. There were temper tantrums, screaming attacks which were uncontrollable.[98]

Another authority described them as follows in 1940:

The moral and social sense of the patient suffers an eclipse. His misdemeanors range over the whole gamut of juvenile depravity, from lying and petty pilfering to offenses against the person. Such changes in conduct seem always to be for the worse. . . . A child of previously responsible character may be so transformed as to seem a different person. Impish, cruel, destructive, abusive, indecent. He may become guilty of any offense, from naughtiness to crime. . . . A creature of impulse, the child's opportunist policy of social offense thrives on the material he finds at hand.[99]

Their lack of emotion and empathy made them indifferent or unresponsive to punishment. But others (probably with unimpaired intelligence) refused to identify themselves with this aberrant behavior and later apologized for it. They sensed their own plight and were depressed by it:

> He feels he is different from boys that haven't been sick and thinks that his whole family thought he was getting dumb.[100]

> In some cases . . . transient but rather severe reactive depressions have occurred as the patients grew older.[101]

> He separates clearly his behavior before he had encephalitis and after it, saying that before his illness he would do what his teacher said and told his father every time he wanted to go out, but that after it he would "holler" at the teacher, eat candy in school, run away from home, and stay out all day.[102]

Remorse could lead to suicide or attempted suicide:

> One such case occurred in the North of England in a boy of fifteen. He nearly strangled a girl who had laughed at him, and afterwards hanged himself.[103]

Intellectual Fragmentation

Their many physical, emotional, and neurologic deficits impose an impossible burden on the development of the intellect. Frank Elliott states: "In clinical practice, impairment of conceptual thought is one of the earliest casualties of diffuse brain damage."[104] The post-encephalitic suffers from the same difficulty as the autistic in attempting to reason conceptually.

Harry Bakwin in 1949 noted that one of the main deficiencies of the child with post-encephalitic brain damage is an inability to integrate perceptions; the difficulty is found in synthesizing the perceptions into a logical whole.[105] Strauss and Lehtinen observed in 1947 that these children are unable to distinguish between essential and unessential impressions—a condition which applies both to their way of thinking and of interpeting visual impressions.[106] They could not draw the figure of a human body, leading Lauretta Bender to conclude that they had a fragmented perception of their own bodies; only by acquiring integrated experience of one's own body can one represent it in a drawing, and this integrated experience was lacking.[107]

Thus they cannot visualize or conceptualize the outside world, cannot abstract, cannot get a rational grip on it, cannot portray it symbolically.

To their other difficulties may be added a defective memory, although sometimes the post-encephalitic child shows a freakishly strong memory.[108]

With so many handicaps, post-encephalitic children cannot acquire experience. Josephine Neal wrote in 1942 that their specific intellectual defects are "based on difficulties in gaining patterned behavior through perceptual experience." Everything that happens to them is confused and uninterpretable; whatever "experience" they acquire is fragmented and unprocessed in their minds.[109]

Since judgment is based on experience, they lack judgment, cannot foresee the consequences of their actions, and are not concerned about them.[110]

Lability and Impulsiveness

Post-encephalitic children were known for their childish lability of mood:

> He was presented to our dispensary with an unusually long history of behavior difficulties. . . . He cried bitterly at the prospect of being taken away from his foster-home, but a few minutes later had attracted attention by spitting over the rail upon the head of a physician below. This we found fairly represented George's mood changes. . . .[111]

> There were times when Roy appeared to be tractable and affectionate. At such times he would put his arms around anyone at the home and act in a tender and loving manner, but a moment later his mood would change, and he would try to injure the object of his former affection.[112]

With lability goes impulsiveness. Far from being premeditated, their actions are often spur-of-the-moment affairs. Impulses are immediately translated into action.

> Case forty-one may be mentioned as an example of this hyperactivity and lack of inhibition together with unpredictable variability in mood. The boy was extremely lively, restless, and destructive, but seemed dreamy at times and neither heard nor saw anything. He had sudden temper tantrums. In many ways he reacted extremely immaturely and primitively; he was completely unpredictable.[113]

Their threshold of frustration is very low:

> Because of his hyperactivity and disinhibition, the brain-injured child appears to be elated: it is astonishing, as sometimes happens, to see him burst into explosive crying when confronted with a difficulty. His reaction is then a state of helplessness and complete despair upon being confronted with a situation which seems insoluble to him. In children it usually appears in the form of crying which may be so intense that comforting or appeasement by verbal efforts is unavailing.[114]

The post-encephalitic is moved by the emotions of the moment. He lacks a superego and manifests the egocentricity and primitive selfishness of a newborn baby—at the mercy of instinctual desires for gratification.

Sometimes they admit to a sensation of being "outside time," which may represent the small baby's lack of a sense of time:

> During her spells, during which she remains fully conscious, she loses completely her sense of time. Unless so informed after the attack is over, she never knows their duration, though she recalls other details with remarkable clarity. This sense of timelessness is very apparent to the patient during her attacks and is very disturbing to her, so that in order to keep in contact and to be correctly oriented with regard to the time element, she repeatedly scans her clock, attempting to concentrate upon each passing minute in order to appreciate more fully its significance which would otherwise be lost to her.[115]

Compensating for Ego Weakness: Resisting Change

These children and adults possess several mechanisms for concealing and offsetting their ego weakness and feelings of inferiority, and for regaining control over their surroundings.

One is argumentativeness, obstinate disobedience, evasiveness, alibis, resistance to questioning, and opposition to authority.[116] Discipline is resented and usually ineffective:

> At first he was reported as doing well in his foster home. Conditions were favorable for a quiet life, such as had been prescribed for him. Soon, however, there appeared such items as: George told long tales that were not true; he did not seem to know what obedience was; he could not be trusted to do simple tasks.[117]

> Following the illness she became irritable and impatient, always wanted her own way, and when not allowed to have it, would kick and scream and bite, acting "like a wild person" and persisting in her disobedience or annoying behavior until she made her mother cry.[118]

When he cannot have his way, the post-encephalitic individual will break down in tears, a regular "cry-baby" (reflecting weakness of the lacrimal nerve).[119]

Another mechanism is whining insistence or "perseveration," reflecting mental rigidity and inability to let go of an idea.[120]

> The boy appeared to be lively and restless but was at the same time extremely rigid mentally. He was unable to adjust himself to any new situation. . . . He showed a marked tendency to perseveration: he drew numerous pictures with exactly the same motif, and at school he often adhered to a question during the entire lesson.[121]

This desire to regain control can also be expressed in a propensity to act willfully, to boss and bully others, to assume leadership.

> Since admission in 1926 she has shown considerable disorder of conduct. She is continually interfering with other children's occupations; she will issue orders to them, try to "boss" them, and a fight will ensue. Her very violent, easily aroused temper produces fierce fights. When her interference with the other children is prevented by anyone, she will attack the latter, striking her and trying to sieze her by the throat. Her interference with other children is governed by a curious maternal or protective feeling for them, which leads her occasionally to order the nurses to carry out this or that treatment for them.[122]

Father reports: "Must have his own way in everything. If he does not, he goes out and cries. All he likes to do is order others about . . . very self-assertive, is certainly not of a retiring disposition."[123]

But bossiness is just a facade for an inferiority complex.

When one of the larger boys left, he took his place as leader. He responded well to the new responsibilities put upon him. He was always interested in anything which gave him a chance to show his authority to others. In making ready for a birthday party for one of the other boys John finally decided he wouldn't go, and got under the bed, explaining that if anything went wrong he would be blamed for it.[124]

Carried to an extreme, bossiness becomes temper tantrums, rage and violence:

His worst fault . . . was his uncontrollable temper. . . . He would on slight provocation kick, bite, scratch, and spit upon others. . . . He was still bossy and at times scrappy.[125]

Her violent outbursts of temper, fighting, or defiance last only a few moments and are of daily occurrence. . . . The ward staff makes this comment on her: "She seems to lose all control and then does not mind what she does to anybody, regardless of consequences." Punishment, reproof, and appeal, although productive of tearful response and promises of good behavior at the time, produce absolutely no effect in the long run.[126]

The child would first grow restless and walk rapidly about the ward, then his face would grow red and expressive of anger. . . . The child would then be very angry and would sometimes actually foam at the mouth. He would try to injure anyone nearby at such times and not infrequently would beat bed-ridden patients with his shoe or any other hard object available. Within a few minutes his anger would have spent itself, and he would be very sorry for his misbehavior. At such times he would be very affectionate and would try to kiss and caress the nurses.[127]

The slightest teasing would irritate him to the point of violence, and his resentment of criticism was extreme. On one occasion, when accused by an older brother of having defaced one of his books, the patient seized a flatiron on the stove and struck his brother with it, fracturing the skull. Since that time the antagonism between them has been extreme.[128]

This behavior, which came to be called the "explosive diathesis," had first been noted in 1899:

> Following the most trivial and most impersonal causes, there . . . may be the most grotesque gesticulations, excessive movements of the face, and a quick, sharp explosiveness of speech; there may be cursing and outbreaks of violence which are often directed towards things. . . . There is an excess in the reaction, with inadequate adaptation to the situation which is so remote from a well-considered and purposeful act that it approaches a pure psychic reflex.[129]

These impulsive acts resembled the facial and vocal tics which these patients also manifested and were just as ungovernable.

> These children are destructive and impulsive. Impulses are immediately translated into action. Inhibitions and fear of consequences are lacking. They steal, lie, destroy property, set fires, and commit sex offenses. They do not evade detection and claim that they cannot help their conduct.[130]

> She was quite conscious of her abnormal behavior, regretted it and said that she could not help it. She could only be kept out of mischief by being put to bed. When reproved . . . said, "I can't help it. I try to be good but I feel I must do it. I will try to stop it. . . ." Sometimes she would say, "Can I stay upstairs by myself until schooltime? I feel I am going to fight."[131]

> They appear to be acutely conscious of the impulse to do wrong, but are quite unable to control it. They frequently express their inability to hold themselves in check. A patient . . . made this remark, "I am a bad boy. I know I am a bad boy, but I cannot help it." A patient of mine sitting down at a table pushed a porcelain vessel out of her reach for fear she might have an uncontrollable impulse to smash it and, having spat fiercely at me, burst into tears and would not be consoled, blaming herself bitterly. Another patient said he often had a "feeling" that he must go into his garden and hurt his dog. . . .[132]

> The patient was admitted to hospital in October 1926. . . . She was quarrelsome and easily upset and was very restless, being unable to sit or stand in any one position for more than a few moments. She showed a violent temper when she could not get her own way, would fight readily, and displayed an uncontrollable

impulse to pinch and slap anyone who came near, which she would obey constantly even if she were hit back in return.[133]

A woman who had recovered from *encephalitis lethargica*:

used suddenly to become conscious of a rising surge within her, a seemingly physical wave which flooded her brain and caused her to clench her fists, set her jaws, and glare in frenzy at her mother: "Had my mother said anything then to cross me, I would have killed her." Her attacks were followed by remorse.[134]

The "irresistible impulse" component is seen in the practice of "gruesome self-mutilation" in some of these children.[135] "In rare cases strange mental states develop which lead to frightful self-mutilation, such as extraction of teeth, avulsion of eyeballs, and gnawing of the fingers."[136]

According to the history, the girl had had severe temper outbursts since the age of four years. Very often she would beat her head against the wall or floor if frustrated.[137]

She would suddenly tear her clothes, or smack someone in the face, or, if nobody were near, smack herself on the head, and she took to blowing at people who went near her and attempting to spit at them, and was constantly spitting when walking about. She was quite conscious of her sins and ashamed and tearful on being spoken to about them, but said, "I can't help it," or "Something makes me do it," and added that it "helped" her to smack someone and that it gave her the same satisfaction to smack her own head if no one else were present.[138]

While some of these individuals were clearly acting under uncontrollable impulse ("psychic reflex"), others seemed to be inherently malign and destructive, motivated by a will to do evil. They were sometimes described as "revengeful," and their violently aggressive behavior could be accompanied by hallucinations and "voices."[139]

Case one—An eleven-year-old boy with no significant medical history and normal premorbid personality had had a four-day influenza-like illness with headache, dizziness, and drowsiness. . . . One month later he was reported to be "hearing voices." When last seen, four months after the original illness, he was still lethargic and worried by aggressive feelings towards members of his family.[140]

The girl expressed many paranoid ideas, and there were evidences of auditory and visual hallucinations. She told that she heard voices which commanded her to kill. She always heard these voices when she was in bed. In her visual hallucinations she saw a small dark woman standing in front of her also ordering her to kill. During one of her temper outbursts the girl attacked one of the workers and tried to kill her. Her conduct during the temper outbursts was extremely violent.[141]

He improved gradually and returned to school, but had to be taken out because he asked so many questions and removed books from other desks to his own. . . . In September 1920, another attempt was made to have him attend school, but this was soon given up as he started to steal at random. He took a diamond ring belonging to his sister and disposed of it for an automobile ride. He began to enter stores and take things which he later gave away. When questioned in regard to his stealing, he invariably replied that he heard a voice in his left ear which forced him to do so . . . he constantly maintained that there were two voices in his ears on these occasions, the one of the devil telling him to run away, and the other of an angel telling him not to do so. . . . He could not play with other children on account of his overbearing manner and his fits of anger. His parents had great difficulty in controlling him, though there were periods in which he appeared perfectly normal.[142]

The same aggressiveness and tendency to violence can often seen in the vaccine-damaged child. Temper tantrums and destructive behavior are rooted in weak ego, emotional lability, and a low threshold of frustration.

She is very emotional. One minute she will be happy and sweet and the next angry and upset.

One minute he will be fine and smiling, and the next minute he will be set off into a spell where he is angry and mean. This past year he went to kindergarten; one day the teacher left for a few minutes, and when she got back, the room was in a shambles. My son and another boy had destroyed the room.

The most difficult thing to cope with right now is her behavioral problems. There are days that she comes out of her room and starts screaming. And we have no idea what brought it on. And it will go away as fast as it came on. Then she will be as sweet and wonderful as any other little kid. But there are other times when you can't even get close to her.

The outcome is often a violent reaction against a hostile world:

She is a real little scrapper. She will pick a fight at a minute's notice. She would as soon tackle her older brother for a fight as someone her own size. She is an agitator. She will make trouble where there wouldn't be any if she would leave it alone.

My daughter is now sixteen. At age fourteen she was hospitalized in an adolescent stress unit for two and a half months. She continues to be a roller-coaster of extremes emotionally—really happy or really sad. There have been days when we have not been able to send her to school because she has such an explosive emotional makeup.

I have great concern with Martin's violent tendencies. I am starting to be afraid because, as he gets older, he could go off half-cocked, and if he does strike out, I am afraid he will strike out at the ones closest to him. The child psychologist has told me she can see violent tendencies in Martin. He is like two different kids at times. When Martin is on medication he is calmer, but when he is off it he gets hyper and very negative. He will be mean and pull the cat's tail and start fights. He doesn't treat his friends very nicely. I had one doctor who would put him on medication during school but take him off it in the summer, and Martin would harass everyone in the family, and we would fight with each other. The whole neighborhood was really angry at him because he was doing abnormal things and getting into trouble. He would call people names and drive everyone crazy.

My son looks perfectly normal on the outside, so it is difficult for people to accept his erratic, violent behavior. Our old doctor told us he was just hyperactive, and so we sent him to a normal preschool for two years. We know now that was the worst thing we could have done for him because the normal children told him he was a "retard" and "dumb," and, of course, he couldn't do the work they were doing. Now we have him in the school for children who have cerebral palsy, multiple sclerosis, learning disabilities, hyperactiv-

ity, etc. When he started he would bite, kick, and hit the other kids, and they had to put him in isolation frequently whenever he became violent.

He was in special-ed. preschool at age three and four. There we noticed a lot of violent behavior, so much so that they wanted to do more CAT scans. He was an adorable child with a sparkling personality, and all of a sudden he started biting, kicking, and scratching. He would pound his head into my chest. I would have to hold him down on the couch. He would do the same to his brothers. He would stay awake until midnight. He did not pick on animals, only people. Lately he has been interested in matches, just recently. We went from violent behavior to now, for the past year, almost uninterested.

There is a strong element of impulse:

When he struck you was he mad at you?

The councilor said that he was and that this was a good sign, showing that he felt comfortable letting his anger show at home with his family.

But what did you think about it?

I thought it was because of the brain damage. I don't think he really knows what he is doing. It's a sort of reflex behavior.

That this violence has an impulsive component is seen in the fact that it is often self-directed, but there are also signs of deliberate malice:

She can go into tantrums. We have had her hurt herself. She has thrown herself against doors. She used to bite herself. She will attack her older sister when things aren't going right.

Especially after a seizure, he will grab the hair of anyone who is in his way. He will bite them or kick them, and you can't stop him no matter what you do—even though he is still very tiny. He will pull his own hair out and bite himself on the arms. If you tell him "No!," he will start screaming and pulling his own hair out. Since he had a really bad seizure last year, his behavior has become even more violent.

Would you say that he is actually malicious?

Yes, sometimes. For instance, last week my husband was rubbing my neck because I had a headache. When he saw it, he wanted to help, but then he pinched me. So I said, "Ow!" And after that he started pinching me some more.

Compensating for Ego Weakness: Hypersexuality

The final compensation for ego weakness in the post-encephalitic population was to seek refuge in heightened sexual activity. In contrast to the delay in other spheres, sexual maturity often seemed accelerated in these individuals, with premature puberty, hypersexuality and precocious eroticism leading to public masturbation, obscene language, exhibitionism, rape and rape attempts, sexual and other assaults on smaller children, and the like. This reflected the type's overall aggressiveness and also a natural craving for affection:

It was unsafe to leave her [age nine] with her younger brothers, as she took delight in twisting their hands and feet unmercifully. Her older brothers she teased and tormented, and when they tried to discipline her, she would bite them and claw at them. At other times she fondled them, was sexually aggressive, and was rather frequently masturbated by one of them. On one occasion intercourse was attempted by the eldest brother who was sixteen years old.[143]

Some children show excessive eroticism and precocious sexual reactions. We have seen a boy of eleven years who was committed because he had been molesting little girls. He masturbated almost constantly throughout the day and at night would steal into the female ward and get into bed with adult women. The strong feeling of shame associated with the sexual life in childhood seems to be quite lacking in these children.[144]

She had an uncontrollable tendency to behave in an over-affectionate way. When she was not pinching or slapping them, she would like to sit with her arm around one of the other patients and longed for caresses. She tried to behave in the same way to the nursing staff. They described her as liking to be petted and "craving for sympathy."[145]

Case one. C.D., age twenty-seven years, male. . . . Patient was admitted to the Neurological Institute where a diagnosis of post-encephalitic (epidemic) Parkinsonism was made. After his discharge, he became involved with the police because of his conduct with young girls and older women. He would approach them and, without any preliminaries, attempt to fondle them, most often putting his hands on their buttocks. This, finally, led to difficulties in the home, the boy on many occasions having annoyed his step-mother and step-sister in this fashion. . . . . He was observed for a time at Grasslands Hospital, where many inmates complained that he tried to put his hands on their buttocks and on their heads. . . . . When interviewed, the patient explained that he desired to have sexual relations with women but had never succeeded in his advances, presumably because of his physical disabilities and unprepossessing appearance. Under these circumstances the presence of women close to him aroused great sexual desires which, wanting expression in socially acceptable forms, led him to place his hands on their buttocks.[146]

Case eight. B.C., born February 22, 1924, had encephalitis at three years, could not keep up with her school work at eight years . . . masturbated, stole, was disobedient, and ran away. . . . She showed numerous tics, she bit her knuckles, showed respiratory disturbances, compulsive masturbation. . . . At the age of twelve . . . she was restless, petulant, dull, had unremitting sex drive, was assaultive if annoyed, and complained of hearing voices saying she was mistreated.[147]

C.D was brought into the hospital at the age of twelve years because of sexual assaults upon little girls. . . . In August 1921, he was arrested with three other boys and charged with sexual assault. It was claimed that the patient had persuaded the other boys to join him in an assault upon a young girl, and investigation revealed that he had been molesting little girls for several months. . . . During his stay in the hospital the child was docile and good-natured. He was always smiling and expressed rather excessive affection for everyone. He masturbated at frequent intervals during the day. On several occasions he crept into the female ward during the night and crawled into bed with a young woman. The next morning he would apologize and promise not to do it again. . . . His subsequent fate is unknown.[148]

Sometimes the genitals are overdeveloped with early manifestation of secondary sexual characteristics.[149]

These individuals may also suffer from confusion of sexual identity, ranging from the boy's desire to wear dresses, to bisexualism or homosexualism.[150]

Case two. N.N., age twenty years, male. . . . At the age of four, in January 1918, he suffered with acute (epidemic) encephalitis leaving no immediate sequelae. Behavior difficulties became apparent a few years later. He constantly stole from other people, ran away from school, was sexually delinquent, stopped strangers on the street and asked them for money. . . . He admitted performance of perverse sexual acts in another hospital. . . . He showed aggressive, impulsive tendencies, was emotionally over-reactive, unstable, irritable, and unpredictable. Occasional homosexual trends were noted early in the course of his admission . . . conduct continues to be abnormal and he has a strong homosexual trend. He will prowl through the wards at night for the purpose of committing sodomy and requires very careful and continued supervision, both day and night. At times, he will try to assault the weaker patients who resent his advances.[151]

Encephalitis, Autism, and Minimal Brain Damage

The three preceding chapters have sought to demonstrate that the conditions known as "autism" and "minimal brain damage" are only parts of a larger entity—the post-encephalitic syndrome—which, in turn, is caused primarily by the childhood vaccination programs.

Richard Schain in 1977 noted the parallels between minimal brain damage and the post-encephalitic syndrome: "The early workers who described the brain damage syndrome consequent to epidemic encephalitis would be surprised at its present prevalence, albeit in an attenuated form."[152] But he did not suspect a connection with vaccination.

The proof that these are all essentially one and the same condition is found in the symptomatic parallels among them.

The areas affected are the central nervous system—especially the cranial nerves—the digestive process, and the immunologic apparatus.

Neurologic involvement is seen primarily in mental retardation, seizure disorders, muscular hypertony or hypotony, cerebral palsy, hyperactivity, and a tendency to left-handedness. When the cranial nerves are affected, the result is weakness of the eyes, ears, voice, and respiratory system, the latter condition being responsible for the cases of "sudden infant death" following upon vaccination.

The principal manifestation of cranial nerve involvement, of course, is the epidemic of dyslexia and other learning disabilities which are already overwhelming the American educational system.

Headaches and sleep disturbances are further ramifications of the overall neurologic destruction accompanying encephalitis.

The digestive and appetite disturbances associated with encephalitis are doubtless responsible, at least in part, for the epidemic of anorexia and bulimia and the weight-gain and obesity problems of Americans in the late twentieth century.

The immunologic sequelae of the post-encephalitic syndrome are discussed in Chapter IV.

The overall impact of encephalitis is "developmental delay" in all areas.

It does not appear that a violent acute case of encephalitis, or a violent acute vaccine reaction, are needed for the development of quite severe long-term neurologic sequelae.

No less important than the physical manifestations of the post-encephalitic syndrome are its intellectual and moral ones. Even the mildly affected individual often shows such symptoms as egotism, narcissism, ego weakness, alienation, impulsiveness, emotional lability, flat affect, anxiety, paranoia, impatience with criticism, rage, depression, and suicidal impulses.

Post-encephalitic individuals have fragmented thinking, and their memory is weak; hence they cannot think rationally and even lack ordinary common sense.

Compensation for these perceived weaknesses often takes the form of aggression against others, hypersexuality, homosexuality, alcohol or drug abuse, and suicide. Very probably these behaviors are also direct manifestations of the underlying neurologic weakness.

The long-term consequence of rage, aggression, premature sexuality, and drug and alcohol abuse in this population is the ongoing epidemic of violent crime in the United States—discussed at length in Chapter V.

While the vaccination program is, of course, not responsible for every instance of the above disabilities and social woes, it nonetheless makes a substantial contribution to them. The full extent of the contribution will become known only after the necessary specialized investigations have been performed to substantiate this working hypothesis.

Awareness of the relationship between these neurological disabilities and the post-encephalitic syndrome has been blocked heretofore by subconscious reluctance to admit that the childhood vaccination program is the only possible cause of a mass epidemic of clinical and sub-clinical encephalitis.

Chapter III Notes

1. Bannister, R., 1978, 408ff.
2. Von Economo, C., 1931.
3. Greenough, Anne *et al.*, 1983, 922. Ravenholt, R.T. and Foege, W.H., 1982, 860.
4. Christian, Henry, A., 1947, 379. Holt, William L., 1937, 1141. Neal, Josephine B., 1942, 6ff.
5. Greenough, Anne *et al.*, 1983, 922.
6. Merritt, H. H., 1979, 104.
7. Neal, Josephine B., 1942, 378–379.
8. Annell, A.L., 1953, 20.
9. Adams, R.D. and Victor, M., 1981, 658–659. Merritt, H.H., 1979, 105.
10. Coulter, H. and Fisher, B., 1985, Chapter 5: Adverse Reactions: An Afterthought? Chapter 7: Long-Term Damage. Ironside, R., 1956, 145.
11. Pittman, M. and Cox, C.B., 1965, 447.
12. Connaught Laboratories, 1986.
13. Coulter, H.L. and Fisher, B., 1985, Chapters 5 and 7.
14. *Ibid.*, 55–56.
15. *Ibid.*, 65–69 *et passim.*
16. Bond, Earl D. and Appel, K.E., 1931, 14.
17. *Loc. cit.* Annell, A.L., 1953, 19, 73.
18. Kennedy, R.L.J., 1924, 168.
19. Bond, Earl D. and Appel, K.E., 1931, 17.
20. Jacob, J. and Mannino, F., 1979.
21. Coulter, H.L. and Fisher, B., 1985, 61–65.
22. Byers, R.K. and Moll, F.C., 1948, 454. Annell, A.L., 1953, 20, 49.
23. Neal, Josephine A., 1942, 347.
24. Ford, Frank R., 1937, 352–353.

25. Connaught Laboratories, 1986.
26. *The Washington Post*, August 19, 1986, C-8: Ann Landers.
27. Kennedy, Roger L.J., 1924, 161.
28. Ford, Frank R., 1937, 356. Kirschbaum, Walter R., 1951, 110.
29. Kirschbaum, Walter R., 1951, 110. Ward, Christopher D., 1986, 219. Ford, Frank R., 1937, 355. Von Economo, C., 1931, 123.
30. Ford, Frank R., 1937, 359.
31. Holt, William L., 1937, 1143.
32. *The Washington Post*, September 1, 1988, B-9: Ann Landers.
33. Annell, A.L., 1953, 75–76.
34. Gibbs, Charles E., 1929/1930, 622.
35. Ford, Frank R, 1937, 355.
36. Bond, Earl D. and Smith, Lauren F., 1935, 32.
37. Cole, Blanche E., 1924, 988.
38. Kahn, Eugen and Cohen, L.H., 1934.
39. *Ibid.*, 750.
40. Neal, Josephine A., 1942, 329.
41. Greenebaum, J.V. and Lurie L.A., 1948, 927–928.
42. Coulter, H.L. and Fisher, B., 1985, 125–129.
43. Byers, R.K. and Moll, F.C., 1948.
44. Kulenkampff, M. *et al.*, 1974, 48.
45. Woody, Robert C. *et al.*, 1986, 2.
46. Neal, Josephine B., 1942, 349–350.
47. Byers, R.K. and Rizzo, N.D., 1950, 889, 890.
48. Annell, A.L., 1953, 67, 199.
49. Gibbs, Charles E., 1929/1930, 625.
50. Cole, Blanche E., 1924, 991.
51. *The New York Times*, April 23, 1986, C-1. Greenebaum, J.V. and Lurie, L.A., 1948, 927, 929. Lurie L.A. *et al.*, 1947, 173–174. *The Washington Post*, October 24, 1989, Health, 18.
52. Neal, Josephine B., 1933, 1147.
53. Holt, William A., 1937, 1143. Ford, Frank R., 1937, 350, 360.
54. Grossman, Morris, 1921, 582.
55. Bond, Earl D. and Partridge, G.E., 1926/1927, 86.
56. Von Economo, C., 1931, 123.
57. Coulter, H.L. and Fisher, B., 1985, 69–84, 110–132. See, also, Hirtz, D.G., Nelson, K.B., and Ellenberg, J.H., 1983.
58. Bond, E.D. and K.E.Appel, 1931, 21. Ford, Frank R., 1937, 356. Hill, T.R., 1928, 3.
59. Ford, Frank R., 1937, 356.
60. Annell, A.L., 1953, 51.

61. *Ibid.*, 69.
62. Greenebaum, J.V. and Lurie, L.A., 925, 927. Annell, A.L., 1953, 70.
63. Nelson, K.B. and Ellenberg, J.H., 1986.
64. Annell, A.L., 1953, 70.
65. Ward, C.D., 1986, 216.
66. Von Economo, C., 1931, 123.
67. Annell, A.L., 1953, 64.
68. Gibbs, C.E., 1929/1930, 627.
69. Ford, Frank R., 1937, 349.
70. Lurie, L.A. *et al.*, 1947, 178.
71. Baker, A.B., 1949, 11.
72. Annell, A.L., 1953, 25.
73. *Ibid.*, 33.
74. *Ibid.*, 17.
75. Bannister, R., 1978, 409.
76. Merritt, H.H., 1979, 104.
77. Coulter, H.L. and Fisher, B., 1985, 66–67.
78. Steinman, L. *et al.*, 1982, 739. Poser, C.M., 1987, 46.
79. Litvak, Abraham, M. *et al.*, 373. Bakwin, Harry, 1949, 375. Bond, Earl D. and Partridge, G.E., 1926/1927, 66.
80. Medical and Surgical Reporter (Lancaster, Pa.) XXI (1869), 3.
81. Hill, T.R., 1928, 4.
82. Bakwin, Harry, 1949, 375.
83. Quoted in Annell, A.L., 1953, 77.
84. *Ibid.*, 75. Cole, Blanche E., 1924, 991. Lurie, L.A. *et al.*, 1947, 172.
85. Cole, Blanche E., 1924, 985.
86. Bond, Earl D. and Appel, K.E., 1931, 17.
87. Ward, C.D., 1986, 219. Grossman, M., 1921, 581.
88. Annell, A.L., 1953, 78.
89. *Loc. cit.*
90. Lurie, L.A. *et al.*, 1947, 174.
91. Bond, Earl D. and Partridge, G.E., 1926/1927, 50.
92. *Ibid.*, 45.
93. *Ibid.*, 63, 87. Greenebaum, J.V. *et al.*, 1945, 1020. Neal, Josephine B., 1942, 337. Grossman, M., 1921, 581.
94. Lurie, L.A. and Levy, S., 1942, 891.
95. Greenebaum, J.V. and Lurie, L.A., 1948, 927–928.
96. Lurie, L.A. and Levy, S., 1942, 891. Hall, A.J., 1925, 111.
97. Elliott, Frank A., 1986, 230.

98. Bond, Earl D. and Partridge, G.E., 1926/1927, 38.
99. Elliott, Frank A., 1983, 87.
100. Bond, Earl D. and Partridge, G.E., 1926/1927, 50.
101. Gibbs, Charles E., 1929/1930, 626.
102. Bond, Earl D. and Partridge, G.E., 1926/1927, 53.
103. Hall, A.J., 1925, 111. See also, Elliott, Frank A., 1976, 299. Grossman, M., 1922, 961.
104. Elliott, Frank A., 1986, 230.
105. Quoted in Annell, A.L., 1953, 55.
106. *Ibid.*, 55.
107. Bender, L., 1940, 286.
108. Annell, A.L., 1953, 15, 29, 55, 61.
109. Neal, Josephine B., 1942, 382. Annell, A.L., 1953, 30. Lurie, L.A., *et al.*, 1947, 177.
110. Annell, A. L., 1953, 31. Lurie, L.A. and Levy, S., 1942, 892. Hill, T.R., 1928, 2. Ward, C.D., 1986, 218.
111. Bond, Earl D. and Partridge, G.E., 1926/1927, 66.
112. Lurie, L. A. *et al.*, 1947, 175.
113. Annell, A.L., 1953, 77.
114. Annell, A.L., 1953, 75.
115. Neal, Josephine B., 1942, 353.
116. Bond, Earl D. and Partridge, G.E., 1926/1927, 80, 88. Cole, Blanche E., 1924, 991. Bond, Earl D. and Appel, K.E., 1931, 17.
117. Bond, Earl D. and Partridge, G.E., 1926/1927, 68.
118. Cole, Blanche E., 1924, 984.
119. Bond, Earl D. and Partridge, G.E., 1927/1927, 83. Lurie, L.A. *et al.*, 1947, 173.
120. Cole, Blanche, E., 1924, 987.
121. Annell, A.L., 1953, 72–73.
122. Hill, T.R., 1928, 4–5.
123. Auden, G.A., 1922, 902.
124. Bond, E.K. and Partridge, G.E., 1926/1927, 48.
125. *Ibid.*, 74.
126. Hill, T.R., 1928, 5.
127. Ford, Frank R., 1937, 360–361.
128. Cole, Blanche E., 1924, 1011.
129. Elliott, Frank A., 1976, 298.
130. Neal, Josephine B., 1942, 364. See, also, Greenebaum, J.V. and Lurie, L.A., 1948, 926–927.
131. Hill, T.R., 1928, 7.
132. *Ibid.*, 4.

133. *Ibid.*, 6.
134. Elliott, Frank A., 1976. 298.
135. Moyer, K.E., 1976, 30.
136. Ford, Frank R. 1937, 357.
137. Lurie, L.A. and Levy, S., 1942, 891.
138. Hill, T.R., 1928, 5.
139. Greenebaum, J.V. *et al.*, 1945, 1019. Neal, Josephine B., 1942, 339. Ward, C.W., 1986, 219. Lurie, L.A. and Levy, Sol, 1942, 893. Bond, Earl D. and Appel, K., 1931, 19. Bond, Earl D. and Partridge, G.E., 1926/1927, 54.
140. Greenough, A. *et al.*, 1983, 922.
141. Lurie, L.A and Levy, S., 1942, 891.
142. Kennedy, Roger, L.J., 1924, 170.
143. Cole, Blanche E., 1924, 985.
144. Ford, Frank R., 1937, 357.
145. Hill, T.R., 1928, 6–7.
146. Neal, Josephine B., 1942, 328–329.
147. *Ibid.*, 374.
148. Ford, Frank R., 1937, 361.
149. *Ibid.*, 356. Von Economo, C., 1931, 123.
150. Kennedy, Roger, L.J., 1924, 160. Bond, Earl D. and Partridge, G.E., 1926/1927, 58, 77. Gibbs, Charles E., 1929/1930, 624.
151. Neal, Josephine B., 1942, 330.
152. Schain, R.J., 1977, 34.

IV

Vaccination and Allergies

Half the American population suffers from skin allergies, allergic rhinitis, bronchial asthma of allergic origin, food allergies, and others. The prevalence of allergies is steadily rising in all industrial societies.

This creeping epidemic could well be one more long-term effect of our increasingly widespread and all-encompassing childhood vaccination programs.

Another aspect of the allergy epidemic is the phenomenon of "autoimmunity," in which the body becomes, so to speak, sensitized to itself. This class of diseases first emerged in the 1950s and has been steadily expanding.

DPT: A Shot in the Dark discussed the allergy component in vaccination reactions, noting that allergic children react more strongly to the DPT shot and that the vaccine seems to heighten existing allergic sensitivities. We concluded, "Certainly the question of whether a personal or family history of allergy puts a child at high risk of reacting to the pertussis vaccine deserves further serious investigation."[1]

Our comment was noted by the manufacturers. At the time of publication (1985) of *DPT: A Shot in the Dark*, vaccine package inserts nowhere mentioned "allergic reaction" as a contraindication to the DPT shot, but in 1986 Connaught Laboratories changed its product insert to warn of "allergic" and "anaphylactic reactions" after DPT vaccination. It advised that "allergic hypersensitivity to any component of the vaccine" is an "absolute contraindication"

151

against further shots.[2]

Some children are apparently born with an allergic sensitivity to milk in the form of a tendency to colic, and they are particularly at risk from a vaccine-induced encephalitis. Others are not allergic from birth but become allergic after the shots. Both groups develop new allergies as they mature and are exposed to allergenic substances in the environment.

> *I took him in to the doctor to have him checked why he was coughing so much, and they did tests, and it came back that he was allergic to milk. So they switched him to soybean, and he couldn't take the soybean formula, so he had to be put on goat's milk. He didn't appear to be allergic to milk until after the DPT shot.*
>
> *Gregory was so allergic to milk he finally had to be put on Isomil, a type of formula. To this day he is fussy about milk. If he drinks certain kinds, certain brands of whole milk, he will go into the bathroom and have diarrhea, and it is a very light yellow color.*

Allergies in Encephalitis, Autism, and Minimal Brain Damage

Our finding of an allergy component in vaccination reactions merely brought to public attention what had always been common knowledge in the medical profession—that encephalitis, especially from vaccination, can give rise to an allergic state, while conversely the existence of an allergic state predisposes to the development of encephalitis after vaccination.

The interrelation among allergies, vaccination, and encephalitis has been an active topic of medical investigation since the 1930s,[3] and a 1954 study on "neurologic sequelae of prophylactic inoculation" summarized state-of-the-art knowledge in noting that the common factor in the pathology of encephalitis from vaccination is "anaphylactic hypersensitivity."[4]

Lawrence Steinman and colleagues at the Stanford University School of Medicine (mentioned in Chapter III) in 1983 performed an animal study indicating that children with allergies may overreact to the pertussis vaccine.[5]

An experiment by Kevin Geraghty, a pediatric immunologist from San Francisco and active critic of the DPT vaccine, is also instructive. He found that one strain of mice reacts violently to the DPT vaccine, while another is quite unaffected. But when mice of the latter strain are first injected with histamine (a cell-released substance which elevates their allergic sensitivity), they then react violently to this vaccine and die in epileptic seizures.[6]

Allergies and other immune-system abnormalities are commonly associated with autism. Four-fifths of autistic children and adults have "severe allergies."[7] Their high levels of serotonin—another substance released by cells during allergic and anaphylactic reactions —point to a chronic allergic condition.[8]

Food allergies are undoubtedly at the origin of the stomach pains, constipation, and diarrhea from which autistics often suffer. These children may have a tendency to colic from an early age, problems with calcium metabolism, and signs of milk intolerance.[9] There may be gastroenteritis, indeterminate stomach pains, flatulence, diarrhea, alternating diarrhea and constipation, etc.[10]

In its most severe form, this becomes celiac disease—severe allergy to wheat products and sometimes to milk products as well. Lauretta Bender in 1953 called attention to the high incidence of celiac disease among patients diagnosed as "schizophrenic" (the distinction between autism and schizophrenia was unclear in 1953), but Rimland was the first to notice the coincidence of autism with celiac disease, writing in 1967 that autistics often manifested "symptoms of gastrointestinal disorder."[11]

Mary Coleman, a physician in Washington, D.C., has also written on the association of celiac disease with autism. Of seventy-eight autistics collected by her for a 1976 study, eight had celiac disease—slightly over ten percent of the sample. This was 200 to 800 times the published frequency of celiac disease in the population, suggesting a strong association with autism. Seven others had a "history compatible with celiac disease."[12]

Sometimes the diagnosis of celiac disease or celiac autism is made after successful therapy through withdrawal of wheat products from the child's diet. Gluten worsens the child's symptoms, and its elimination leads to improvement.[13]

Rimland has written in this connection:

> Wheat is a common and powerful disruptor of behavior in some children. We have case histories of certain autistic children whose behavior becomes completely wild for several days after he or she eats any wheat. Too much wheat can mean the corner of a soda cracker, a chicken leg rolled in flour, a few Wheaties flakes, a hamburger patty to which some of the bun has adhered. . . . Some of these children, including several who later became textbook cases of autism, were diagnosed as having celiac disease in infancy.[14]

Hyperactive and minimally brain-damaged children also manifest a high incidence of allergic manifestations.[15] Doris Rapp, a pediatric allergist practicing in Buffalo who was interviewed for this book, stated her opinion that two thirds of hyperactive or minimally brain-damaged children suffer also from severe allergies. She stated further:

> I have repeatedly noted in the history of many of the small children whom I treat for allergies that they get a DPT, and then within a month or two they begin to regress. Their allergies will have gotten better, and they will have started to learn well and easily, and then they get their DPT, and a short time later their allergies come back, and they stop talking, or they don't walk as well. The parents keep giving me this history and they ask, "Is it related?"[16]

She has written two valuable discussions of this connection: *Allergies and the Hyperactive Child* and *The Impossible Child*.[17] Another important discussion of allergies, autism, and hyperactivity is *Allergies, Your Hidden Enemy* by Theron G. Randolph and Ralph W. Moss.[18]

The autoimmune diseases—rheumatoid arthritis, systemic lupus erythematosus, allergic rhinitis, celiac disease, pernicious anemia, and others which came to prominence in the 1950s—are thought to result from the body's allergic reaction "to itself," or to some component of "self."

As already noted, Norman Geschwind found a tie between

autism, dyslexia, and autoimmune diseases.[19] Some authorities have gone so far as to call autism an autoimmune disease, and Israeli researchers in 1982 found autistic children to have a "cell-mediated immune response to brain tissue," suggesting that an "undetectable brain lesion associated with autoimmunity may play a role in the pathogenesis of autism."[20] Researchers in France and the United States have found abnormally active immune-system reactions in autistic children, suggesting a state of hypersensitivity.[21]

It is highly probable that autoimmunity and developmental disabilities are interlinked by way of a vaccine-induced encephalitis.[22] In 1970 G.A. Rosenberg wrote: "An autoimmune allergic mechanism has been postulated as the cause of the uncommon occurrence of postvaccinal encephalitis, possibly with an initial invasion of the nervous system by a virus, with a subsequent antigen-antibody reaction."[23] If this line of research is followed up, the interrelations among these conditions will doubtless be substantiated.

Myelin and Demyelination

The key to these relationships is the myelination process and its interruption.

Myelin is the tough, white, fatty, waterproof substance that coats the nerves like insulation on an electric wire and has the same function.

Development of the child's nervous system during pregnancy and after birth occurs in two stages. First the nerve fibers (neurons and axons) appear. Only when they are all in place does the process of coating with myelin commence.

Prior to myelination the nerve fibers are vulnerable, as nerve impulses travel more slowly through unmyelinated than through myelinated fibers, and they can short-circuit from fiber to fiber.[24]

But at the moment of birth myelination has only just commenced. In some nerves it does not even start until eight months of age or later.[25]

It proceeds at different rates in different neurologic areas *for the next fifteen years*, and in some nerves myelination continues to age 45![26]

It starts in the phylogenetically older parts of the brain (those areas which humans share with the lower animals) and then moves to the phylogenetically more recent parts (which distinguish the human from animals). Since the cerebral hemispheres and the cerebral cortex (the locus of memory and higher activities of the mind) are the phylogenetically newest parts, they are the last to be completely myelinated—in the *fifth year* of life or later.[27]

Anything that interferes with myelination hinders the child's neurologic development and maturation. If myelin is prevented from being deposited or, once deposited, is removed (demyelination), the nervous system remains undeveloped and immature. The newborn infant, *especially if premature*, is clearly very much at risk.[28]

To be precise, a vaccination-associated encephalitis sometime during the first year of life could easily interrupt the myelination process and thus cause neurological damage. Charles M. Poser of the Harvard Medical School Department of Neurology writes:

> Almost any . . . vaccination can lead to a noninfectious inflammatory reaction involving the nervous system. . . . The common denominator consists of a vasculopathy that is often . . . associated with demyelination.[29]

In 1947 Isaac Karlin suggested—with great prescience, it would appear—that stuttering is caused by "delay in the myelinization of the cortical areas in the brain concerned with speech."[30] In 1951 he extended this idea to "congenital word deafness."[31] More recently Roland Ciaranello suggested that the link between autism in the child and German measles (rubella) in the pregnant woman might be through "impaired myelination"—children dead of rubella have inadequate myelination in various areas of the brain—but he did not develop the point further.[32] Quite recent research (1988) by Rosalind B. Dietrich and colleagues, using magnetic resonance imaging of the brains of infants and children from four days to thirty-six months of age has found that those who were developmentally delayed had immature patterns of myelination.[33]

Researchers also find that impairment of myelination alters neural communication without necessarily causing severe central nervous system damage.[34]

Now the meaning of "delay"—as in "developmental delay"—becomes obvious. It signifies physical immaturity of the nervous system, due to impairment of the myelination process—or even its undoing.[35]

The mother who exclaims, "Sam is a child, in the body of a man!" is speaking the literal truth.[36]

Experimental Allergic Encephalomyelitis

The association between the post-encephalitic syndrome and demyelination or incomplete myelination of the brain seems quite secure. And the fact that encephalitis—*including that caused by vaccination*—can cause demyelination has been known since the 1920s![37]

But precisely how this occurred, i.e., the role of the allergic reaction in encephalitis, became understood only after the 1935 discovery by the prominent American scientist, Thomas Rivers, of the phenomenon known as "experimental allergic encephalomyelitis."

Prior to this time physicians had assumed that encephalitis was caused by direct viral or bacterial infection of the nervous system. But when, in the 1920s, they started searching for these infective microorganisms, none were to be found, and the causal factor for a while remained an enigma. The mystery was solved when Rivers produced brain inflammation in monkeys merely by injecting them repeatedly with extracts of sterile normal rabbit brain and spinal cord material.[38]

Encephalitis was now seen to be an *allergic* phenomenon, and this explains the association of allergies and autoimmune states with a prior case of encephalitis.

Experimental allergic encephalomyelitis remains even today the prime research model for studying the evolution of autoimmune diseases and their effect on the nervous system.[39]

Peculiar allergic skin rashes had often been observed during infectious diseases associated with encephalitis, as well as after certain vaccinations.[40] So Rivers' famous experiment provided an explanation for this phenomenon also. No longer was encephalitis attributed to viral or bacterial infection of the brain. After 1935 physicians looked increasingly to the allergy model to understand encephalitis and the post-encephalitic syndrome.[41]

This "experimental allergic encephalomyelitis" (EAE), is identical to encephalitis after infectious diseases such as measles and whooping cough and, by extension, after vaccination—with myelin playing the role of antigen.[42] While the precise mechanism is not fully understood, the myelin dissolved in the blood and other fluids by the inflammation of encephalitis seems to act as an additional antigen, intensifying the inflammatory reaction.[43]

The two aspects of encephalitis feed upon one another.

Usually, some discrete portion of the nervous system is involved: the meninges (the membrane around the brain and spinal cord), the brain itself, the brainstem, the spinal cord, the nerves, or a combination of some or all of these.[44]

But the reaction can extend to any part of the brain or central nervous system, explaining the heterogeneous symptoms and sequelae of these diseases.[45] "Atypical" cases of postvaccinal encephalomyelitis may "mimic" meningitis, viral encephalitis, or poliomyelitis.[46]

Autopsies after postvaccinal encephalitis show many small yellowish-red lesions in the white matter of the cerebrum, cerebellum, brainstem, and spinal cord. Their characteristic feature is loss of myelin: staining shows "complete or incomplete destruction of myelin sheaths within the lesions . . . [the nerves] are affected to much less extent than the myelin sheaths."[47]

If the functions of the human brain were to be replicated by a modern computer, it would occupy two city blocks of circuits and synapses. Even a single neuron can transmit several messages simultaneously (just as several telephone or telegraph conversations can be passed along a single filament).

The effect of encephalitis on the brain can be likened to dropping heavy weights through the roof of one of these computers here and there at randomly selected points. The resulting damage cannot always be categorized or described with precision, despite heroic efforts by the American Psychiatric Association.

The pertussis vaccine itself was awarded a bit part in this ongoing drama when, in 1959, it was found to have a peculiarly powerful allergenic effect on all sorts of laboratory animals. Experiments to produce anaphylactic shock are facilitated by addition of pertussis vaccine to the solution: the mice (or rabbits, or hamsters, or whatever) die more rapidly and in larger numbers.[48] By the same token, addition of vaccine to the sterile brain and spinal cord solution greatly enhances its ability to generate an allergic encephalitis.[49]

For these reasons pertussis vaccine is the preferred "adjuvant" in experiments to produce allergic encephalomyelitis.

U.S. vaccination authorities seem steadily oblivious to the danger of injecting U.S. children with an "adjuvant" which, of all those known to the world of biochemistry, has the most pronounced ability to produce allergic sensitization.

James D. Cherry, a prominent specialist in the vaccine field and professor at the UCLA School of Medicine, observes, "There is no evidence that any of the experimental adjuvant activities of pertussis vaccine . . . occur in vaccinated children."[50] But that is only because these "experimental adjuvant activities" have never been sought. Small babies differ in many ways from mice, rabbits, and hamsters—but not in their vulnerability to anaphylactic shock or allergic encephalitis.

This point should be investigated further.

Increasing Allergic Hypersensitivity of Modern Man

The discovery of EAE clarified an important issue which had been puzzling physicians. Prior to World War I, the infectious diseases of childhood had rarely been complicated by encephalitis. After 1920, however, physicians noted a steady rise in the numbers of such cases. The rabies vaccine had always yielded a high incidence of encephalitis (one in 750 cases, with twenty percent mortality), but soon encephalitis was found after other vaccinations as well.[51]

In 1922 the smallpox vaccination program, for the first time in history, caused an outbreak of encephalitis; one of the more malevolent after-effects was an ascending paralysis, often ending in death, known as the Guillain-Barre Syndrome.[52] Annell wrote in

1953:

> During the past few decades certain of the epidemic children's dis-
> eases—measles in particular—have shown an increased tendency
> to attack the central nervous system. . . . Up to the 1920s only
> isolated cases were, as a rule, described. After this time a large
> number—not uncommonly occurring epidemically—were
> reported.[53]

Other perceptive researchers at length realized that "the increased incidence of cerebral involvement may be due . . . to a special reaction, e.g. *of an allergic nature.*" [emphasis added][54]

Roger Bannister, a leading British neurologist, stated the same in 1978: these acute demyelinating diseases have become more serious because of "some abnormal process of sensitization of the nervous system."[55]

"Sensitized" is the technical term for "allergic." The greater reactivity of today's children to vaccinations and to ordinary child-hood diseases—expressed as a tendency to encephalitis—is due to the emergence of an allergic dimension that had not been there before. But why are children today more allergic than they used to be?

Quite probably because the level of allergic sensitization of the American population is being steadily enhanced by the vaccination programs which commenced in the beginning of the century. Prior to 1900 encephalitis from childhood diseases was an almost negligible danger. After 1920 it was encountered more and more frequently.

And today the threat of encephalitis from whooping cough or measles is the main justification for vaccination programs.

Thus the medical profession is in the curious position of urging vigorous measures against a health threat created largely by itself.

Genetic Predisposition?

An aspect of autism and minimal brain damage that has steadily puzzled researchers is the finding that related conditions are fre-quently found in other family members.

These range from stomach aches, diarrhea, and colic to far more serious conditions. In one study fifteen autistic children were randomly selected from twenty-three cooperating families. Eight families reported two mentally handicapped children apiece, including six pairs that were autistic; of the twelve autistics seven also had gastrointestinal disorders. In four other families five children had been diagnosed autistic, schizophrenic, and celiac; seven had combinations of autism, schizophrenia, celiac disease, eczema, and learning disabilities, and four a gamut of autism, schizophrenia, eczema, food intolerance, and learning disabilities. One family of four had diagnoses of autism, celiac-like symptoms, learning disabilities, and neurosensory hearing loss.[56]

Other studies find that autism, pervasive developmental disorder, developmental language disorders, stuttering, academic skills disorders, developmental articulation disorders, and many other "Disorders Usually First Evident in Infancy, Childhood, or Adolescence" are clustered in the same families and their close relatives.

Often the connection among the conditions has been the red thread of allergy or autoimmunity running through all the cases.[57]

This has stimulated a search for genetic factors supposedly predetermining the child to become autistic, celiac, learning-disabled, autoimmune, or the like.

However, this search is misguided. The genetic factor to be sought is the child's *predisposition to react to vaccination.* No child of healthy parents and an uneventful pregnancy is born to become autistic. But a perfectly healthy baby can be constitutionally vulnerable to the effects of vaccination. When this enhanced vulnerability encounters the hypodermic needle, the outcome is autism, minimal brain damage, or some other neurologic disorder.

There is, without any doubt, a genetic link among all of these conditions. The family clustering evidence is overwhelming. But, as Steinman's research has shown, clustering is due to the genetically determined predisposition of members of the same family to react violently to vaccination.[58] If that factor could be spotted, and those children not be vaccinated, there would be no more family clustering of developmental or autoimmune disorders, and a tiny incidence of these disorders generally.*

---

*Steg and Rapoport in 1975 claimed to have found that certain minor physical abnormalities—relating to head size, shape of ears, height of palate, length of the toes and gap between toes, and curvature of the

Dietary Treatment of Allergies

Since multiple allergies are common in both autism and minimal brain damage, it stands to reason that treatment of the allergic state—specifically by refraining from allergenic foods—would benefit these children:

Q. My three-year-old son has a number of idiosyncrasies that concern me.

He has always banged his head before going to sleep or when he is tired, even in his car seat. In a department store he will lie down on the floor and bang his head. I thought he'd outgrow this by now.

He also bites his hand. He has a large callus area, which is continually peeling, because he chomps on his hand whenever he gets excited.

He has other disturbing habits. He stuffs socks down the front or back of his shirt, and he piles the blanket, the pillow, and the top sheet on a hill on his bed and sleeps on them.

Am I unduly concerned or not concerned enough? . . . He goes to nursery school two mornings a week and does fine, but at home he is rough, loud, volatile, cries easily, and becomes frustrated quickly.

A. You're right to be concerned about your little boy . . . First you should rule out neurological problems and particularly allergies and sensitivities. Many, many parents have written to say that these cause temper tantrums, frequent crying, sleeplessness, and head-banging—in their children. . . . You can test his diet simply by eliminating all forms of milk, wheat, corn, eggs, sugar, cocoa, peanuts, pork, beef, yeast, preservatives, and colors—the most common allergens—for five days. The child is then challenged by reintroducing a food each day.[59]

Even in the 1920s researchers had noted the relationship

---

fingers—distinguish learning disabled or "severely disturbed" children from normal controls. This is an interesting approach and should be followed up. Of course, researchers will have to ensure that these abnormalities are not themselves the consequence of vaccine damage (see Steg, J.P. and Rapoport, J.L., 1975).

between encephalitis, food allergies, and behavioral disturbances: allergy-prone children were seen to be "restless, irritable, unruly, peevish, out-of-sorts, high-strung, and difficult to manage . . . because of anaphylactic reactions to food proteins to which the patient is sensitized."[60] But this knowledge was largely lost, to be revived decades later by Linus Pauling, Theron Randolph, Benjamin Feingold, and a few others with a broader perspective.

Probably the most widespread dietary treatment for hyperactivity, and for allergies generally, is the Feingold Diet, now propagated by the Feingold Association which has twelve chapters in the United States and seven or eight in other countries.

Feingold held that hyperactivity is worsened by foods containing certain artifical (petroleum-based) colors, flavors, and preservatives as well as natural salicylates. The diet stipulates a five-day fast to eliminate these substances from the organism; thereafter all foods containing such substances are avoided.

Humphrey Osmond, Abram Hoffer, Bernard Rimland and others have called for dietary and vitamin treatment of autism and other "mental illnesses" according to the principles of "orthomolecular psychiatry," a concept first introduced in 1968 by Linus Pauling and defined as "treatment of mental disease by the provision of the optimum molecular environment for the mind, especially the optimum concentration of substances normally present in the human body."[61]

They have emphasized vitamin C and nicotinic acid (one of the vitamin-B complex), but many other combinations of vitamins are used as well; allergenic foods or clothing are replaced by hypoallergenic foods and household articles.

In addition, they urge a program of allergy desensitization.[62]

Many case reports have been published indicating success with these various treatments:

> When she was eight years old, I became interested in nutrition after reading several of Adelle Davis's books and began, on my own, to give Terry [autistic] large doses of vitamin C. We noted improvement in her behavior immediately . . . through diet and our own vitamin program we have been able to control her behavior—except for occasional uncontrollable lapses, always traceable to sweet-food binges.[63]

One of 100 children in a megavitamin control program conducted by Dr. Bernard Rimland, Aaron showed immediate improvement. He was nine years old then, and we had all suffered six useless years of Freudian psychotherapy with no result other than compounded confusion and guilt. . . . We feel the vitamins reduced the established pattern of ritual play and general tension.[64]

Skin testing to about a dozen substances served as a guide to several trials of food elimination. Avoidance of orange, corn, wheat, and eggs led to reports from his parents and school that he had improved urinary control, better sleep, more direct gaze, and a more affectionate affect.[65]

Paul was noisy, incontinent, and destructive. . . . On a gluten-free diet, his appetite returned, his weight increased, his autistic symptoms decreased, and he began to share play and meal times with other patients.

A brief severe relapse occurred when a normal diet was ordered in error. Reinstitution of the gluten-free regime restored · his previous course. . . . Paul displays increasing friendliness and presents few management problems.[66]

The theory of food allergies hypothesizes that the body craves precisely the substances which are most harmful to it:

the foods he was most allergic to were the very ones he had seemed so addicted to at home and had craved so badly and enjoyed so much. Apparently the initial feeling of stimulated well-being appealed to him, and when it wore off, he tried to restore it by quickly trying to obtain more of that same food before the unpleasant symptoms began. It seemed to have been a vicious cycle.[67]

In 1978 Dan O'Banion published a careful study of the effects of certain foods on "levels of hyperactivity, uncontrolled laughter, and disruptive behaviors" in an eight-year-old autistic boy. The floor of the child's room was taped off into six equal-sized rectangles to measure the general activity level. Frequency data were recorded on screaming, biting, scratching, laughing, and object-throwing.[68]

The results showed that foods such as wheat, corn, tomatoes, sugar, mushrooms, and dairy products were instrumental in producing behavioral disorders with this child.

But, despite encouraging results, dietary and megavitamin treatments of autism and minimal brain damage have not been accepted with enthusiasm by the medical profession, some of whose members (writing in establishment medical journals) suggest that parents seeking this for their children need psychiatric treatment themselves:

> One must always keep in mind the sequence that families go through when informed they have a developmentally disturbed child. . . . Search for Magical Cure (I know mega-vitamins and chiropractic manipulations will cure my child). . . . In the face of these reactions, appropriate supportive counselling may be necessary. (*Pediatric Annals*)[69]

> Five days of starvation is a serious stress for a young child. The laxatives given if the child takes a forbidden food might be considered punitive. The establishment of special diets based upon additive-free organic foods is both expensive and inconvenient. Eliminating synthetic fibers from clothing, bedding, and furnishings is both difficult and expensive. Altering all of these things would certainly alter family dynamics. . . . The anecdotal evidence offered, while interesting, should not be accepted by parents or other physicians until much more substantial evidence is made available. (*Journal of Autism*)[70]

> I know of no good data demonstrating that niacin or megavitamin therapy does anything for autistics, although there is much talk about its effectiveness. . . . To my knowledge the data have not been published for critical review, and until they are, the citation implies that this has been demonstrated and accepted, whereas in fact it has not. This may create hope and eventual disappointment. (*Journal of Autism*)[71]

U.S. government literature on hyperactivity also tends to belittle the data from nutritional studies: "Many studies, including those supported by the Food and Drug Administration and the Nutrition Foundation, have been unable to support the Feingold claims."[72]

Only very recently has a standard text (*Nelson's Textbook of Pediatrics*) managed to say something positive about dietary and megavitamin treatment.[73]

Caution in accepting new modes of treatment is always well-advised, and if physicians had been equally cautious in accepting central nervous system stimulants and depressants and other substances for treating these children, they would deserve all credit. Unfortunately, they were not. Dozens of drugs—amphetamines, barbiturates, chlorpromazine, phenobarbitol, fluphenazine, methylphenidate, lithium carbonate, benzodiazepine, haloperidol, and others—together with milieu therapy, aversive therapy, psychotherapy, hormonal treatment, electrical and insulin shock, frontal lobotomy, and other modes of treatment have been endorsed enthusiastically by physicians, even though they have had less justification than is offered in favor of dietary and megavitamin treatment.

Physicians have three reasons for disliking dietary treatment (lack of therapeutic efficacy is not one of them): a) They know comparatively little about nutrition, having almost never studied it in medical school, and feel ill-equipped to use nutritional techniques, b) Advising the patient to change his diet, or buy some bottles of vitamins, seems somehow undignified—unsuited to a professional with eight or ten years of training, c) Dietary treatment must be tailored to the specific child or adolescent—*individualized*—which takes time and understanding.

For all these reasons physicians much prefer treating with drugs. They learn a little pharmacology in medical school and feel competent in this area. Prescribing a powerful prescription drug seems more consonant with the physician's elevated professional status. Finally, drugs can be prescribed rapidly, and time is the physician's most precious commodity.

Drug treatment is quick because drugs are developed for broad classes of diseases ("autism," "learning disabilities"), and once the diagnosis is made, the prescription follows automatically. This is then justified as "scientific" because "scientific" is understood to be that which is applicable to a large class of patients.

But prescribing powerful medicines to broad categories of poorly defined patients inevitably generates side-effects which would not occur if the prescriptions were more precise.

Treatment that must be adjusted to the patient (e.g., diet or vitamins), and is almost never harmful, may be seen as "unscientific," when, in actuality, it is just more trouble and more time-consuming.

The treatment of millions of minimally brain-damaged children and adolescents with powerful pharmaceutical substances is making its due contribution to the national scourge of drug addiction, as described in the next chapter.

Chapter IV Notes

1. Coulter, H.L. and Fisher, B., 1985, 208.
2. Connaught Laboratories, 1986.
3. Finley, K.H., 1938. Miller, H.G. and Stanton, J.B., 1954. Warren, W.R., 1956. Neal, J.B., 1942, 77. Bakwin, H., 1949, 376.
4. Miller, H.G. and Stanton, J.B. 1954.
5. Coulter, H.L. and Fisher, B., 1985, 132. Steinman, L. *et al.*, 1982.
6. Geraghty, K. C., Zahalsky, A.C., and Novotny, A. (to be published).
7. Freeman, B.J. *et al.*, 1984, 286. S.M.Baker, 1984, 14. E.G. Stubbs *et al.*, 1977, 50. M. and W. Goodwin, 1969, 559, 563.
8. Coleman, M., 1980, 11.
9. Coleman, M. *et al.*, 1976, 202–204, 214, 222. Bergman, P. and Escalona, S.R., 1949, 337. Lewis, S.R. *et al.*, 1960, 510.
10. Gillberg, C. *et al.*, 1984, 355. Stubbs, E.G. *et al.*, 1984, 186. Goldberg, T.E. *et al.*, 1984, 766. Mnukhin, S.S. *et al.*, 1975, 106. Goodwin, M.S. *et al.*, 1971.
11. Sullivan, R.C., 1975, 180.
12. Coleman, M., 1976, 197–205, 214–215. O'Banion, D. *et al.*, 1978, 327.
13. Dohan, F.C, 1970, 897.
14. Quoted in Coleman, M., 1980, 198.
15. Geschwind, N., 1982, 19. Routh, D.K., 1977, 421. Kaplan, B.J. *et al.*, 1987, 309. Backman, Z.M., 1985.
16. Interview with Doris J. Rapp, M.D., October, 1989.
17. Rapp, Doris J., 1979, 1986.
18. Randolph, T.J. and Moss, R., 1981.
19. Geschwind, N. *et al.*, 1982.
20. Sullivan R.C., 1975, 178, 185. M. Coleman, 1976, 4. Weizman, A. *et al.*, 1982.
21. *Science News* 130 (July 26, 1986). See, also, Stubbs, E.G. *et al.*, 1976. 1977, and 1980. Warren, R.P. *et al.*, 1986.
22. Menkes, J.H., 1980, Chapter 7: Autoimmune and Postinfectious Diseases.
23. Rosenberg, G.A., 1970.

24. Ciaranello, R.D. *et al.*, 1982, 136.
25. *Ibid.*, 137. Dobbing, J., 1968, 184. Dietrich, R.B., 1988, 893.
26. Dobbing, J., 1968, 184, 196. Dietrich, R.B., 1988, 893. Elliott, Frank A., 1986, 232.
27. Laufer, M.W. *et al.*, 45. Dietrich, R.B., 1988, 893.
28. Amiel-Tison, C., 1973, 6. Dobbing, J., 1968, 196. Menolaschino, F.J. et al., 247.
29. Poser, C.H., 1987, 45–46.
30. Karlin, I., 1947.
31. Karlin, I., 1951, 66.
32. Ciaranello, R. D., 1981, 187. Ciaranello, R.D., *et al.*, 1982, 136.
33. Dietrich, R.D., 1988.
34. Ciaranello, R.D. *et al.*, 137.
35. Younes, R.P. *et al.*, 1983. Shaywitz, S.E. *et al.*, 1984. Schain, R.J., 1977, 2. Money, J., 1966, 59. Laufer, M.W. *et al.*, 1957, 469. Clements, Sam D. *et al.*, 1981, 185. Satterfield, J.H., 1973, 47.
36. *J. Autism* 7 (1977), 291.
37. Adams, R.D. and Victor M., 1981, 658. Bender, L., 1943, 75.
38. Rivers, T.M. *et al.*, 1935.
39. Arnason, B., 1987, 406. Menkes, J.H., 1980, 375.
40. Neal, Josephine A., 1942, 461–462, 477. Annell, A.L., 1953, 11, 16, 131.
41. Neal, Josephine A., 1942, 77. Bakwin, Harry, 1949, 376.
42. Arnason, B., 1987, 406. Hemachudha, T. *et al.*, 1987.
43. Menkes, J.H., 1980, 375. Weizman, A. *et al.*, 1982. Bannister, R., 1978, 408. Poser, C.M., 1987, 46, 52, 55.
44. Adams, R.D. and Victor, M., 1981, 659.
45. Merritt, H.H., 1979, 104.
46. Adams, R.D. and Victor, M., 1987, 659.
47. Merritt, H.H., 1979, 102–103.
48. Cherry, J. *et al.*, 1988, 943.
49. *Loc. cit.*
50. *Loc. cit.*
51. Bannister, R., 1978, 408. Adams, R.D. and Victor, M, 1981, 658.
52. Neal, J.B., 1942, 444; 1933, 1148.
53. Annell, A.L., 1953, 15–16.
54. *Ibid.*, 16.
55. Bannister, R., 1978, 408.
56. Goodwin, M.S. *et al.*, 1971, 49. Also, Folstein, S. *et al.*, 1988. Coleman, M., 1976, 215, 221. Kanner, L., 1954, 381.
57. Sullivan, R.C., 1975, 177. F.C.Dohan, 1970. Money, J. *et al.*, 1971.

58. Steinman, L. *et al.*, 1982.
59. *The Washington Post*, January 15, 1987, C-5: "Family Almanac."
60. Bakwin, H., 1949, 376.
61. Hawkins, D. and Pauling, L., eds., 1973. Hoffer, A., 1974. Campbell, 1973, 360–361. O'Banion, D. *et al.*, 1978. A general discussion of dietary treatment for allergic states is found in L.D. Dickey, 1976.
62. Egger, J. *et al.*, 1985.
63. *J. Autism* 8 (1978), 109.
64. *Ibid.* 7 (1977), 298.
65. Baker, S.M., 1984, 19.
66. Goodwin, M.S. and W.C., 1969, 561.
67. *J. Autism* 6:1 (1976), 82.
68. O'Banion, D. *et al.*, 1978, 325.
69. Freeman, B.J. *et al.*, 1984, 290.
70. *J. Autism* 6:1 (1976), 91.
71. *Ibid.*, 5:2 (1975), 185.
72. USDHHS PHS, 1984, 9.
73. Behrman, R.E. *et al.*, 1989.

V

The Sociopathic Personality and Violent Crime

Children, adolescents, and adults who are mentally retarded or autistic, or have some other serious neurologic disability, cannot make their way in society. Their adjustment problems are resolved, or left unresolved, in mental hospitals and insane asylums, where they spend the rest of their days out of sight and mind. Bizarre, destructive or dangerous behavior is handled within the walls of these institutions.

But what of the post-encephalitic individual who is not put away in some back ward?

Every biological phenomenon occurs on a spectrum from the near normal to the pathological. For each post-encephalitic individual who requires institutionalization hundreds of others remain at large.

The marginal autistic, the epileptic with occasional seizures, the slightly retarded, the severely dyslexic—all must still make some accommodation with society.

But since they cannot compete successfully with the neurologically sound, they lapse easily into the life of crime. This neurologically defective population commits a disproportionate share of the mounting wave of murders, assaults, rapes, robberies with violence, physical abuse of wives, sexual abuse of children, and other myriad infractions of the social code which in the past two decades have become so widespread as to merit designation by former Surgeon-General Everett Koop as a "public health problem."[1]

It is, indeed, a "public health problem," but not in quite the sense intended by the Surgeon-General.

An epidemic of violence started in this country in the 1960s and is still intensifying—to the despair of clogged judicial systems and overcrowded prisons.

Psychologists, psychiatrists, ministers of the gospel, and criminologists have offered myriads of causal explanations—usually laying the blame at the door of an "uncaring" society and thus ignoring the fact that this civic breakdown is occurring at a time of unmatched economic prosperity.

No one has yet directed attention to the huge contribution made by the emergence into the limelight of the first two vaccinated—post-encephalitic—generations.

Increasing Crime and Violence in America

The modern era of American violence began on November 22, 1963, with the assassination of President John F. Kennedy by Lee Harvey Oswald—a man who, by weird coincidence, was himself a dyslexic and neurologic defective.

Since that day every indicator of social and civic peace and order has shown a steady deterioration.

The figures are startling and unsettling and, like autism itself and the associated congeries of developmental disabilities, devoid of any adequate explanation.

The murder rate doubled between 1960 and 1980, from four to eight per 100,000 inhabitants, for a total of more than 20,000 in 1987, giving the United States the highest incidence of homicide of any industrialized country. The largest increase occurred between 1960 and 1970. Murder today remains the leading cause of death for black males aged fifteen to thirty-four.[2]

Meanwhile the West European and Japanese rate remains stationary at 1/100,000.

The number of physical assaults is not known but is estimated at more than 100 for each case of murder, i.e., perhaps 2,500,000. The total actually reported in 1980, for persons over the age of twelve, was 1,600,000.

FBI statistics show a fifty percent increase in crimes of all categories (violent crime, arson, robbery, burglary, and property crime)—from 4000/100,000 inhabitants in 1971 to 6000/100,000 in 1980. This index subsequently declined marginally but has remained stable at 5500—well above the figures for the 1940s and 1950s.[3]

Between 1970 and 1980 the number of fires attributed to arson rose 325 percent.[4]

In 1933, the depth of the Depression, the incidence of "violent crime" (a category which includes murder, forcible rape, robbery, and aggravated assault) was 200 per 100,000 persons in the population. By the 1940s it had declined to 100, but in 1963 it was back at the Depression-era level. Thereafter it climbed steadily, reaching 500 in 1978 and over 600 in 1987.[5]

Those who would blame today's epidemic of violence on poverty should explain why it is three times higher today than in 1933 and six times higher than in the 1940s. Has the United States really become a poorer country since 1933?

Louis J. West, Professor of Psychiatry at the UCLA School of Medicine, stated in 1985: "If you had morbidity and mortality rates like that from any infectious disease, there would be millions of dollars spent on it. This epidemic makes all the rest of what the Centers for Disease Control is doing pale by comparison as an epidemiologic problem."[6]

Women are often objects of assault. Between a fifth and a quarter of the women in the country have been beaten at least once by a male family member or acquaintance. Officially reported rapes have risen five times in twenty-five years—from 17,000 in 1960 to 91,000 in 1987. And probably as few as ten percent of rapes are actually reported.[7]

But women are themselves participating in violent crime in an unprecedented way, for the first time engaging in armed robberies and other crimes of violence:

When Charlie T. Deane found himself at the scene of a bank robbery Thursday, he did what any ordinary policeman would do. He investigated, apprehended suspects, and made arrests . . . he arrested Paulette Lisenby, 32, of Alexandria. At the same time he took in Robin Diane Cash, 33, of Woodbridge, an alleged accomplice in the robbery. . . . Yesterday afternoon, two armed women robbed another bank in the same Route 1 area and fled with a third woman accomplice.[8]

They are also performing acts of "extraordinary brutality" which used to be the exclusive reserve of males. In 1969 only twelve percent of female adolescent criminals had committed "more violent" acts, but by 1979 the total had risen to forty-eight percent—approximately equal to the rate in male adolescents.[9]

Child abuse is showing an even steeper rise in incidence. This became a public problem in the early 1980s:

> The wife of a man accused of murder in the death of his three-year-old daughter testified yesterday that her husband told her "he snapped" and strangled the crying child with a bandana, then struck her with a brick "to make her pass out." . . . Alicia Seefeldt said that in the days after Lindsay's death she twice visited her husband in jail, where he admitted to killing their daughter after becoming enraged by her crying. "He said he was sorry, it was an accident, it shouldn't have happened," said the mother. . . .[10]

> John M. Malvin, thirty, a maintenance worker from Annandale charged with murder in the death of his three-month-old son was arraigned yesterday in Fairfax County juvenile court. . . . An autopsy showed that the baby died of multiple internal injuries. . . . Raymond F. Morrough, deputy commonwealth's attorney, said the child's most recent injuries included a bruise on the chest, a ruptured liver, and a ruptured kidney. . . . X-rays revealed old injuries. "There were some old breaks, in the ribs and the arms and the legs." Morrough said. "These aren't fresh." The infant was wearing a cast for a fractured leg, and the cause of that break is under investigation. . . . In fiscal 1986-1987, there were twenty-seven fatalities of children in Virginia as a result of abuse or neglect. . . . This was nearly double the four-teen cases in the two previous years. . . In the fatal cases of abuse . . . the mother was the perpetrator about thirty percent of the time, the father in about thirty percent of the cases, and both parents in fifteen percent. Two-thirds of the child abuse deaths occurred in infants less than a year old.[11]

In 1986 there were 2.1 million reports of child abuse in the United States—up 200 percent since 1976. New York State authorities estimated in 1987 that 100-150 children in that state die every year from abuse, with 2000-5000 deaths nationwide (up almost twenty-five percent over 1986). The majority of cases are never reported. An estimated 123,400 cases of child sexual abuse were reported in 1984, up one-third from 1983.[12]

The U.S. prison population has *doubled* since 1970; in California it *tripled* between 1977 and 1988. Today we have 250 people in prison per 100,000 of the population; in 1850 the figure was 29/ 100,000.[13]

Particularly disturbing are the randomness and unpredictability of this epidemic. Murder used to be a family affair, but between 1963 and the early 1980s the incidence of murder at the hands of a stranger increased nearly twice as rapidly as murder by relatives, friends, and acquaintances.[14] This makes the risks unforeseeable and the planning of one's own physical safety impossible.

An eighteen-year-old male at a rock concert is stabbed to death in front of friends by another adolescent to whom he has refused to give a ride home. A young man attacks an elderly female acquaintance, crushes her skull with a hammer, stabs her several times with a kitchen knife, and then tries to set fire to her dead body. An eighteen-year-old girl is shot to death while embracing her boyfriend at a Grateful Dead-Bob Dylan concert; the fifteen-year-old boy who did it stated that he "just wanted to shoot someone." During the course of a summer twenty-three drivers of automobiles on Los Angeles freeways are shot at by unknown assailants, who apparently view these passing cars as the equivalent of migrating ducks. Four drivers are killed, and twelve wounded.

The crimes themselves are becoming more gruesome: a man is killed by a single knife blow to the heart; then his assailant delivers thirty more knife blows to the dead body. A fifteen-year-old Massachusetts high-school student lures a classmate to a secluded spot and beats him to death with a baseball bat as his victim is screaming for help. "Afterwards Matthews walked to a friend's house, got into a snowball fight, and offered to show his pal the body." His defense attorney said Matthews had told classmates "he wanted to know what it was like to kill someone before the crime was committed." A psychiatrist testified at his trial that Matthews ". . . doesn't internally know right from wrong. He knows the theory, but can't perform the action . . . so that he is morally handicapped."

> Just a month before, seventeen-year-old Kendall Merriweather
> had looked down the barrel of a gun and surrendered his radio to
> robbers. The second time, two weeks before last Christmas, he
> said no.
> Merriweather died seconds later, shot once, then a second
> time in the back with a .357 Magnum—in broad daylight on a
> busy street. His killer and an accomplice, Merriweather's fellow
> students at the Frank W. Ballou High School in Southeast
> [Washington], were arrested a half-hour later, listening to their
> new radio at a friend's apartment. . . . The "boom box" killers
> . . . were convicted yesterday after a two-week trial. . . . Jarrell
> D. Allen, seventeen, and Rodney Prophet, seventeen, were found
> guilty of first-degree felony murder and armed robbery. . . . Attor-
> neys for Prophet, who had argued that he was "borderline men-
> tally retarded" . . . appeared distraught by the outcome.[15]

Six black adolescents, seventeen to twenty-one years old, rob
and beat a forty-eight-year old black woman; two of them then hold
her legs apart while another kills her by shoving a pole up her
rectum. At the trial one of the six defendants convicted of first-
degree murder complains at the severity of the sentence, saying, "I
only beat and kicked the lady."[16]

A "wolfpack" of eight black and Hispanic fourteen-year-olds
attacks a young female bank executive jogging at night in New
York's Central Park. According to the press account, "The woman
was kicked and beaten with fists, hit with a pipe, struck in the face
with a brick, bound and gagged, and raped several times." Although
surviving the rape and a skull fractured in two places, she was left
with serious, and probably permanent, brain damage.[17]

Violence takes new and bizarre forms.

While driving his car to work, a man is so incensed at another's
cutting in front of him that he screams with rage and slams his fist
through the windshield. The reaction of another driver in the same
circumstances is to cut off the other car (a small Volkswagen), get
out, reach down, and overturn it on the highway shoulder.

A young woman of twenty-five severely bites a policeman who
has given her a parking ticket.

A thirty-one-year-old New York woman turns seventy-five frustrated airline passengers into a screaming mob, then knees a cop in the groin when he tries to restrain her. The trigger? A four-hour delay in a flight to Newark—a flight that is not even hers.

Inexplicable attacks of rage happen to the most normal people:

> Jim Kelter is not a violent man. He works hard at his accountant's job, loves his wife and infant son, and generally has "a soft answer," as the proverb calls it, for all who come his way. At the moment, however, he is using grievous words loudly in a major New York department store, where a little plastic anti-shoplifting device, erroneously left on his merchandise, has just triggered an alarm that screams "Thief!" at the top of its electronic lungs.
>
> Swinging the shopping bag, Kelter slams it at the feet of an approaching security guard. . . . "Pick it up!" he screams. "You want to see what's inside, you pick it up!"
>
> The guard glowers, his own blood pressure beginning to rise. . . . "It was the third time in a week they'd done that to me," Kelter fumes. . . . "An hour or two later, after we got home, I started feeling embarrassed. I felt I'd acted like a child, but at the time, it was the only way to vent my frustration."
>
> There seem to be no "soft answers" left in urban America. Wrath is the name of the game and, increasingly, those who dwell in metropolitan pressure cookers from New York to Los Angeles are playing it with perilous intensity.[18]

The crime age is going down. In California a ten-year-old baby-sitter strangles the child she is caring for. In Texas a ten-year-old boy is convicted of stabbing and beating a 101-year old woman.

Adolescents, and even children, are committing crimes of sexual violence of which in the past they were hardly physically capable.

> A thirteen-year-old boy weighing 100 pounds pulls a knife on a twenty-two-year-old woman in downtown Seattle, pushes her into the walkway of an auto dealership, and rapes her. Later he tells the judge he's sorry, but he doesn't know what for.
>
> A twelve-year-old Auburn boy ties his former baby-sitter, a thirty-two-year-old mildly retarded woman, to a schoolyard fence, burns her with matches, and sexually assaults her.
>
> Mountlake police warn the community that a sexual predator has been released from a juvenile institution into their midst.

While in custody for burglary, the eighteen-year-old devised a detailed plan to abduct, molest, and photograph elementary-school children. He was freed because he had served his time for the burglary, and officials believed he could not be legally committed as mentally ill.

Eventually state officials got an order to have him committed to Western State Hospital for evaluation, where he remains while the state decides what to do with him.

These incidents all happened within the past year.[19]

Barry was sent to Echo Glen two years ago—a sullen child, a murderer, and rapist.

Barry readily admitted stalking and strangling the six-year-old girl who lived down the street in his Eastern Washington hometown. In fact, since he came to Echo Glen he has admitted to all sorts of sex offenses involving eleven other victims—cousins, brothers, and sisters—starting when he was about six.[20]

In the borough of Queens, New York City, a twelve-year-old faces twenty-seven charges, including first-degree rape, robbery, aggravated assault, and grand larceny in a series of crimes committed with another twelve-year-old and an adult. In 1985 youths aged fifteen and younger committed 381 murders and non-negligent manslaughters, 18,021 aggravated assaults, 13,899 robberies, and 2645 rapes. Children twelve years old and younger committed 21 killings, 436 rapes, and 3545 aggravated assaults.[21]

The contrast between then and now was emphasized in a 1987 report on school discipline by the New Jersey Human Rights Commissioner. In the 1940s the most frequent school problems were: talking, chewing gum, making noise, running in the halls, getting out of turn in line, wearing improper clothing, and not putting paper in wastebaskets. In the 1980s they were: drug and alcohol abuse, rape, robbery, assault, burglary, arson, bombings, murder, absenteeism, vandalism, extortion, gang warfare, abortion, and venereal disease.[22]

Evidence indicates that many, perhaps most, of these crimes and offenses are being committed by neurologic defectives—i.e., the hyperactive generation, now giving vent to its drives and compulsions and begetting a new generation which is probably even more defective. The post-encephalitic syndrome, and ultimately the childhood vaccination programs, must bear a share of the responsibility for this new "public health problem."

Criminal Behavior in the Post-Encephalitic Population

The historical record supports the view that persons with the post-encephalitic syndrome gravitate toward violence and crime.

In the 1920s and 1930s such behavior had often been noted in individuals recovering from encephalitis—who were called "apaches." The typical outcome was described as: "'good' boys made 'bad' and 'bad' boys made 'worse'."[23] "This encephalitis . . . may produce an intellectual, tormented, and cruel monster out of a gentle girl or boy." "A child of previously responsible character may be so transformed as to seem a different person . . . cruel, destructive, abusive, indecent."[24]

There was argument over whether encephalitis actually changed the individual's character or merely intensified preexisting traits. L.A. Lurie wrote in 1947:

> According to some, the encephalitis merely brings out character defects and abnormal personality traits that were already present but had been dormant. According to others—and we agree with them—encephalitis does not necessarily accentuate the premorbid personality. . . . The tragic feature of encephalitis is personality change, not personality exaggeration.[25]

A different spiritual being was occupying the familiar physical form. Sometimes it almost seemed to resemble demonic possession:

> Two years after an attack of encephalitis, a boy, aged nine, had so changed in personality as to be barely recognizable to his mother as her own child. He had "bouts of miserable weeping, followed by uproarious laughter, singing, and whistling. He was cruel to his brothers and sisters and to his playmates" . . . and developed the habits of kicking animals in the street, stealing, and "lying cleverly."[26]

> G.M. was a normal, well-behaved child until January 1920, when he had a febrile illness of about ten days' duration. He was aged eight years at the time. . . . Within a few weeks of this illness

the child seemed to be a bit restless and irritable. He quarreled a great deal with his baby brother and seemed to grow angry more readily than usual. . . . Late in the spring of 1920 his rages became more frequent, and he displayed a tendency to mistreat other children when he was angry . . . he soon became a danger in the home. On one occasion he was found preparing to stab his baby brother with a carving knife, and on another he inflicted a small cut on his mother's throat with a piece of glass. Finally the child attempted to set fire to the house, and the parents brought him to the hospital. . . . The child's intelligence was apparently quite normal if allowance were made for his difficulty in concentration.[27]

M.E., a white girl aged fourteen, was referred because she presented a severe behavior problem both at home and in school. Lately she had had terrific outbursts of rage, during one of which she attempted to choke her mother and her aunt. According to the history the girl had had severe temper outbursts since the age of four years. Very often she would beat her head against the wall or floor if frustrated. She had always been cruel to children and especially to animals. She was an inveterate liar. . . . During one of her temper outbursts the girl attacked one of the workers and tried to kill her. Her conduct during the temper outbursts was extremely violent.[28]

Earl D. Bond and Kenneth E. Appel wrote in 1931:

Twenty-one boys had records roughly as follows: They were good, obedient, well-behaved, bright children, either lively or shy, up to a certain age, which varied from three years and a half to eleven years, and was usually about six years.

Then, "all of a sudden," often after an attack called "the flu," or sometimes after a head injury, appeared such symptoms as crossing of the eyes or seeing double, paralysis of legs, headache and nausea, outpouring of saliva, disturbed breathing, or wetting the bed. . . .

Following the first physical symptoms, immediately or after a lapse of years, came changes in behavior. The boys became disobedient, unmanageable, restless; they got into many fights; they stole rides on trains and in automobiles. One little fellow of seven curled himself up in the spare tires of cars which he hoped were bound for a long run. One amused himself by letting the air out of the tires of parked cars. All lost their fear of punishment or other consequences of their conduct; but curiously, they often manifested other most unusual and foolish fears. One boy who was brave enough to steal rides on freight-trains and defy a policeman, was afraid of "the Ghost" at night—sometimes he called it "the Holy Ghost." Another, willing to fight much larger boys, was afraid of imaginary pirates and Indians and giants. Others had frequent nightmares which woke them screaming. They lied and stole and often were caught. They stole canaries, kiddy-cars, money, watches, toys, rifles, the Book of Knowledge, spectacles, flowerpots, and Victrola records. They characteristically gave away what they stole.[29]

These children were often of normal or near-normal intelligence—"moral rather than mental imbeciles."[30]

Many of them embarked on a life of crime. Post-encephalitic patients appeared repeatedly in the criminal courts for criminal or antisocial behavior—such offenses as stealing, cruelty, sexual assaults, and murder.[31]

Often their criminal behavior seemed provoked by an overpowering impulse—a manifestation of the "explosive diathesis." They were "indifferent to punishment."[32] And although sometimes contrite, they repeated the offenses over and over again.[33]

The "explosive diathesis" has reappeared in our days under the name of "episodic dyscontrol syndrome" and is discussed further below.

In the 1920s and 1930s these post-encephalitics were an almost invisible minority, their depredations being known only to medical and legal specialists. Today they probably constitute the majority of offenders in all categories of violent crime.

Criminal Behavior and Autism: Asperger's Syndrome

The autistics, despite a tendency to impulsive violence, have little opportunity, since, by definition, they spend their days in institutions. If out on the street, they are probably not diagnosed as autistic, so the data are skewed. But one would expect autism in its milder form of Asperger's Syndrome to manifest aggressive proclivities, as in the following case from England.

Researchers there in 1985 reported on a link between Asperger's Syndrome and violence.[34] The forty-four-year-old son of a prosperous engineer had displayed marked autistic features from the earliest age. Even before his third birthday "he was unusually placid, his face was expressionless, and his voice monotonous." After that he developed many typical autistic features, including a series of obsessions: people's hair, the plumbing in the house, a fear of dogs. He rocked repetitively as a child and to this day suffers from enuresis and encopresis. *In adolescence this withdrawn and even prim young man started a series of impulsive attacks on women.* At sixteen "he had become 'girl mad' and had attempted to strangle a girl . . . later telling his headmaster that he had completely lost control of himself." "At eighteen he dropped a firework into a girl's car and then stabbed her in the wrist with a screwdriver. . . . Eight months later he jumped on the back of a girl in a park, and said this was because of the way she was dressed." "He explained another attempt to stab a girl in the following terms: 'I thought she was indecently dressed—she was wearing shorts.'"

Committed to a mental hospital at age twenty-nine with the diagnosis of "more able autistic adult," he remains there to this day. Recently "he became increasingly preoccupied with women and, for the first time ever, started to keep a collection of pictures of naked women, which he carried openly. . . . This . . . soon led to behavior problems: he showed frank sexual interest in a female teacher and got as close to her as possible at every opportunity, sometimes following her about inappropriately. . . . Recently a preoccupation with witchcraft and cutting up babies was elicited. He said he would like to poison or shoot actresses, and admitted that were he married, his wife would be at risk; thoughts of violence to actresses occurred on most days, he claimed, but could be dispelled by turning his attention to thoughts of gear levers and steering columns. His attitude toward women varies in this manner from concern with them as adored sexual objects, to their being potential victims of homicidal violence."

The authors conclude: "This association between Asperger's Syndrome and violent behavior is more common than has been recognized."

Criminal Behavior and Minimal Brain Damage: Conduct Disorder

The *Journal of the American Medical Association* observed in 1988, "Adults with a history of attention-deficit hyperactivity disorder appear to be overrepresented in the ranks of felons."[35]

Probably the most common neurologic feature encountered among violent criminals is hyperactivity. Whatever the study, a large majority of the subjects will have been hyperactive in childhood:

> R.J., a twenty-three-year-old unemployed mechanic, had a history of truancy and hyperactivity as a child. He left school at thirteen and had been jailed several times since for assault and drunken driving. One night, several months before referral, his wife noticed that he "went into a blank stare"; he proceeded to beat her severely with a metal candlestick causing lacerations and unconsciousness. Several weeks later, after drinking five or six cans of beer, he became engaged in an altercation and, grabbing a hunting rifle away from a close friend, shot him to death. Two weeks thereafter, out of jail on bond, he threw his two-year-old daughter from the window of a moving car after she "talked back."[36]

Hyperactivity often declines in late adolescence, being "replaced by aggressiveness and hair-trigger temper, with the individual showing destructive impulsive behavior."[37]

Another common feature of the violent criminal is a short attention span.[38]

Dyslexia and other learning disabilities are found very frequently in all surveys of prison inmates.

Various studies have shown that almost ninety percent of delinquents have disabilities in reading and other school subjects: dyslexia, dysgraphia (extremely poor handwriting), dyscalculia (inability to perform basic mathematical calculations), poor spelling, defective sequential memory (cannot remember the order of the letters of the alphabet), etc.[39] Dorothy Lewis writes, "Reading disabilities abound in the delinquent population. This is one of the few facts about delinquents for which there is consensus in the literature. The research to date indicates that the majority of juvenile delinquents are at least two years, and perhaps as much as five to seven years, below grade expectancy in reading achievement."[40] Whereas four percent of the population as a whole suffers from reading retardation, Rutter and his colleagues found in 1970 that fully one-third of children with conduct disorders were reading-disabled.[41]

These learning disabilities contribute to a high level of illiteracy, or partial literacy, among the prison population. A 1976 study by the Virginia State Department of Education found that half of the incarcerated juvenile delinquents in that state read two or three years below acceptable reading levels, while one third were three or more grades below the acceptable level.[42]

In 1986 Virginia instituted a policy denying parole to any prisoner who could not read or write, aiming to combat the illiteracy which prevents released convicts from reading want ads, filling out job applications, and holding jobs.[43]

A 1988 pilot study by the Brooklyn Family Court found that forty percent of the juveniles appearing before that court had learning disabilities; the majority were aged seven to seventeen, had failed in school or dropped out, and then engaged in various kinds of criminal behavior, from robbery and drug dealing to murder.[44]

In 1984 Ernest T. Bryant and coworkers examined the relationship between "neuropsychological functioning, learning disability, and violent behavior" in 110 prisoners incarcerated for violent crimes:

> The results support the contention that violent criminal offenders have serious neuropsychological deficits. On four of the [learning] scales (Writing, Reading, Arithmetic, and Intellectual Processes) the mean scale scores of the violent group were within the pathological range.
>
> The violent group demonstrated impaired performance on tasks requiring complex integration of information from the visual [and] auditory . . . processing systems . . . the ability to create, plan, organize, and execute goal-directed behaviors, and sustained attention and concentration.[45]

Psychiatrists and social workers usually explain the attraction of this group to the criminal life by their unsuitability for a normal existence, their inability to compete with their peers. As the AMA

Journal opines: "The stress of trying to fit into a society that is intolerant of them is said to cause many to be very sad or depressed adults."[46]

This surely is an important factor: high-school graduates with second- or third-grade reading skills are hardly equipped to handle the challenges of late twentieth-century industrial society. And they sense their own inadequacy and inability to compete. But, as we have frequently noted, the cause-and-effect relationship should not be turned upside-down. The ultimate causal factor—the one which society has the power to eliminate or mitigate—is the preexisting neurologic disability.

Furthermore, these individuals often seem malevolent as well, enjoying inflicting pain on others or at least oblivious to it ("no concern for the feelings, wishes, and well-being of others, as shown by callous behavior").

They feel "different" from others, hence outlaws, and admire the outlaw type. This may well predispose them to the criminal life. Many resemble the six-year old with minimal brain damage described by his mother as

> *obsessed with the bad guys on TV etc. He is very upset that the bad guys always lose. He thinks they look better, have better musculature, etc., and can't understand why they always lose. He doesn't think things should be black and white. He was so obsessed by this that the school called us in once, worrying that he was taking the side of the bad guys always in school. So they allowed him to construct his own world, and he did it with the bad guys' headquarters in the center. And then he began to taper off.*

The six-year-old's partiality for the bad guys on television becomes admiration for the neighborhood pimp, drug-runner, or gunman ten years later.

Psychiatry has names for the intermediate stages between minimal brain damage and criminal behavior. We have already encountered "oppositional disorder" as a subvariety of minimal brain damage. When carried to an extreme of aggressiveness, this, in turn, becomes "conduct disorder"—"a persistent pattern of conduct in which the basic rights of others and major appropriate social norms are violated."

Physical aggression is common. Children or adolescents with this disorder usually initiate aggression, may be physically cruel to other people or to animals, and frequently deliberately destroy other people's property (this may include fire-setting). They may engage in stealing with confrontation of the victim, as in mugging, purse-snatching, extortion, or armed robbery. At later stages, the physical violence may take the form of rape, assault, or, in rare cases, homicide. . . . Regular use of tobacco, liquor, or nonprescribed drugs and sexual behavior that begins unusually early for the child's peer group in his or her milieu are common. The child may have no concern for the feelings, wishes, and well-being of others, as shown by callous behavior, and may lack appropriate feelings of guilt or remorse.[47]

In the United States *nine percent of males under the age of eighteen, and two percent of females, are estimated to suffer from "conduct disorder."*

Associated features are low self-esteem ("though the person may project an image of 'toughness'"), poor frustration tolerance, irritability, temper outbursts, provocative recklessness, anxiety, and depression. "Attentional difficulties, impulsiveness, and hyperactivity are very common, especially in childhood, and may justify the additional diagnosis of Attention-Deficit Hyperactivity Disorder."

This nine percent group of young males, and two percent of young females, are easily tempted by the life of crime. Starting with lying and cheating in school and stealing money from the mother's purse, the individual goes on to "borrowing" others' possessions, joyriding in the family's or a stranger's car, breaking into a neighbor's house, shop-lifting, or arson.[48]

Involvement with alcohol and drugs from an early age, of course, exacerbates their other problems in a variety of ways.[49]

The Sociopathic Personality

The minimally brain-damaged child promoted to "conduct disorder" in adolescence may graduate with a full-fledged "sociopathic personality" upon reaching adulthood. This syndrome is defined by the American Psychiatric Association as persistence into adult life of a pattern of antisocial behavior that began before the age of fifteen. . . . The antisocial behavior is not due to either severe Mental Retardation, Schizophrenia, or manic episodes. Lying, stealing, fighting, truancy, and resisting authority are typical early childhood signs. In adolescence, unusually early or aggressive sexual behavior, excessive drinking, and use of illicit drugs are frequent . . . failure to accept social norms with respect to lawful behavior. . . . Despite the stereotype of a normal mental status in this disorder, frequently there are signs of personal distress, including complaints of tension, inability to tolerate boredom, depression, and the conviction (often correct) that others are hostile toward them. . . . Almost invariably there is markedly impaired capacity to sustain lasting, close, warm, and responsible relationships with family, friends, or sexual partners.[50]

An estimated three percent of U.S. males and one percent of females suffer from "sociopathic personality" (reflecting the customary 3:1 or 4:1 ratio of males to females afflicted by these various neurologic conditions). It is found in all social classes but is thought to be marginally more common in lower-class populations, "partly because . . . fathers of those with the disorder frequently have the disorder themselves, and consequently their children often grow up in impoverished homes."[51]

This group has become the leading social, economic, and legal problem of American life.

Tommy Colella, of Garden Grove, California, who made history in 1988 when his adoptive parents annulled the adoption, is a classic study in the sociopathic personality.

What the caseworker didn't tell them, according to the Colellas, was that the [seven-year-old] boy had a long record of sociopathic behavior and had just been removed from another would-be adoptive home when he tried to pour urine over the couple's daughter. . . .

At first Tommy seemed subdued. "He was withdrawn and quiet," says Tom. "He gave you that kind of beaten-puppy feeling." The quiet did not last. A few days after he arrived, Janice told Tommy to stop watching TV and get ready for school. "He attacked me," she says. "He pulled my hair out, gouged me, and hit me with his fists. I had bruises all over my face and breasts."

A week later Janice asked him to make his bed. She recalls that Tommy became enraged and swung a croquet mallet—an eighth birthday gift—at her head. "If I hadn't ducked, it would have hit me," she says. "It went right through the wall."

The Colellas called the Social Services Agency with the idea of sending him back. "They kept saying he's a misunderstood child that needs a lot of love and affection," says Tom. "When you have professionals tell you its going to work out, you figure maybe this isn't as bad as you think.". . . They asked Social Services for more information. Tommy's medical records, they were told, were incomplete.

Tommy mutilated a hamster. . . . "We'd have company over," says Janice, "and he'd take his feces and smear it all over everything. And he'd get the 'stares.' He'd gaze blankly into the distance. When he'd come back, he was either violent or depressed."

Still the Colellas wouldn't quit. Janice tutored him in reading and writing several nights a week. "Working with Tommy became our whole lives," says Tom. They taught him to use silverware— when he arrived, he ate only with his hands—and they completed the eight-year-old's toilet training. Once Tommy even told Janice he loved her. "But then he said he couldn't let himself love me because I wasn't his real mom," she recalls, "and that if he ever told me that again, he didn't mean it."

To ease the strain Tommy was creating in their family the Colellas went into therapy.

After a year, the Colellas say, the Social Services Agency began to pressure them to finalize the adoption proceedings. . . . Despite grave qualms, the Colellas consented, and the adoption was completed in February 1979. . . . But Tommy immediately got much worse. The stares became a daily occurrence. He began cutting himself and drawing designs with his blood. He'd walk down the middle of the street as traffic whizzed by. Then the Colellas discovered he was practicing Satanism. "We caught him chanting," says Janice. "He'd light candles and call to the powers of darkness. It was really scary. . . ."

Tommy's violence escalated. On occasions, "too many to count" says Janice, he tried to hang or stab himself. Despite taking prescribed psychotropic drugs—"enough to stop a charging elephant," said the pharmacist—he nearly strangled a boy to death. "He tried to kill the paperboy in our front yard," says Janice. "When I got there, he wasn't breathing. I had to revive him." In

November 1980, the Colellas checked Tommy into a psychiatric unit of the Huntington Beach Inter-Community Hospital. Janice recalls Tommy saying to a staff psychiatrist, "I think I need the hospital because I think I'm going to kill somebody. . . ."

The Colellas say a caseworker at the hospital showed them some of Tommy's medical records that they'd never been allowed to see. One report concluded, "The youngster's dependency (and subsequent rage) are very deep and need to be dealt with. . . ."

After four months at Huntington Hospital, despite lack of any real improvement, Tommy was sent home. . . . His rages grew even more violent, his suicide attempts more frequent and earnest. Finally, after he tried to hang himself in April 1981, the Colellas summoned the police. . . .

[Tommy's natural mother, Barbara] remembers him as a difficult child. "Even as a small baby, he'd just sit and stare with this empty, faraway look in his eyes." When he was four, she caught him urinating on his two-year-old half-sister. One afternoon Barbara came home to find him "playing" with the family cat. "I walked into the bedroom," she says, "and he's twirling the cat by the tail. The cat's screaming and Tom just thinks it's the neatest thing.". . . Tommy became even more unmanageable. He developed a fascination with matches and fire. One morning, after Barbara sent him upstairs to his room, a blaze broke out there. "I knew he needed psychiatric help. And I knew I couldn't afford it."

One day Barbara found herself in a rage, pinning Tommy down on a bed, shaking him. "He looked at me with this hateful look in his eyes," she recalls, "and he told me, 'I want to be adopted.' I said, 'You want it, you got it.' I couldn't take it anymore. . . ."

Little Tommy Colella is now nineteen and, at 6'1", 240 pounds, little no longer. . . . He says there are warrants out for him, "nothing major," for driving without a license and disorderly conduct. "It's kind of ridiculous for people to portray me as the devil incarnate," he says. "I don't remember doing a lot of the things the Colellas said I did. I do remember being scared a lot and not knowing what was going to happen next." He appears perfectly conventional: he rents an apartment, works as assistant manager of a fast-food restaurant in California, has earned his high-school equivalency diploma, and would like to go to college. . . .

Tommy's feelings about the Colellas seem generally warm. "They were nice to me," he says. "They tried everything to help me." He pauses. "I don't love them, but I like them. I could see getting together with them sometime."

The Colellas can't. . . . They last saw Tommy four years ago. . . . Janice brought her child, then a year old. "Tommy sat in the car with our son," she recalls. "He gave him a gift—I can't remember what—but it clearly meant a lot to Tommy that he picked it up and played with it."

Three weeks later the telephone threats started. "It's like something snapped," says Tom. "Tommy said he was going to burn our house down and kill us and our son." We decided to move when his social worker called and said, "There's something I have to tell you: Tommy means it!"[52]

This account highlights many of the hallmarks of a syndrome between not-so-minimal brain damage and moderate autism, showing the progression to sociopathy. Tommy had "blank staring" as a small baby (i.e., a type of mild epileptic seizure), severe withdrawal, fearfulness, anxiety, and depression, and the "triad" which predicts later violent behavior (fire-setting, cruelty to animals, and enuresis). He was fascinated by urine and feces. He probably had learning disabilities (needing constant tutoring in school). He was oblivious of personal danger ("He'd walk down the middle of the street as traffic whizzed by."). His anger and hostility had a sexual component (Janice Colella's breasts were severely bruised). He was always emotionally remote, repelling both his mother and his adoptive mother, with worsening episodes of rage, self-mutilation, severe depression, and suicide attempts. He was afraid and confused (remembers "being scared a lot and not knowing what was going to happen next"). He is fascinated by evil (Satanism) and sympathetic to it. And today he has amnesia for much of what happened to him. Also he is overweight, suggesting post-encephalitic obesity.

Although we know nothing definite about Tommy Colella's vaccination history, he probably received the shots more than once. His natural mother was eighteen and unmarried; he went to an adoption agency, then to his first adopted family, back to the adoption agency, and then to the Colellas. Shot records are always chaotic in such cases ("Tommy's medical records . . . were incomplete"), and children are repeatedly revaccinated in case some shot has been overlooked.

That sociopathic behavior in adults is the continuation of minimal brain damage in childhood has been demonstrated by numerous studies.

A basic technique is to select a group of young adults in trouble with the law and diagnose them for evidence of neurologic damage in childhood. Several of these "retrospective" studies have been done; all "strongly support the idea that there is a link between the presence of the [MBD] syndrome in childhood and significant anti-social behavior in adolescence and later life."[53]

A 1982 study of 200 consecutively admitted incarcerated male juvenile offenders from prisons in New Jersey found that one in three had a "personality disorder," while one in five had attention-deficit disorder and/or some specific developmental disability; half had an IQ below 85; one in three had schizoid, paranoid, or other personality disorder. Incarceration for violence was significantly associated with borderline IQ, conduct disorder, and personality dis-order, but not with family structure or receiving welfare assistance.[54]

The authors concluded that "poverty, although a defect in the social structure, does not cause delinquency . . . ninety percent of poor families are law-abiding."

Similar is the "prospective" follow-up study: interviewing chil-dren when they are young and following them for some years through life. James Satterfield performed such a study on 110 min-imally brain-damaged youngsters, comparing them with a control group of eighty-eight normals: "Rates of single and multiple serious offense and of institutionalization for delinquency were significantly higher in the [MBD] subjects."[55]

Mendelsohn and coworkers in St. Louis interviewed the mothers of eighty-three children aged twelve to sixteen who had been diagnosed some years earlier as hyperkinetic. Antisocial behavior of a marked degree was a common finding: twenty-two per-cent of the children had long histories of such behavior and were considered likely to be sociopathic as adults; nearly sixty percent had had some contact with the police, seventeen percent on three or more occasions; nearly twenty-five percent had been referred to the juvenile court. By the time of follow-up fifty-one percent were involved in fighting and stealing; thirty-three percent had threatened to kill their parents; fifteen percent had set fires; seven percent had carried concealed weapons; five percent exhibited significant drug abuse, and fifteen percent were becoming alcoholics; fifty-five of the eighty-three were considered incorrigible. "The picture emerging from this study was one of children who had difficulty conforming to rules, whether the rules were set by society or by their families."[56]

A 1974 study by Hussey of eighty-four hyperactive children, adolescents, and young adults (nine to twenty-four years of age), who had been followed from eight to ten years, found a school dropout rate five times higher than the state average; they were twenty times more likely than the population at large to end in a reform school.[57]

A lengthy study of MBD children was made by Gabrielle Weiss at the Montreal Children's Hospital. In 1971 she published interviews with mothers of sixty-four adolescents ten to twenty years of age diagnosed as hyperkinetic four to six years earlier; one-quarter had a history of antisocial behavior, while fifteen percent had already been in the courts.[58]

She did follow-up studies of this group ten and fifteen years later and found: "While about half the children seem to outgrow the symptoms of the syndrome, half continue to be disabled to a varying extent by continuing symptoms. The childhood condition . . . leads to antisocial personality disorder in a significant minority of the subjects."[59]

These findings led Michael Aman to comment in 1984:

> These follow-up and comparison studies suggest that children originally identified as hyperactive do not merely grow out of their problems, as was once widely believed to be the case. Instead, it appears that *manifestations* of the disorder tend to change over time. These studies suggest that there is a shift from an emphasis on overactivity and inattention as children to academic failure, social incompetence, and lower self-esteem as adolescents and young adults.[60]

Of great interest are family studies which suggest a genetic factor in the MBD syndrome. They find, for instance, that the parents (especially the fathers) of hyperkinetic or sociopathic children were more likely to have themselves been sociopathic or alcoholic, while the mothers were more likely to have been hysterics.[61]

When a criminal has a twin, that twin is at least twice as likely to be a criminal himself if he is an identical rather than a fraternal twin; and there is a relation between criminality in parents and in children —even when the children have been given away for adoption.[62]

We have already seen that susceptibility to vaccine damage is undoubtedly under genetic control. This raises the possibility that a whole family, due to encephalitis from vaccination, can be involved in a life of crime. Take the Bolden brothers of New York, the children of a respectable middle-class black Baptist minister of the gospel:

In June of 1979, Robert, Ernest, Henry, and Curtis Bolden [given the diagnosis, "anti-social personality disorder" by a court-appointed psychiatrist] ranged in age from seventeen to twenty-one. They lived in the Bronx, and, among them, had been arrested approximately a hundred and twenty-five times . . . the police say that the Bolden brothers were responsible for "anywhere from 1200 to 6000 crimes." All were street criminals, and Henry, then nineteen years old, was serving eight to twenty-five years in jail for a 1977 robbery conviction. It was no ordinary robbery. While an accomplice held a knife to the throat of a seventy-four-year-old woman, Henry Bolden was said to have ripped the teeth from the mouth of her eighty-four-year-old husband. On the day Henry was sentenced . . . he "entered the Bronx courtroom laughing." Robert Bolden, then seventeen, had been arrested eighteen times before his sixteenth birthday . . . and the charges included robbery, grand larceny, jostling (picking pockets), possession of stolen property, and burglary. He was then in jail. Ernest Bolden, then eighteen, was back on the streets after completing a ninety-day sentence for drug possession and criminal mischief. In the eighteen months before his incarceration, Ernest had been arrested sixteen times. Before his sixteenth birthday he had been arrested twenty-three times. The oldest brother, Curtis—then twenty-one—had been indicted for the rape of three Bronx women, one of them an eighty-two-year-old widow, who had been kicked by her assailant with such force that an impression of his sneaker sole was implanted on her left cheek. He had previously been arrested at least twenty times and served two years in prison for robbery. In March of 1980, after having been convicted the previous month for two of the rapes, Curtis Bolden was sentenced to thirty years in prison.[63]

The Criminal Class, the Underclass

Two social formations have come to prominence in American life during the past decade—the "underclass" and the "criminal class."

The members of the "underclass" are poor, either because they cannot find work or are unable or unwilling to work. Many are illiterate. Often they have lost contact with their relatives and are simply unsuited for normal human intercourse. They reject society's laws and values, become drifters, dealers and takers of drugs, petty criminals, asocial alienated beings with no ties to family, friends, or society. The "homeless" who clog the public parks and bus stations are drawn largely from this underclass.

Still unexplained is why this apparently permanent class of unemployed should have arisen in a time of economic prosperity.[64]

The "criminal class" includes both the poor and the well-to-do; they have in common a preference for an alienated and sociopathic way of life involving aggressive attacks on other members of society.

While many in the "criminal class" are poor, and their depredations may be attributed to being "disadvantaged," many others are not. Sociopathic crime is rather evenly distributed across the American class structure. Joel Steinberg, the New York lawyer who in 1988 was convicted of beating his adopted daughter to death, was not economically disadvantaged. And the gang of black and Hispanic adolescents which raped and brutalized the young female bank executive in 1989 were from stable, working-class families, not from a background of slums and drugs.

Lee Robins, professor of sociology and psychiatry at the Washington University School of Medicine in St. Louis, who studied the life histories of 524 persons seen in child guidance clinics and then interviewed thirty years later, found sociopathy, with associated criminality, in all social classes:

> In our group of offenders, the white-collar criminals, just like the burglars, thieves, and vagrants, were predominantly men who showed the whole spectrum of behavior diagnosed as sociopathic personality. Two-thirds of the white-collar criminals were so diagnosed, as were sixty percent of the thieves, burglars, and robbers.[65]

Indeed, "Traffic offenders, persons arrested as drunk and disorderly, and persons arrested on suspicion were the only groups with police records in which the sociopaths did not constitute the majority of cases."

Robins concluded that the career criminal whose "occupation" is separate from his personal life—in other words, who does not have sociopathic traits—"must be either extremely rare or seldom apprehended."

The "criminal class" includes, in particular, the "repeat criminal."

An important discovery of modern criminology has been the realization that a large part of the crime wave presently engulfing our cities is due to these "hard-core" or "repeat" criminals.

A New Jersey study in the 1970s found that five percent of juvenile offenders (1200 out of 24,000) committed fifty percent of the crimes for which juvenile arrests were made.[66]

They have been singled out for special attention by law-enforcement authorities, and an effort is made to see that they receive long sentences when apprehended.

The underclass and the criminal class are not entirely coextensive with one another but overlap in a significant way. Not all of the underclass are aggressive criminals; some are passive drifters. Not all of the criminal class are poor. But the two groups have in common a feeling of alienation and unsuitability for life with other humans, of being separated from society.

This alienation is often associated with the very neurologic disabilities discussed in the preceding pages.

Take the case of Dwayne Gosso, who was born in a New York prison and given up to foster care by his inmate mother. He is "learning-disabled but not retarded; anti-social but not mentally ill; drinks too much and has used drugs, but is neither an alcoholic nor an addict; views himself as a victim, but whose behavior is frequently self-defeating." At age twenty-seven he has spent nearly his whole life in prison or in custody. When released he commits some incompetent burglary or other minor infraction and is promptly remanded to custody. At latest count he had been before the courts nineteen times in eighteen months. Since he is not diagnosed as retarded or psychotic, those services are not available to him, and society's only recourse is to remand him to prison. His social worker said of him, "Dwayne is not a bad person. He's just not socialized enough to cope with the pressure of society. I don't think he's dangerous. But one day he's going to march into someone's apartment, he's going to surprise them or they're going to surprise him, and something terrible is going to happen."[67]

At that point Dwayne Gosso, member of the underclass, will become Dwayne Gosso, member of the criminal class.

While the other factors that can unsuit an individual for life in society should not be ignored or belittled—and Dwayne Gosso is a textbook example of these other factors—the contribution of the post-encephalitic syndrome to these individuals' alienation, aggressiveness, and inability to adapt to society's norms should no longer be ignored.

The Black Adolescent

The problems of black youth are, of course, notorious. In all educational categories they perform worse than whites, and society's production of an uneducated, seemingly uneducable, mass of blacks generates much of the crime and drug-abuse which today disfigure the social landscape. Is there a possibility that blacks could be disfavored even more than whites by the vaccination programs?

Little research has been done on this, but what there is suggests that vaccination has an even more destructive effect on the neurologic status of blacks.

A few reports have suggested that blacks suffer disproportionately from whooping cough. A 1964 controlled study in Baltimore found that black children suffered greater intellectual impairment from this disease than white children, and a greater tendency to behavioral disorders.[68] In France it is common knowledge, and discussed in the medical texts, that African blacks suffer more seriously than whites from such infectious diseases as measles and whooping cough.

If this is so, they doubtless suffer disproportionately also from the pertussis vaccine.

Blacks are also known to suffer more than whites from conditions which are recognizably the sequelae of an encephalitis, such as epilepsy and asthma.[69] The incidence of asthma in American black children is two and a half times what it is in whites; and the death rate from asthma is three times higher.[70]

Norman Geschwind was of the opinion that dyslexia is higher among American blacks than whites.[71]

The increased vulnerability of black children is due, in part, to their markedly lower birth weights which in turn reflects the breakdown of the black family in the United States and the astonishingly high incidence (*fifty* percent) of illegitimacy in this group. When adolescent black girls become pregnant outside marriage and have little family support, their babies will very often be premature and/or of low birthweight (the two conditions are not easy to distinguish).

Low birth weight and prematurity are known to predispose to a variety of disabilities, including, as we may assume, vaccine damage through demyelination of the immature nervous systems of these babies.[72]

These suggested lines of research should be investigated more thoroughly.

Violence and Epilepsy

Epilepsy and seizure disorders are among the most common sequelae of encephalitis. They are common in autism and the more severe forms of minimal brain damage. And they are also encountered with greater than normal frequency in the criminal class and the underclass.

For more than a century scientists have debated the relationship between epilepsy and violence. And while opinions have been expressed on both sides, the consensus today, to quote K.E. Moyer's *The Psychobiology of Aggression*, is that "there is a significantly greater probability that disorders of impulse control and aggressiveness will be found in the population of epileptics than in a normal population."[73]

Several surveys of prison populations done in 1975—the Cook County Jail in Chicago, the New York City prison system, and the

Dade County Jail in Miami—have found that five percent of prisoners have a history of seizures according to their own accounts, or have been taking anti-seizure medications.[74] This is five to ten times higher than the prevalence of epilepsy in the population at large (estimated at 0.5-1.0%). It is also probably underestimated, since diagnosing a seizure disorder in this population requires a degree of skill and patience. Frank Elliott describes the difficulties of detecting seizures in apparently normal individuals suffering from "episodic dyscontrol syndrome":

> Few had typical grand mal convulsions or dramatic attacks of unconsciousness. In most cases the seizures were infrequent and in many were so slight that their epileptic nature went unrecognized by both patient and physician. This is especially likely to happen in the more seriously disordered patients, because it is easy to confuse some manifestations of psychomotor epilepsy with psychogenic hallucinations, illusions, and emotional disturbances. It is not enough to ask the patient whether he has had seizures, convulsions, or attacks of unconsciousness, and to leave it at that. History-taking in these cases demands a meticulous search for the more subtle types of temporal lobe attack which sometimes provide the only supplementary evidence of organic damage.[75]

Among the poor, uneducated, and marginal population groups that furnish the bulk of the prisoners filling American jails, few will have had this sort of meticulous examination, and the incidence of seizure disorders in this class may well be twenty or thirty times higher than in the population at large.

Dorothy Lewis in 1979 found an association between psychomotor (temporal lobe) epilepsy and criminal or delinquent behavior. The study group was composed of ninety-seven male juvenile delinquents in a Connecticut correctional school, of whom nineteen were classified as "less violent" and seventy-eight as "more violent." Of the ninety-seven, twenty-five had four or more symptoms of psychomotor epilepsy, and the "more violent" had more symptoms than the "less violent."[76]

In 1988 Lewis examined juveniles sentenced to death for homicide and other capital offenses. All had such neurologic disabilities as severe headaches, absence seizures, dizzy spells, psycho-motor symptoms, epilepsy, or impaired memory.[77]

She attributed these neurologic symptoms to severe blows to the head, falls, automobile and motorcycle accidents, etc.—which nearly all of these young men had experienced. Eleven of the four-teen bore notable facial scars as evidence. But hyperactivity makes children accident-prone and predisposes parents to violence directed at the child, and this factor should also have been considered.[78]

Studies have been done of other violence-prone population sub-groups.

Frank Elliott found in 1982 that thirty percent of 286 patients with "episodic dyscontrol" had had complex partial seizures at some time in their lives. "In many the seizures had not been recognized as epileptic because of their subtle form and rare occurrence."[79] He later expanded this study and told the Fourth World Congress of Biological Psychiatry in 1985 that of 321 excessively violent indi-viduals, *most of middle-class background and ninety-five percent white, more than ninety percent showed evidence of brain dysfunction and neurologic disabilities.* "This was a great surprise to me," he said. "I had expected twenty percent maybe." The defects noted included "evidence of past brain injury, medical history compatible with a form of epilepsy, and physical abnormalities in portions of their brains."[80]

The electroencephalograms of sociopaths, criminals and vio-lence-prone individuals, although not altogether reliable, also suggest a difference between the normal and the criminal population.*[81]

The so-called "6 & 14 dysrhythmia" discovered in 1951 has come in for a good deal of attention. It is seen to be associated clin-ically with attacks of rage: "The patient with 6 & 14 per second positive spikes . . . usually has a normal personality, and his family complains chiefly of his episodes of meanness and cruelty."[82] A 1956 survey of 1000 cases with the "6 & 14 dysrhythmia" noted:

---

*An EEG can be negative even in the presence of epileptic fits; about ten percent of the population has an EEG compatible with grand mal epilepsy, while 0.5% has the epilepsy; and twenty percent of those with grand mal have a normal EEG.

The control by rage is so absolute that parents fear for their lives and those of others. Typical complaints are: extreme rage outbursts, larceny, arson, violent acts without motivation, sexual acts (aggressive), threats to stab, shoot, mutilation of animals, and total inability to accept correction or responsibility for the act.[83]

The authors concluded that this sort of aggression can no more be curbed by the individual than a *grand mal* seizure can be suppressed by an epileptic.

In 1959 Peter Kellaway and coworkers in Houston, Texas, found this dysrhythmia in 2.3 percent of a 1000 normal children. It was associated with attacks of headache or abdominal pain, behavioral disturbances, and seizures.[84] Sherwyn Woods, of the University of Wisconsin Medical School, in 1961 found it associated with "firesetting, aggressive sexuality, murder, and other acts of violence."[85] Other investigators subsequently have found the "6 & 14" cropping up in EEG surveys of violent criminals.[86]

Steve, the hyperactive adolescent who murdered his middle-aged cousin in an episode of rage because she nagged him, manifested the "6 & 14 dysrhythmia" and was described as having autistic features.

A connection between violence and epilepsy is also seen in the positive response of individuals with episodic dyscontrol to dilantin and other seizure medications.[87]

Violence, Mental Retardation, and Cranial Nerve Palsies

The criminal class suffers from cranial nerve palsies, a low IQ and tendencies to mental retardation.

As already noted, the Hollander and Turner study found that half of the male juvenile offenders in their New Jersey sample had an IQ lower than 85. (What is more, offenders with IQ below 70 could not be included in the sample for administrative reasons; if they had been included, an even larger proportion of the prisoners would have manifested the low IQ.) Offenders with a low IQ were involved predominantly in violent crimes against persons; those with an average IQ were property offenders.

Other studies have supported this conclusion.[88]

The cranial nerve palsies from which the criminal class also suffers, with the accompanying harvest of learning disabilities, contribute to their deficit in intelligence.

In this class one finds such visual disturbances as: crossed eyes (strabismus), poor eyesight in one eye, visual illusions and hallucinations, inability to move the eyes from side to side, inability to follow movements with the eyes, poor coordination between hand and eye movements, seeing double (diplopia), blurred vision, episodes of blindness, and photophobia—often leading the individual to wear dark glasses.

There is also inability to interpret what is perceived with the eyes. The individual sees colors but cannot name them; he sees the expression on another person's face but can't interpret it. He cannot recognize forms (astereognosis) and thus cannot follow maps, cannot copy designs on paper or with building blocks, cannot do jigsaw puzzles.

They manifest the full range of learning disabilities.

Disturbances of hearing include hyperacusis (too-acute hearing), exaggerated startle reactions to sudden noises (unexpected noises will sometimes precipitate an attack of rage), tone deafness, and audiomotor incoordination (inability to dance in step to music).

Speech problems involve simple inability to pronounce and use language, inability to pronounce certain sounds (aphasia), syntactical errors, poor vocabulary, temporary loss of voice, difficulty giving verbal reports, stuttering, and a tendency to get lost in unimportant details. The individual talks too loud, and his voice is unmodulated.

Another cranial palsy affecting this population is inability to move the facial muscles. Frank Elliot's patients with uncontrollable rage manifested

> inability to show the teeth properly; inability to wink one eye by itself; inability to whistle; difficulty in wrinkling the brow to order, though it can happen spontaneously; and inability to project the tongue to order. Emotional immobility of the face can occur in frontal and brain stem lesions (as after encephalitis).[89]

Violence and Minor Neurologic Disabilities

The minor neurological peculiarities already discussed in connection with encephalitis, autism, and the MBD syndrome are encountered with disproportionate frequency in violent criminals.

Of these the most common is hyperactivity, as already mentioned. Criminals often have memory weaknesses as well, especially of short-term memory.

This group manifests a variety of "hard" and "soft"" neurological signs.

The individual may be clumsy—dropping things, bumping up against furniture, and unable to perform tasks requiring fine coordination. His movements are awkward and lacking in grace.

He may be unable to perform alternating movements in rapid succession and has defective control over muscular coordination, leading to "jerky" movements, starts and twitches of various kinds, grossly abnormal posturing of the arms or upper body, twistings and turning of the hands (athetoid movements), tremors, temporary paralysis, trouble walking, and inability to learn certain motor skills. A man who walks normally may be extremely clumsy in running, falling over if he tries to go too fast. A man of normal athletic ability may be unable to jump rope.[90]

The pain threshold, especially in the hands and feet, is lowered —"which may help [them] to be impervious to physical punishment."[91]

They have slower than normal responses to aversive stimuli.[92]

Another disorder is "disturbance of laterality," meaning tendency to left-handedness, ambidexterity, or difficulty in telling right from left, suggesting damage to the left hemisphere of the brain (which governs the right side of the body).[93]

Several studies, including one conducted in 1979 in Alberta, have found that psychopathic criminals (convicted of homicide, rape, physical assault, etc.), persons with learning disabilities and conduct disorders, persons who are simply aggressive, alcoholics with personality disorders, mentally handicapped adults with behavioral disorders, sex offenders, and non-psychopathic violent male criminals frequently manifested dysfunction of the left hemisphere.[94]

The triad of enuresis, pyromania, and cruelty to animals, which in children is regarded as a predictor of adult crime, is encountered with unexpected frequency in patients with episodic dyscontrol syndrome (note the case of Tommy Colella).[95]

Arson today is a serious social problem. In 1975 fire caused 7,500 deaths, 310,000 injuries, and $13.4 billion in property damage in the United States; eleven percent of this was estimated to be caused by arson, and another five percent by "children playing with fire." In the decade 1970-1980 the number of fires attributed to arson increased 325 percent.[96]

Arsonists are often described in ways showing a relationship to the postencephalitic syndrome. Such "pathological firesetters" are described by one authority as "psychotics, children with atypical ego development, neurologically handicapped children, delinquents, and the retarded."[97] They cannot "deal with impulse expression," they "manifest high anxiety," are "violent children," have "sleep disturbances," cannot "control aggression resulting from frustration, loneliness, and inadequacy." One study of thirty males found that "twenty-two of the children were diagnosed as psychotic or prepsychotic, and eight had a conduct disorder. Only eight were at their proper grade level [in school]. The authors noted other behaviors present to include rage reactions, hyperactivity, and impulse problems." "Others have also noted a high incidence of physical abnormalities in firesetters, including allergies and especially respiratory problems in children." "Case material also tells of psychotics who are 'told' to set a fire to purge a building of evil."[98]

In the past arson had rarely been committed by females, but this changed in the 1960s. Kenneth R. Fineman finds "firesetting in adolescent females to be indicative of rather severe psychopathology." One study found serious sexual disorders in female arsonists, including a high prevalence (thirty-three percent) of prostitution.[99]

Enuresis is common in violence-prone individuals. According to Frank Elliott, "Adults with MBD often give a history of bed-wetting until early adolescence," while those with episodic dyscontrol may have "incontinence of urine and/or feces."[100]

Another problem is unusual sleep patterns. Sleep can be too deep and is often combined with bed-wetting, sleepwalking, trouble falling asleep, and the like.[101]

There is a tendency to headaches, whether migraine or other-wise.[102] Attacks of rage are sometimes preceded by an intense pain on one side of the face or head, or by a "bursting" or "piercing" headache; the ensuing act of aggression then relieves the pain.[103]

C.E. Climent and coworkers examined ninety-five female pris-oners for a history of violence, depression, and suicide attempts. They found a significant association with loss of parents, especially of the father, but "other early life history variables found to be associated with the later presence of violent behavior are: severe headaches and convulsions before age ten, extreme stubbornness, and severe temper tantrums as children. These factors might be con-sidered to be early predisposing conditions which increase the prob-ability of later violent behavior. They suggest the possibility of neurological predisposing variables for later violent behavior."[104]

The histories of violence-prone adults have also been found to include appetite troubles with anorexia, gastrointestinal pains, nausea and vomiting, and bowel trouble with weight loss.[105]

Personality of the Sociopath: Childish Egotism

The effects of encephalitis are often described in terms of develop-mental or maturational "delay." This illness retards the growth of the organism and its neurological system. The victim remains neurologically and sensorially immature.

This means that he is also immature emotionally and intellec-tually. An early paper on antisocial aggression stated that these delinquents "exhibit a definable syndrome, a parody of immature egotism and aggressiveness that would be bound to bring the indi-vidual into conflict with any community."[106] Harvey Cleckley, a major authority on the criminal mind, writes: "The psychopath is always distinguished by egocentricity. This is usually of a degree not seen in ordinary people and often is little short of astonishing . . . a self-centeredness that is apparently unmodifiable and all but complete."[107]

The parallel with the self-absorption of autism, of course, is striking.

Being still a self-centered child, the repeat criminal feels, thinks, and acts like a self-centered child.

He is incapable of mature long-term emotional relationships with family, friends, sexual partners. He is incapable of empathizing with others, of putting himself in another's place.

> Vexation, spite, quick and labile flashes of quasi-affection, peevish resentment, shallow moods of self-pity, puerile attitudes of vanity, and absurd and showy poses of indignation. . . . But mature, whole-hearted anger, true or consistent indignation, honest solid grief, sustaining pride, deep joy, and genuine despair are reactions not likely to be found.[108]

Sociopathic criminals show "a general callous disregard for the feelings or rights of others, and are blatantly manipulative." They cannot be trusted to react in the sense of "one good turn deserves another." They cannot be counted on to demonstrate appreciation. There is a "lack of conscience, no sense of guilt, senseless lying, no capacity for affection or empathy. . . . Many . . . are reported by their mothers to have been different from other children from birth onwards; they were *resistant to cuddling, emotionally remote*, and *impervious to correction*." [emphasis added][109]

They have no capacity to see themselves as others see them. "The psychopath shows not only a deficiency but apparently a total absence of self-appraisal." Instead, they are full of grandiose illusions and delusions. For this reason they often lack an ordinary sense of fear, an ordinary awareness of obstacles and pitfalls; they are big risk-takers.[110]

Ted Bundy, the young university graduate who was executed in Florida in 1989 after having raped and murdered probably eighty young women (and who is discussed at greater length below), fits the above description perfectly. According to the court-appointed psychiatrist, he "really and truly did not have a sense of the enormity of what he had done." "I don't know why everyone's out to get me," he said. "Do you think it could have something to do with the number of victims?" The day before his execution he asked: "Will I get into heaven?"[111]

Their threshold of frustration is very low; as children they have severe temper tantrums (as did Bundy).[112]

They have no sense of responsibility, no feelings of remorse or shame, and are "callously indifferent to the grotesquely brutal murders for which they were convicted."[113] The Asperger's Syndrome case mentioned earlier "showed manneristic behavior, his affect was flat, but, although admitting that the various attacks on the children and girls had been wrong, he did not appear to be at all distressed or remorseful."[114] Bundy never showed regret but was described as "detached" from the brutal murders he committed.

Former Bronx District Attorney Mario Merola: "They'll kill you for nothing. . . . They'll stare through you. They're cold and callous. They have no remorse."[115]

The judge who sentenced Curtis Bolden to thirty years in prison told the court:

> The attacks inflicted upon aged and defenseless women defy description. They are almost too horrible to relate. So vicious, so cruel, so lacking in sensitivity and compassion. I am totally bewildered as to how one human being can treat another human being in this manner.[116]

Reporting on the adolescent who murdered his middle-aged female cousin, one investigator noted:

> There is always a striking flattening of affect while discussing the incident. He appears indifferent and unable to fully appreciate the significance of his behavior, and there is a notable absence of remorse or regret.[117]

The Washington Post editorialized about the six young black men mentioned earlier who were convicted of first-degree murder:

> None of those six seemed to possess that internal moral compass that rules out certain actions—that, even before any calculation of gain or of the risk of being caught and punished, simply refuses to take part in a crime because it is deeply wrong. Can there be a more rudimentary transgression than an attack on a defenseless woman on her way to the store?[118]

When the fourteen-year-olds who attacked the female jogger in New York were being arraigned, one of them "laughed, joked, and carried on in the precinct house, not showing the least bit of remorse. In his statement to police Salaam admitted hitting the woman with a pipe and said, 'It was fun.' "

And even when these criminals do express remorse, it does not prevent them from repeating the same behavior.[119]

Usually they lack insight or intuitive sense about others. An extreme case was the woman who invariably gave the names of people she had stolen from as references for job applications.[120]

But sometimes they can mimic emotions and pretend to possess feeling which they do not have—the typical ploy of the "confidence man." These criminals are sometimes able to size up people quickly and skilled at manipulating others when it serves their purposes; Bundy was described by his interviewers as a "consummate gamesman" with an "innate need to manipulate."[121]

Their lack of a sense of humor (although they can be witty) is perhaps a minor point, but still worth making as a sign of emotional and intellectual childishness.[122]

The Gang That Couldn't Think Straight

The psychopathic criminal often thinks like a child. Maturing means learning to perceive the world with some degree of objectivity, ceasing to take wishes for realities, understanding events as part of a pattern and making plans accordingly, applying logic to the analysis of affairs. But the post-encephalitic criminal can do none of these things. He is still at the prerational stage (the "preoperational" stage as defined by child psychologist Jean Piaget).

Dorothy Lewis writes:

> For example, the "loose, rambling, illogical" thought processes of the delinquent youngsters could be seen as manifestations of the egocentric language and autistic logic characteristic of young children. According to Piaget, children prior to approximately eight years of age may successively adopt different, mutually contradictory opinions. Their explanations for behavior and events lack coherent order or a logical sense of causality. Thus an ostensibly psychotic symptom, "loose, rambling, illogical" speech, can also be understood as a manifestation of an extreme delay in cognitive maturation.[123]

The sociopath's mode of thinking is "anti-conceptual." His intellectual processes are overly concrete and fragmented, with little capacity for abstraction.

But the power to conceptualize is what enables us to act on principle, to think in terms of long-range goals, and to learn from experience.

Curtis Bolden was described by the psychiatrist:

> On direct examination he appears mentally dull. His responses are quite slowed. His affect is very flat. He attempts to answer questions relevantly, but appears unable to bring any judgment or insight to his situation. His responses are impoverished. He is unable to elaborate on anything.[124]

Like the autistic and the minimally brain-damaged, these criminals cannot organize their thoughts, their perceptions, their lives. When combined with memory weakness, this prevents them from associating the present event with past experience, as is essential for "thought as trial action" or the "reflective delay" needed for a considered adaptive act.[125] The amount of information coming in, or its complexity, may exceed the memory span of the temporal lobes, and the subject cannot retain it.[126]

Thus they *cannot accumulate experience, cannot accumulate wisdom.*

This has three consequences: (1) They do not plan ahead, (2) They have poor judgment, and (3) They act on impulse. "The psychopath shows a striking inability to follow any sort of life plan consistently, whether it be one regarded as good or evil. He does not maintain an effort toward any far goal at all."[127] "The defects . . . include . . . poor judgment, a genius for doing and saying the wrong thing, a reduced sense of fear." "They lack foresight as regards their own affairs and proceed from one egregious folly to another."[128] "The psychopath continues to show the most execrable judgment about attaining what one might presume to be his ends. . . . This is not particularly modified by experience, however chastening his experiences may be."[129]

Life to these individuals has no pattern, no meaning, and no purpose—just one thing after another. Their tiny attention span prevents them from taking a long-range view of their lives. They live in the moment and see no value in long-term rewards, such as family or career. To these criminals the "straight" life is a series of boring concrete acts.

Their fragmented thought processes prevent them from seeing the contradictions in their behavior. They show total disregard for the truth and are often very convincing liars.[130]

The inability to foresee consequences, ordinarily a weakness, can become a strength and aid to the violent criminal in the form of "cut-off"—a withdrawal from conceptual thinking that enables him to blank out his fears and doubts.[131]

In the midst of an episode of dyscontrol the individual may feel "disorganized," "in an altered state of consciousness," "depersonalized," "in a dream state," "something seems to go wrong in my head," "unreal,"—as though someone else is committing the act and not he himself.

Sometimes there is complete amnesia afterwards. Tony Colella continued to profess ignorance of the numerous violent assaults he committed against his adopted family.

The most notorious manifestation of these weaknesses is impulsive behavior, specifically, the "irresistible impulse." Inability to resist impulse and the demand for immediate gratification are the main components of the "episodic dyscontrol syndrome." "There was a driven quality to the actions, eliciting such comments from the patients as 'I just couldn't help what I was doing even though I knew that it was wrong.' "[132]

The impulse, of course, is often one of aggression. Sherwyn Woods observed as early as 1961 that crimes committed out of "irresistible impulse" were already presenting a serious problem for forensic psychiatry.[133]

The best example of the "irresistible impulse" is the case of Ted Bundy, discussed in detail below.

Personality of the Sociopath:
Ego Weakness, Losing Control

The excessive assertiveness, egotism, and "toughness" of the criminal often masks what is in reality "ego impoverishment" "low self-esteem," and absence of self-confidence.[134]

Jean Lion, who founded the first center for the study of violence at the University of Maryland in the 1970s, stated in a 1985 interview that many aggressive patients are "frightened—angry people often are. But if you could get past their fright and your own reaction to what they did, you would often find helplessness and fear."[135]

A study of 130 violent patients by George Bach-y-Rita found

> a sense of being useless and impotent and unable to change the environment. . . . The individual episodes were marked by a total breakdown of ego function and disorganization of thought process. . . . The patients can be seen as having inadequate ego defenses that are insufficient to deal with stresses. . . . The key difference between these patients and other persons is that they make themselves noticeable because they react with violent or anti-social behavior rather than with withdrawal, alcohol, etc.[136]

Thus these criminals are in the same paradoxical situation as the autistics: their grandiose and childish egotism is transformed into ego impoverishment after repeated rebuffs by the world of reality.

The feelings of worthlessness and impotence are often concretized in a *fear of losing control*, leading to panic. In this anxious state a chance occurrence can be misconstrued as an aggressive insult, or a friendly remark perceived as a homosexual advance.[137]

This ego weakness and self-contempt—sometimes called the "zero state"—is always just below the surface. The criminal may protect against it by grandiose visions of himself as a superman effortlessly achieving great ends by unconventional means. He sustains the image primarily by forcing others to bend to his will—sometimes through manipulation but most commonly through violence. Various investigations have come to the conclusion that the weaker the ego, the greater the tendency to violence.[138]

Loss of control over a situation is perceived by these individuals as a serious threat. It brings the "zero state" to the surface and can lead to erratic outbursts. This was described graphically by a young street criminal in discussing an aborted attempted mugging by friends of his. The victim refused to give up his credit cards but kept his hand in his pocket, was shot by them, and died on the spot:

They were afraid. The man might not have had nothing in his hand, but they didn't care. . . . And by him making that sudden move to reach, dig, they didn't think to look in his hand. They just shot him. . . . This is how I used to be, you know, because I used to be a stickup kid . . . I was always scared. . . . The dude was supposed to be in control of the situation. And by his saying, "Give me back my credit cards," as far as I can understand it, he snatched it back, his wallet back. That's like him rebelling. . . . When you robbing somebody, you supposed to be in control of everything at all times. That gun make you the boss.[139]

Ultimately, these criminals know they are losers:

The psychopath . . . seems to go out of his way to make a failure of life. By some incomprehensible and untempting piece of folly or buffoonery, he eventually cuts short any activity in which he is succeeding, no matter whether it is crime or honest endeavor. At the behest of trivial impulses he repeatedly addresses himself directly to folly.[140]

It is the subconscious desire to fail which makes him such a risk-taker. "He will commit theft, forgery, adultry, fraud, and other deeds for astonishingly small stakes, and under much greater risks of being discovered than will the ordinary scoundrel."[141]*

Personality of the Sociopath: Depression and Suicide

A pervasive depression, with inclination to suicide, is often found in these individuals between bouts of violence.[142] Ted Bundy, who suffered from fits of extreme depression, is an example.[143]

The effect is intensified when combined with alcoholism. Women tend to commit violent crimes during the week before menstruation, when they are feeling depressed and paranoid.[144]

---

*Whether the pathological gambler, who subconsciously wants to lose, also has the characteristics of the post-encephalitic syndrome, would be worth investigating. Quite recent research shows that chronic gamblers often suffer from disturbances of the central nervous system. (*The New York Times*, October 3, 1989, C-1, 11).

Suicide is merely another manifestation of impulsive rage—directed this time against the self. Tommy Colella, who was permanently depressed and attempted suicide on numerous occasions, is typical. Many will threaten suicide and make suicidal gestures. In one study of episodic dyscontrol, eighteen of the twenty-two subjects manifested "suicidal ideation."[145]

The amphetamines which have for years been prescribed for symptoms of minimal brain damage may potentiate the suicidal impulses of these individuals.*

The teenage suicide rate in the United States jumped seventy-five percent between 1968 and 1979—from 5 to 9/100,000 (in 1950 it was 4.5). By 1986 it had climbed to 13. This translates into 5000 adolescent suicides per year, and there are fifty or 100 attempts for every successful suicide.[146]

Defenses and Compensations: Paranoia, Sex

The sociopath is often aware of his personality weaknesses and develops techniques for protecting his ego and elevating his self-esteem.

One is to cast blame on others. The sociopath is instinctively paranoid, feels unfairly treated, and blames the rest of the world for his troubles. He rejects responsibility for his repeated difficulties with the law and consistently offers rationalizations for his own behavior.[147]

Dorothy Lewis has found paranoid ideation to be one of five characteristics predicting a tendency to commit murder (the others: having inflicted violence as an adolescent, severe neurological impairment, abuse by parents as a child, a first-degree relative with a psychiatric/neurologic disability).[148]

Paranoia is often directed against persons in authority. They are resented and viewed in a derisive and disparaging manner.[149]

Other compensations for ego weakness are perseveration and stubbornness. A study of ninety-five violent female prisoners found "extreme stubbornness" to be a common associated characteristic.

---

*See below, pp. 217–228.

The man who stabbed his dead victim thirty more times would be an example of perseveration.[150]

Intense sexual activity at an age "unusually early for their peer group" is a common finding in future sociopaths.[151] A 1977 study in Cambridge, England, of 411 working-class males, of whom 128 had a criminal record by the age of twenty-one, found that as adolescents they manifested excessive sexual promiscuity.[152]

This predilection has numerous manifestations: a casual attitude toward sexual matters generally, involvement with pornography, more frequent use of obscene language, incest, continuous masturbation, coprophilia (smearing of feces: "an astonishingly ambivalent attitude in which the amorous and excretory functions seem to be confused").[153]

> Bundy . . . was such a compulsive masturbator, he once told a psychiatrist, that he masturbated in school closets, where other boys found him and taunted him, dashing him with ice water.[154]

Other serial killers have reported that they fueled their fantasies while young by masturbating as they imagined sexual murders.[155]

This sexual behavior substitutes for their impaired ability to form lasting, close, warm, and responsible relationships with family, friends, or sexual partners.[156]

Confused sexuality, bisexualism, and homosexualism are further features of the post-encephalitic syndrome. Von Economo noted that post-encephalitics "indulge in sexual misbehavior of every kind and make themselves willing partners to such. . . . Sexual delinquencies . . . remain the common practice of these patients."[157] In general, their attitude toward sexual matters is impulsive and superficial, their sex life "impersonal, trivial, and poorly integrated."

Bach-y-Rita and coworkers studied 130 violent patients and found forty-one admitting to gross sexual difficulties such as impotence, total abstinence, or severe hypersexuality; sixteen had had adult homosexual encounters, six were sterile by surgical sterilization, two had Klinefelter syndrome (the individual appears to be male but has large breasts, small genitalia, atrophied testes, and is sterile), two were transvestites, and one had committed incest.[158]

When studies are done of temporal lobe epilepsy, often a component of the episodic dyscontrol syndrome, sexual disorders become apparent there also: most are hyposexual, with impotence and frigidity; some are markedly hypersexual; while another group deviates into bisexualism, homosexualism, transvestism, or fetishism.[159]

Bach-y-Rita found that patients with episodic dyscontrol were "generally outwardly hypermasculine and intent on physically defending their masculinity against other men." But, at the same time, they are usually dependent on some female figure placed in a mothering role, and their sense of masculine identity is poor.[160]

Barry Maletzky described a group of twenty-two males with episodic dyscontrol syndrome as "'hypermasculine' yet tremulous."[161]

While paranoia and excessive sexual preoccupations are not to be understood as invariably linked with the post-encephalitic syndrome, in this latter group they often serve as ego-boosters and outlets for overwhelming feelings of depression and frustration.

Defenses and Compensations: Child Abuse

Another outlet is found in the abuse of children.[162] This mounting social plague reflects the growth of sociopathy in American society and the need of these individuals to compensate through violence for their underlying ego weakness. Children are the innocent and helpless victims of the parents' ungovernable impulses.

Consider the following case of a twenty-year-old divorced woman with minimal brain damage who sought therapy

> because of her concern that she was abusing her child. She related this to her excessive temper and poor ability to tolerate frustration. She also suffered from chronic anxiety and the abuse of alcohol. . . . As an infant and young child she was extremely active, belligerent, and hot-tempered. These symptoms persisted more or less constantly through grade school. When she entered junior high school, her family began to live with her grandparents, a change that was followed by a marked increase in family discord and a deterioration in her adjustment. She now started to cut classes and to run away from home. This was shortly followed by first experimentation with and then abuse of several drugs. During this time she fell in love and wanted to marry, contrary

to her parents' wishes. Frustration and discord led to two suicide attempts. The issue with her parents was forced when she became pregnant and married during her junior year of high school. In a short time arguments and fights led to a separation from her husband. During this period she became concerned about her quick temper and her inability to deal with the stress of being a mother. One manifestation was her excessive punishment of the child, which extended—by her own report—to physical abuse.[163]

But the contribution of the children themselves should not be neglected. If, as we assume, vaccine vulnerability has a genetic component, the hyperactive parent may have a hyperactive child.

William Heffron and coworkers in 1987 found that abused children were often originally hyperactive and suggested that "hyperactivity may either contribute to, or result from, physical abuse. The behavior of the child is one of the causative factors leading to abuse."[164]

The stress of family life becomes greater than even a neurologically normal parent can easily bear—much less one with the typical sociopathic impatience, short attention span, and tendency to impulsive violence.

This is one more area of social analysis in which "emotional" etiological theories have had free play. But the chain of causation has been misunderstood, with effects being mistaken for causes and causes for effects.

Starting from the observation that the future child abuser was himself, or herself, often abused as a child, researchers conclude that said childhood trauma *transformed* him or her into a child abuser.[165]

While it is a commonplace that children repeat as adults the behavior which they have experienced as children, the question is rarely asked *why* they were abused in the first place. The child may well have been abused because he or she was unbearable to live with (those who have never had to raise a hyperactive child should refrain from passing judgment).

Thus the more common scenario may be one of pathological interaction between a minimally brain-damaged parent and a minimally brain-damaged child.

In this way the family pattern degenerates from generation unto generation.

Even if the brain-damaged child was never abused, he would still have a low threshold of tolerance for frustration, and thus little talent for dealing with his own hyperactive children.

What should be investigated is the extent to which child abusers are themselves neurologically damaged—i.e., learning-disabled and hyperactive—and thus from childhood drawn inexorably into the cycle of violent family interaction.

Defenses and Compensations: Alcohol and Drugs

Finally, the post-encephalitic sociopath tends to cope with his manifold problems through alcoholism or drug abuse. "Adults with a history of attention-deficit hyperactivity disorder appear to be overrepresented in the ranks of . . . substance abusers," states the *Journal of the American Medical Association*.[166]

The relationship of alcoholism and drug abuse to criminality is notorious and hardly needs elaboration. Drug abuse, especially, is an intimate part of the almost unimaginable increase in criminality of all kinds registered in this country since the 1960s.

Criminals kill and steal for funds to purchase drugs; and when under the influence of drugs they kill and steal for other reasons. A third of all serious crimes are committed under the influence of alcohol. A 1988 U.S. Department of Justice survey found that up to seventy-nine percent of persons arrested for serious crimes in various American cities were using illegal drugs. The nationwide average was over fifty percent. Those consuming multiple drugs were even more likely to be involved in crime.[167]

If factors in the post-encephalitic syndrome predispose to alcoholism and drug abuse, the vaccination program then becomes one of the causes of these two vices, and of the associated criminality.

In fact, an association with the post-encephalitic syndrome is more than likely on general grounds. A major cause of alcoholism and drug abuse is inability to sustain normal personal relations. These substances compensate for the lack of human contact. And, as we have seen, the marginal autistic, the minimally brain-damaged, the adolescent with a sociopathic personality, and all other post-encephalitics with neurologic damage have a terrible insufficiency of human contacts.

Other causes of alcoholism and drug addiction are depression and anxiety, according to recent research at the New York State Psychiatric Institute. The director of the project observed that their findings run against conventional wisdom—that depression and anxiety are the *results* of drug and alcohol abuse.[168]

Depression and anxiety are, of course, widespread in the post-encephalitic population.

Alcohol and Drug Abuse by Autistics and the Minimally Brain Damaged

The problems of the sociopath with alcohol and street drugs find a parallel in the autistics and minimally brain damaged.

Alcoholism and drug addiction among autistics are difficult to research and complicated by the fact that most are in institutions and deprived of a choice, but it would be astonishing if they did not use these to prop up their felt inferiority and difference. Tony W., for instance, the twenty-two-year-old marginal autistic whom we have already encountered, states that he smoked marijuana and drank in the ninth and tenth grades "to be normal like everybody else." After spending time in the army, he came home, "got drunk a lot and did destructive things, magnified fears and paranoia on pot." He also had "difficulties with various symptoms of anxiety, periodic alcohol abuse . . . occasionally used substances other than alcohol in an attempt to diminish his pervasive anxiety and to feel more socially adequate."[169]

This sort of account must be typical.

Children with minimal brain damage are attracted to alcohol and "recreational drugs" while still very young.[170] They are said to have a "calming" effect on the jittery and impulsive hyperactive youngster.

The modern literature of alcoholism distinguishes "primary" alcoholics, who commence in childhood or early adolescence, from "secondary" alcoholics who start drinking to excess as adults. "Primary alcoholism" has been linked with minimal brain damage and hyperactivity and is (of course!) thought to be genetically determined.[171] In fact, it is probably linked to the post-encephalitic syndrome, and this hypothesis should be investigated.

Adults with minimal brain damage have a high incidence of alcoholism and drug abuse.[172] Females may manifest the so-called "St. Louis triad" of alcoholism, sociopathy, and hysteria.[173]

The MBD syndrome transformed into "conduct disorder" is also associated with "unusually early smoking, drinking, and other substance use." "Psychoactive Substance Use Disorder" is a commonly associated diagnosis. And when "conduct disorder" degenerates into "sociopathic personality," "these kinds of behavior continue."[174]

The sociopathic criminal cannot tolerate even mild depression, anxiety, boredom, or tension and welcomes the relief provided by these habit-forming substances.[175]

But alcohol itself leads to crimes of violence; there is a "pathological reaction to alcohol without reference to the amount consumed." [176] "Pathological intoxication" and "episodic dyscontrol" can be triggered by very small quantities of alcohol, especially if the individual is feeling irritable, trapped, or insulted. [177] In many cases a single drink might set a subject off if he happened to feel angry at the time.[178] Afterwards he may not remember anything.[179]

Ted Bundy often drank before committing one of his murders, in order to calm his inhibitions.[180] He was also a pothead:

> I'm strictly a marijuana man. . . . I love to smoke reefer. And I haven't, never have tried anything but reefer. And valiums. And, of course, alcohol.[181]

If the fifteen or twenty percent of schoolchildren with minimal brain damage are predisposed from an early age to alcoholism and drug abuse, they are contributing far more than their share to the current drug and alcohol epidemic. Not only do they form a sizable contingent of themselves, but, as Gresham's Law of social behavior dictates, they set the standard for the rest.

This is scarcely ever emphasized in the public and professional discussion of this issue.

Equally ignored by the professional literature is the role of purely medicinal drugs in attracting children to a life of addiction. Since the 1950s medicinal drugs have been administered systematically to hyperactive and minimally brain damaged children to make their behavior bearable and to ward off a total collapse of the educational system.

Today at least a million children are being given such medicinal drugs by their physicians or by the school, to keep them from disrupting the classrooms.[182]

Pervasive awareness that children are being drugged for "behavioral" or "emotional" disorders creates an atmosphere in which drug use for reasons other than medicinal is seen as licit.

In these three ways hyperactivity and other manifestations of the post-encephalitic syndrome, as well as the therapeutic drugs prescribed to combat them, have contributed, and are still contributing, to American society's overall problem of drug involvement and addiction.

For many years the major class of drugs for treating hyperactivity were stimulants, known as "uppers," with the amphetamines in the lead.

Especially in the form of Benzedrine or Dexedrine, they had been used in child psychiatry since the 1930s and were initially recommended with enthusiasm for both autism and the MBD syndrome.[183] Their use increased explosively during the 1950s.

Their impact was often labelled "paradoxical," in the sense that it seemed illogical to give hyperactive children a drug whose effect is to stimulate activity. In fact, the mechanism of action of amphetamines on the central nervous system is still a mystery:

> There is neither specific evidence which clearly establishes the mechanism whereby amphetamines produce mental and behavioral effects in children, nor conclusive evidence regarding how these effects relate to the condition of the central nervous system.[184]

Whether or not they were understood, the amphetamines at first seemed to benefit many children with hyperactivity and were even seen as "specific" for this disorder.[185] "Most striking is the child's newly found ability to maintain his attention on things for longer periods. He is less driven in his behavior and is in general easier to get on with."[186]

But an uninviting negative side soon became apparent.

One child in three failed to respond or became even more hyperactive; the reasons for this are not understood.[187] And the list of adverse reactions is extensive: appearance and exacerbation of tics, heart palpitations and tachycardia (rapid heart beat), increased blood pressure, restlessness, insomnia, dizziness, tremor, headache, impotence, change in libido, urticaria, abdominal pains, and growth retardation.[188]

When amphetamines were used to treat autism, their disagreeable and incapacitating side effects became evident even sooner. They were found to "exacerbate preexisting autistic symptoms, leading to increased activity, irritability, explosiveness, and stereotypies." The autistic often became more psychotic and disorganized, even on very low doses.[189]

Often the old symptoms returned in a more serious form after discontinuation of therapy—"symptom rebound."[190] There was an increase in components of the hyperkinetic syndrome, including heightened hyperactivity, irritability, easy tears, headaches and stomachaches, tremor of the fingers, and others. Often the child or adolescent took on the "amphetamine look"—"a pale, pinched, serious facial expression, with dark hollows under the eyes." [191]

The appetite is depressed by amphetamines (they are often used as "appetite suppressants"), and anorexia—already a common symptom of minimal brain damage—is intensified.[192]

In 1983 an amphetamine-like diet pill, PPA (phenylpropanolamine), was the leading drug prescribed for weight reduction, with sales of $200 million annually.[193] To what degree has this practice helped perpetuate and intensify the plague of anorexia in American adults?

The risk of addiction was quite evident and well known. While amphetamines and other drugs for hyperactivity were supposed to be administered in a controlled setting, this rarely occurred.[194] They have been prescribed by physicians, and consumed by patients, more or less ad libitum.

The long-term effect of amphetamine addiction could be a suicidal depression or a schizophrenia-like syndrome combined with paranoid and hallucinatory phenomena ("amphetamine psychosis").[195]

And individuals with an amphetamine psychosis have attacks of "episodic dyscontrol."[196] Bach-y-Rita found that twelve of 130 patients in a study of episodic dyscontrol suffered from chronic amphetamine use (seventy-two were chronic alcoholics).[197] Jeffrey MacDonald, the "Green Beret doctor" convicted of stabbing and bludgeoning to death his wife and two daughters in a fit of "episodic dyscontrol," had been taking amphetamine-based diet pills during the preceding days and weeks.[198]

Thus the vicious circle is complete: children with minimal brain damage who have uncontrollable tempers are given amphetamines to calm them down, but these very pills predispose to attacks of "episodic dyscontrol." Of course, the precise ratio between these two factors as causes of violence is a matter of conjecture, as is the extent to which Benzedrine and Dexedrine, whose effect has been likened to that of cocaine, predispose to addiction with the latter substance.[199]

Amphetamines are still used today to treat hyperactive children.[200] But in the late 1950s parental resistance led to introduction of Cylert (pemoline) and Ritalin (methylphenidate)—two new stimulants which now dominate the market. Their "mechanism of action" is as mysterious as that of the amphetamines.[201]

They were and are said to be "non-amphetamine" drugs but are structurally similar to amphetamine and have a virtually identical pharmacologic effect.[202] As with the amphetamines, one child in four does not benefit at all.[203] And the other three are in no way cured by methylphenidate, although it has the same addictive potential as the amphetamines. "Chronically abusive use," according to the *Physicians' Desk Reference*, "can lead to marked tolerance and psychic dependence with varying degrees of abnormal behavior. Frank psychotic episodes can occur."[204]

The "abnormal behavior" which can accompany Ritalin use was illustrated by the case of Rod Matthews, the fifteen-year-old Massachusetts boy who killed his classmate with a baseball bat and then engaged in a snowball fight. He was found to be taking 10 mg.

of Ritalin twice daily for hyperactivity, fire-setting, and "social withdrawal." A month before committing the murder he had written his health teacher that he experienced urges to set his house on fire and was afraid he was going to kill someone.[205]

An equally serious dimension of childhood drug abuse is the psychological dependence it encourages. Taking responsibility for one's behavior is part of growing up. The child who shifts responsibility to a pill is evading an essential stage of development. Carole Whalen and Barbara Henker, who interviewed hyperactive children taking Ritalin, observed: "Magical 'fix-it' properties are often attributed to the pills, the assumption being that positive changes occur regardless of—and perhaps even despite—the child's own efforts and actions. Children often refer to their medication as 'smart pills' or 'good behavior pills'. . . . One concern is that the prescription of medication to facilitate the behavior . . . that most children are expected to accomplish on their own may interfere with this . . . progression toward . . . personal responsibility."

> Child: I didn't at all have hardly any friends. I only had two, and that was it. And last year I didn't take Ritalin in the afternoon, but the last time I saw my doctor he said, "Why don't you have her start taking it in the afternoon?" And since I've been doing that I've gotten about twenty more friends.
>
> Interviewer: How can you tell when you forget to take Ritalin?
>
> Child: When I can tell that I'm not concentrating in school. Like the teacher'll give us a half hour to do a math page, like there's about twenty problems, and I'll get about six done in twenty minutes, a half hour. But if I take it, I can get them all done in ten minutes, twenty minutes, and have ten minutes free. . . . They'd ask me, like "What does it do?" I'd just tell them, "Well, it helps you concentrate, get more friends, and you want to join in the games more. And you'd be invited more places."
>
> Interviewer: You were giving me a good example of times when you take an extra pill. Can you think back to another time?
>
> Child: Yes, at Catalina. Another fishing story. . . . In the fishing I got bored, 'cause we didn't catch them, and I got bored waiting for another Catalina perch. We were bored, and I needed a pill— so I had to have another pill. And I didn't have one that morning.

Then I had two. My Dad brought a case of them.

Interviewer: He carries them with him?

Child: Yeah.

Interviewer: So, how did he know you were bored and that you needed a pill?

Child: 'Cause my legs started kicking and my hands got all loose . . . then my feet started kicking all around and stuff. . . . My body gets all out of control, and I need another pill.[206]

Is it any wonder that many of these children, once grown up, still reach for a pill to cure whatever ails them—physicially, morally, or spiritually?

How about the children (one fourth) who are not benefited? Sometimes there is no effect at all, but more often the symptoms are intensified: tics, schizophrenia, depression, autistic features, and various developmental disorders are all aggravated.[207] There can be "rebound"—return of the symptoms in an intensified form—when treatment is stopped.[208] And Ritalin has other side effects, similar to those of the amphetamines: "Nervousness and insomnia . . . hypersensitivity (including skin rash . . . fever, arthralgia, exfoliative dermatitis. . .), anorexia, nausea, dizziness, palpitations, headache . . . cardiac arrhythmias, abdominal pain. . . . In children, loss of appetite, abdominal pain, weight loss during prolonged therapy, insomnia, and tachycardia. . . ."[209]

In the 1960s Ritalin was banned in Sweden because of widespread abuse by young people, who were injecting it like heroin. When the Ciba-Geigy company in 1971 decided to market Ritalin in the United States, the decision was roundly criticized by the Swedish Medical Association. A company spokesman denied that a similar problem would arise in the United States. " 'The drug was easily obtained in Sweden, which is not the situation in the United States, because of the controls we have here,' he said."[210]

In contrast to the methylphenidate family, which stimulate the central nervous system ("uppers"), the phenothiazine derivates—chlorpromazine (Thorazine), trifluoperazine (Stelazine), fluphenazine (Prolixin, Permitil), haloperidol (Haldol) and several others—are depressants ("downers").

They are also known as "neuroleptic" drugs, meaning "acting on the nerves."

Their psychotropic effects were discovered accidentally in the late 1940s when they were being used to treat allergies.[211]

How they operate is, again, not well understood. The *Physicians' Desk Reference* tells us: "The precise mechanism whereby the therapeutic effects of chlorpromazine are produced is not known. . . . Chlorpromazine has actions at all levels of the central nervous system—primarily at subcortical levels—as well as on multiple organ systems."[212]

They have been prescribed since the 1950s for hyperactivity—"particularly," according to one author, "where parents are affected by adverse publicity concerning the use of amphetamines by juveniles, delinquents, etc. Then amphetamine may be tried later, first in combination and then alone."[213] The effect of phenothiazine derivatives on the MBD syndrome is mixed—sometimes apparently helpful, sometimes not. Sometimes, in fact, the patients get worse.[214]

However, the adverse reactions to these central nervous system depressants have been truly spectacular. Among the short-term ones are: decrease in white blood cells ("increasing the likelihood of infections"), accelerated heart beat, jaundice, akathisia ("constant motor restlessness . . . body rocking and shifting, inability to sit still, and other behaviors often mistakenly identified as being self-stimulating [stereotypic] or hyperactive"), dystonic reactions ("abrupt spasms of the head, neck, and upper back muscles. . . . Muscles of the face, throat, and tongue may also spasm. Retrocollis—head tilted back—and torticollis—head turned to a side—often result. Dystonic reactions may resemble and be mistakenly identified as seizures"), Parkinsonian reactions ("body rigidity, masklike facial expression, and shuffling gait"), and withdrawal dyskinesias ("involuntary movements of body parts and musculatures. The facial musculature—particularly, oral, buccal, lingual—is most likely to be affected. . . . Early indications include involuntary smacking and sucking of the lips, dartings and tremors of the tongue, lateral jaw movements, and purposeless movements of the extremities such as the fingers and wrists").[215]

The last symptoms are known as "tardive dyskinesia"—"an iatrogenic, often unremitting disorder characterized by involuntary bucco-lingual-masticatory movements, facial grimaces, blepharospasm [excessive winking], involuntary respiratory grunting, choreoathetoid movements [twisting of the fingers and hands], and occasionally truncal dystonias [spasmodic jerking of the body]." According to Stewart Tepper and Joanne Haas, of Cornell Medical College, "Increase in the use of neuroleptics, the causative agents, has made tardive dyskinesia a serious iatrogenic problem, the magnitude of which has not been fully defined."[216]

For years physicians, pharmaceutical manufacturers, and the National Institutes of Health denied that tardive dyskinesia could occur. A 1964 document produced by the NIH National Clearinghouse for Mental Health Information announced: "There is nothing in the NCMHI document collection which refers to permanent movement disorders due to phenothiazines, nor incidence of brain lesion occurring after phenothiazine administration."[218]

But, as often happens, with the passage of time disorders did appear. And they rarely go away. Joseph DeVeaugh-Geiss, professor of psychiatry at the State University of New York, states, "There is no treatment for the involuntary movement disorder and it is usually irreversible. . . . Prevention is the only effective method of dealing with this problem."[217]

Dyskinesia is merely another unintended consequence of technological progress. Studies of patients taking these drugs find dyskinesias of various kinds occurring in *twenty-four to fifty-six percent* of cases (one researcher reported *sixty-seven* percent). In a study on autistic children, over one in five taking these drugs developed such "neuroleptic-induced dyskinesias."[219] Children with minimal brain damage can develop tics, even the severe form known as the Tourette Syndrome, after taking Ritalin. Tourette Syndrome is not a benign condition, but makes the individual's life insupportable, causing many to commit suicide, and these new symptoms can also be irreversible.[220] It is never possible to predict who will be affected, as the effect is not dose-dependent but idiosyncratic.[221] T.I. Lidsky in 1981 suggested that "the full range of risks associated with drug-induced brain disorders has not been established."[222] This remains true today.

In 1988 Stephen E. Breuning, who published some of the above information, entered a guilty plea to charges of falsifying data in studies from 1980 to 1984 showing Ritalin and Dexedrine to be more beneficial in hyperactive retarded children, and with fewer side effects, than the medications used previously. A colleague stated that he was pressured by the "publish or perish syndrome. . . . In the research world, there's a great deal of pressure on those guys to produce, to get the grants . . . He wasn't getting any results, so he made the stuff up." A NIH panel report stated that Breuning became "one of the frequently quoted workers in this field" and that several states adopted new drug treatment policies on the basis of his findings. "The effect of Breuning's now-questioned research is not known, experts in the field said." He could have received a ten-year sentence but was sentenced to sixty days in a halfway house, with five years of probation, and fined $11,352. He also agreed to stay out of the field for ten years.[223]

Even though Breuning's data were falsified, Ritalin and Dexedrine are still used today in the same quantities as before. What else can parents and schools do, after all? Programs exist which educate parents in the "lifelong nature" of hyperactivity and train children in behavior modification—but at a cost of $3000/child/year. A special institution for the child costs ten times more. The pills cost pennies a day.[224]

As new theories are promulgated about autism and minimal brain damage, resourceful clinicians devise new medications and new modes of treatment. The availability of unlimited research funds in the National Institutes of Health further stimulates production of such studies.

Sometimes there appears to be a rationale. Sometimes the researcher seems to be trying out a drug just because it is on the shelf.

Following the observation that anxiety is a component of the MBD syndrome, various tranquilizers and anti-anxiety drugs have been employed: Librium, Miltown, Atarax, and others. These, in turn, produced their own side effects, including "paradoxical" attacks of rage.[225]

On the theory that autism resembles manic depression, lithium carbonate (the standard treatment for manic depression) has been used.[226] On the theory that it resembles schizophrenia, Benadryl (diphenhydramine) was explored.[227] The anti-Parkinsonian drug L-dopa was used on the theory that autism resembles Parkinson's Disease, and also because it lowers blood levels of serotonin (which are high in autism, as discussed in Chapter IV); indeed, the serotonin was lowered, but no clinical benefit was observed.[228]

Because the hyperactive child often feels depressed and has poor bladder control, the anti-enuretic antidepressant Tofranil (imipramine hydrochloride) has been prescribed.[229] As we have found with the other drugs, "the mechanism of action of Tofranil is not definitely known." But, "the action of the drug in controlling childhood enuresis is thought to be apart from its antidepressant effect."[230]

The "leading theory" on this and other "tricyclic antidepressants" suggests that they restore normal levels of neurotransmitters, as depressions are thought to be caused by "a relative deficiency of neurotransmitters." [??]

Rauwolfia serpentina (Reserpine, Serpasil), classified as an antipsychotic and used in schizophrenic, paranoid, and manic states, was another common medication for hyperactivity in the 1950s and early 1960s.[231] It had a calming effect on some children; others were unaffected or reacted merely with drowsiness, while a significant number became worse from Reserpine and Serpasil.[232]

One sometimes thinks it would be better to leave these unfortunates alone rather than fill them with drugs whose "mechanism of action" is so perplexing.

In the early 1970s half a million to a million children in the U.S. public school system were taking one or another drug every day for hyperactivity, with the number steadily increasing. Today the figure is probably over a million. Manufacturers more than doubled their output of methylphenidate between 1982 and 1988.[233]

This abuse of drugs for "medicinal" purposes in school children cannot help but predispose them to amphetamine, marijuana, heroin, and cocaine addiction later in life. If over a million schoolchildren are taking Ritalin or an amphetamine every day from the teacher in the classroom, why should they not take something stronger from the stranger in the street?

Today—thirty years after these programs were started!—parents have come to realize that these medicinal drugs contribute mightily to the American "drug culture."

A lawsuit was filed in 1987 in Atlanta, Georgia, against the local school district and the American Psychiatric Association by the mother of a minimally brain-damaged child who claimed that four years of Ritalin treatment had made him violent and suicidal. Her lawyer stated in an interview: "Personally, I think it's horrifying. . . . The psychiatric community thinks it's perfectly okay to give drugs to children. At lunchtime in schools there is a line of little children waiting to take psychiatric medicine."[234]

At a 1987 meeting of a professional society of psychiatrists in Minneapolis, an airplane was seen circling overhead with a banner reading, "Psychs, Stop Drugging Our Kids." At another such meeting the same year in Canada a group passed out leaflets under a banner stating, "Psychiatrists Are Making Drug Addicts Out of Our Children."[235]

Indeed, psychiatrists and pediatricians are major pushers of psychoactive and neuroleptic drugs.

The incipient parental resistance has made a few dents in the armor of physicians' aloof self-assurance. Richard Roberts, chairman of the American Academy of Pediatrics Committee on Drugs, stated, "I don't remember as much furor over any other issue" and reported numerous telephone calls from fellow pediatricians concerned about possible side effects of Ritalin treatment. And when Barry D. Garfinkel, Director of the Division of Child and Adolescent Psychiatry at the University of Minnesota, was asked if these drugs are overprescribed, he admitted, "We just don't have a good way to judge that."

But other physicians and psychiatrists shrug off the criticism. Judith Rapoport, M.D., chief of the Child Psychiatry Branch, National Institutes of Health, announced, "The data are very good that stimulant drugs are one of the mainstays of treatment. Although there are individual cases of overuse or misuse, properly used stimulant drugs can be good treatment."[236]

The Irresistible Impulse: the Case of Ted Bundy

Mention has already been made of the repeat criminals who make up a sizable portion of the criminal class.

In the early 1970s American criminologists discovered that such repetitively violent criminals were often diagnosed with "episodic dyscontrol syndrome"—a tendency to "uncontrollable storms of aggression"—which is a major cause of unplanned homicides, wife and child abuse, criminally aggressive driving, pointless destruction of property, and savage attacks on animals.

But "episodic dyscontrol" is merely a new name for the "explosive diathesis" associated with the post-encephalitic syndrome since the late nineteenth century and already discussed in Chapter III.

It is a violent manifestation of the "irresistible impulse."

It affects males more than females, at the usual ratio of 3:1 or 4:1.

Psychologists and psychiatrists today have apparently forgotten the "explosive diathesis" and its association with encephalitis. So the origins of the irresistible impulse have been cloaked in obscurity. While it is seen to be linked to hyperactivity and minimal brain damage in childhood, as well as to many other neurologic features encountered in autism and minimal brain damage, the source of these other neurologic states has also remained a mystery and could throw no light on the irresistible impulse.

The topic has been given over to doctors of the mind who have no trouble rooting it in traumatic episodes from childhood, illegitimacy, sexual maladjustments, poverty, "racism," and the like.

This has led to a radical misunderstanding of this condition and consequently to inappropriate measures for treating it.

This riddle can be deciphered by noting the parallel with other kinds of compulsive behavior associated with encephalitis. The oculogyric crisis, for instance, and post-encephalitic respiratory disorders, have tic-like properties in addition to an element of obsession or compulsion; they can be suppressed voluntarily only for brief periods and are closely linked to the individual's emotional state.[237]

Or take the neurologic disease mentioned above known as

Tourette's Syndrome (also of encephalitic origin and associated with hyperactivity, attention deficits, and various obsessions and compulsions).[238] Here the impulse takes the form of verbal tics, barks, and grunts:

> Sounds varied from expiratory noises, throat clearing, snorting, etc. to barking, echolalia [repeating the words and statements of others], and coprolalia [use of obscene language]. . . . The . . . vocal utterances are characteristically sudden, abrupt, and explosive in nature. They may interrupt normal conversation only briefly in a staccato-like style.[239]

Persons with Tourette's Syndrome are, in their great majority, neither retarded nor mentally deficient. *But they cannot prevent themselves from emitting these grunts, barks, and verbalisms:*

> They may be minimally influenced by voluntary efforts of inhibition. It is not infrequent that a patient can control coprolalia [spoken obscenities] until he reaches the safety of a men's room, whereupon he will emit a stream of words and subsequently feel some relief until the next episode. Some patients can disguise mild involuntary noises by forced laughter or similar accepted forms of vocalization. Voluntary inhibition of symptoms, however, frequently causes an explosive build-up of other symptoms. Symptoms . . . commonly increase with states of anxiety, anger, silence, or prolonged periods of emotional stress.[240]

The mother of one young man with Tourette's Syndrome described his plight as follows:

> *He had an arrangement in school where he could go out of the room whenever the nervous tension got too great. Then he would have one tic after another outside. Or, if he was trying hard to control them in school, he would have a whole string of tics when he would come home.*

Thus the tics and grunts of Tourette's Syndrome are not under the individual's conscious control. They are not rooted in traumatic episodes of childhood or in sexual maladjustments. They cannot be prevented by effort of will.

The irresistible impulse emerges in a more tragic and brutal form when it involves acts of aggression. Sherwyn Woods described it as follows:

> The particular aggressive act is described by the patient as impulsive, though considerable time and planning may have intervened between impulse and action. During this time there is an obsessive preoccupation with the impulse, and the feeling of an overwhelming and uncontrollable urge whose tension cannot be relieved until the act is fully completed. Once started there is a sense of an inability to stop or deflect the direction of the impulse. If the act is assaultative, it is usually compulsively repetitious, sometimes to the point of the bizarre.[241]

This is illustrated by the story of Ted Bundy.

He has attracted particular attention because he was from a middle-class family and enjoyed considerable success in both school and college, graduating "with distinction" from the University of Washington with a B.A. degree in psychology.

However, while pursuing a successful academic career, dating sorority girls, and having affairs with some of them, he was at the same time prowling the streets of Seattle, Tacoma, and smaller towns in Washington and Oregon, picking up young girls, raping, and murdering them in the most brutal ways imaginable.

An enormous amount has been written about his case, and several interpretations of his aberrant behavior have been proffered. No one, however, has yet suggested that he was suffering from post-encephalitic syndrome.

Bundy did not have a seizure disorder and was not mentally retarded. He was left-handed and stuttered. But in him the post-encephalitic syndrome came out most strikingly in the form of an uncontrollable urge to rape, mutilate, and kill young women.

His case is very important if only because there are certainly many others like him waiting in the wings. Their future detection will be facilitated by a correct understanding of Bundy's disorder.

In numerous interviews with journalists Bundy disclosed a great deal about himself and, in fact, displayed considerable understanding of his compulsion. These materials give us an accurate picture of his personality and its dynamics.

The results of neurological examinations to which he was subjected during his years in prison showed an extraordinary gap between his superior verbal IQ and a very inferior ability to perceive spatial relationships. This condition, according to psychiatrist Dorothy Lewis, is highly suggestive of central nervous system dysfunction.[242]

Such dysfunctions are usually caused by an encephalitis which, as we have seen, is most commonly due to vaccination. While we know nothing about Bundy's vaccination history (his mother refused to release records from the home for unwed mothers where Ted spent the first three months of his life), analysis of his personality profile shows close parallels with that of the post-encephalitic individual.

Bundy had the same low self-esteem (even though he was, in fact, handsome, charming, and intelligent), the same feeling of being surrounded by "chaos" and "confusion," the same mounting stress levels, and the same tendency to discharge this stress through outbursts of uncontrollable violence.

He felt alienated from his earliest years ("I have absolutely no desire to relate to people") and once stated that he would have preferred to be a lumberjack: "I'd have as little contact with modern society as possible."[243]

His alienation meant that he could not understand other people's emotions and motivations. He had trouble "learning what the appropriate social behaviors were," hence an "outright fear of socializing." "I wasn't sure what was wrong and what was right. All I knew was that I felt a bit different." "When people were genuinely interested in me I seldom picked up on it."[244]

He disliked unstructured situations where he did not know what was expected of him. In high school, for instance, he could not adapt socially but enjoyed his classes. "It's a formalized setting, and the ground rules are fairly strict. And your performance is measured by different rules than what happens when everybody is peeling off into little cliques down the hallway."[245]

In his early twenties, he participated enthusiastically in a political campaign. "It's a sort of built-in social life. Which I never had."[246]

And for the same reason he even claimed to find some satisfaction in prison:

I feel comfortable, so much more confident when I talk to people. I *know* who I am. . . . I used to be very intimidated by situations. And people. Not understanding motivations. I can now speak my mind and be not at all self-conscious about it.[247]

His alienation and social incompetence caused him great stress.

"Stress" was the first topic he mentioned when interviewed by journalists Michaud and Aynesworth.

Stress is a very ambiguous word in that it includes both the physical being and the emotional self. With respect to this personality, stress influenced development over a number of years.[248]*

You take the individual we're talking about—a unique personality with certain defects, if you will—and then you subject him to stress. Stress happens to come up randomly, but its effect on the person is *not* random; it's specific. That results in a certain amount of chaos, confusion, and frustration. That person begins to seek out a target for his frustrations.[249]

We have to go back to the root causes of the person—the causes we can identify in trying to determine why any individual would undertake to kill persons in this way. And we said that this person was reacting inappropriately to stress from his own environment. We're talking about stress as an umbrella label for any number of things. Stress in his personal life. Let's say, a financial situation . . . his own sense of self-esteem and fulfillment. The failures in his life . . . other forms of anxieties.[250]

When asked what he meant by "chaos," Bundy responded:

I guess it is probably no more or no less than any young person would experience today who is going to college or just growing up. Nothing special, nothing peculiar, and nothing that is peculiarly related to the ultimate conduct that we are interested in. We could be talking at this point about anyone. A lot of things he understands, and a lot of things he doesn't. A lot of things make him happy; some things make him sad. That's basically the kind of things I am trying to get across.[251]

---

*In these interviews Bundy usually referred to himself in the third person.

In other words, Bundy was saying that what normal young men found easy to cope with was for him a source of "turmoil" and "chaos." This is a precise description of the post-encephalitic's reaction to the hurly-burly of everyday life.

The feeling of being under stress had a purely neurologic component, since it waxed and waned independently of Bundy's external circumstances:

> We talked about stress and the way passage of time would build up tension, but also he would suffer from periodic fluctuations that were more biologically or biochemically based than from any environmental explanation or psychological reasoning. It came as a rise in intensity, and these periods had no regularity.[252]

Bundy's feelings of stress demanded some sort of release:

> When people have—are—unable to cope with some part of their life—the feelings of discontent, loneliness, alienation, [low] self-esteem, or whatever it is—they usually attribute their state of mind to one degree or another to society at large. And they finally choose some way of venting what they have inside.[253]

He analyzed this need for release in terms of an "urge" or "entity" which, at periodic and increasingly frequent intervals, took possession of him.

He was not able to define this "urge" with precision:

> You're talking about a man who has a type of, what will we call it . . . "personality disorder"? I *still* don't know what in the world to call it . . . this part of him that is compulsive and uncontrollable.[254]

> We may have a situation here where the individual is *seeking* to satisfy certain urges . . . unconsciously or whatever . . . but it's the absence of this *fulfillment*, to use a different word, that we would expect to drive him to . . . that kind of futile exercise.[255]

> It could be . . . an aberration, caused by a great deal of pent-up frustration . . . of rage, or whatever.[256]

As a small child Bundy was notorious for his temper tantrums. He had also manifested incipient inclinations to sadism at age five, as seen by his inserting three butcher knives one night into the bed of his fifteen-year-old aunt. Even at this early age, he had been fascinated by stories of murders, murderers, and death.[257]

This violent streak in his makeup obviously contributed to his chosen mode of tension release.

As an adolescent he had sought escape by visiting pornography stores and devouring girlie magazines, being drawn, in particular, to scenes of sexual violence. He ransacked neighborhood trash cans for the same reason, but for years he ventured no further:

> This condition is not immediately seen by the individual or iden-
> tified as a serious problem. It sort of manifests itself in an interest
> concerning sexual behavior, as sexual images. . . . For most every-
> one that would simply be a sign of healthy interest, normal. But
> this interest, for some unknown reason, becomes geared toward
> matters of a sexual nature that involve violence. I cannot empha-
> size enough the gradual development of this. It is not short-term.
>
> The individual does not particularly see himself as the actor
> where the violence is directed toward women. But he *is* fascinated
> by this kind of literature that depicts this kind of action.[258]

As Bundy grew older, he came closer and closer to acting out his fantasies of violence. Finally,

> on one particular evening, when he had been drinking a great deal
> . . . and as he was passing a bar, he saw a woman leave the bar
> and walk up a fairly dark side street. And . . . something seemed
> to seize him! . . . The urge to do something to that person seized
> him—in a way he'd never been affected before. And it seized him
> strongly. And to the point where, without giving a great deal of
> thought, he searched around for some instrumentality to attack
> this woman with. He found a piece of two-by-four in a lot some-
> where and proceeded to follow and track this girl. . . . And when
> he reached the point where he was almost driven to do something
> —there was really no control at this point.[259]

The girl, fortunately, turned into her driveway and escaped him. But this aborted assault changed Bundy forever:

> The sort of revelation of that experience and the frenzied desire
> that seized him, really seemed to usher in a new dimension to
> the, that part of himself that was obsessed with, or otherwise ena-
> mored with, violence and women and sexual activity.[260]

Within a few years, by his mid-twenties, he had already committed a string of rape-murders.

After an assault the "urge" would subside, even for months at a time, and at first Bundy felt extreme contrition:

> What he had done terrified him. Purely terrified him. And he was full of remorse and remonstrating with himself for the suicidal, uh, nature of that activity . . . the ugliness of it all. . . . He was horrified by the recognition that he'd done this, the realization that he had the capacity to do such a thing, or even attempt—that's a better word—this kind of thing.[261]

But then the crimes came at shorter and shorter intervals

> . . . until it didn't take him any time at all to recover from what always was the horror and repulsion and disgust. Whatever it was, you know, fervent desire and a serious attempt to suppress this kind of behavior. Whatever. But now what happened was that this entity inside him was not capable of being controlled any longer—at least not for any considerable period of time.[262]

Bundy was at a loss to understand why he was attracted by pornography and fantasies of violence against women:

> Michaud: In this person there are no identifiable shocks, traumas?

> Bundy: No . . . and none associated physically with women. There is really no trigger. It is truly more sophisticated than that.[263]

> He has no hatred for women; there is nothing in his background that happened that would indicate he has been abused by any females. The only explanation would be that there is some kind of weakness that gives rise to this individual's interest in the kind of sexual activity involving violence that would gradually begin to absorb some of his fantasy.[264]

In fact, Bundy had several extended sexual relationships with women at the same time that he was committing his murders. And he did not assault the women with whom he was having affairs.[265]

He denied that anything in his childhood or upbringing had driven him down this path (the fact, for instance, that he was illegitimate and never knew his father).

There's nothing in my background—I swear to God and I know it—I've analyzed my own background and I know . . . there's no doubt in my mind that there's nothing in my background, no one factor or collection of factors that would explain, or would otherwise lead one to believe that I was capable of committing murder.[266]

I think you could say that the influence of this person's family history was positive. But not positive enough—not enduring, perhaps not strong enough to overcome the urges or compulsions that resulted . . . positive, but not so positive as to prepare this individual to totally avoid failure.[267]

He did not believe that the primary reason for the rapes was sexual:

The sexual act—in the larger scheme of things—was sort of obligatory conduct. Not in itself, you know, the sexual act was not the, the . . . principal source of gratification. Being satisfied.[268]

Most heterosexual persons—homosexuals, whatever—would probably agree that the most satisfying sex is that which is had with responsive, willing partners. . . . So I think it would be fair to say that engaging in an act of sex with a person who is injured or frightened or whatever—or [un]conscious or whatever*— would not be satisfying sexual contact, okay?[269]

He vehemently rejected the idea that he was insane or schizophrenic. This he backed up by refusing to plead insanity—which would very likely have spared him the electric chair:

I said I wouldn't have *anything* to do with an insanity defense. . . . I was strongly opposed to even, you know, even considering the idea because I *knew* I wasn't crazy. I *know* I'm not crazy! insane, incompetent, or anything else. And I was insulted by even the suggestion by my attorneys that we should consider the defense. They knew damn well I wasn't crazy.[270]

If you can't see that the great bulk of my personality is alert and vital and reality-oriented and *normal*, then there's really something wrong with your analysis.[271]

---

*Bundy probably practiced necrophilia.

What then compelled him to rape and murder eighty innocent young women (he confessed to thirty of these murders before his execution)?

The psychiatrists Samuel Yochelson and Stanton Samenow, who have written extensively on the criminal personality, suggest that the psychopathic criminal most fears his own sense of profound worthlessness (the "zero state"). He protects his nonexistent ego by exerting control over others. By subjecting them to his will, the psychopathic criminal makes society affirm a view of his potency that he cannot affirm by looking within.[272]

This analysis seems to cover the Ted Bundy case. Thus, he explained his behavior as an effort to exert "control." By raping and killing young women, that is, by "possessing" them, a person who was not in control of himself or his life, who felt oppressed by his surroundings—in a state of "chaos" or "turmoil"—could strike back and restore a measure of control:

> With respect to the idea of possession, I think that with this kind of person, control and mastery is what we see here.[273]

> I mean, had he been raised in a different background, maybe he would have taken to stealing Porches and Rolls-Royces.[274]

Killing the victim was a way of finalizing control, of truly possessing something of social value:

> In the beginning—the act of killing—we would *not* expect it to be the goal. Remember, it was the *possession* of this desired thing which was, in itself—the very act of assuming possession was a very antisocial act—was giving expression to this person's need to *seize* something that was . . . highly valued, at least on the surface, by society . . . sought after, a material possession, as it were.[275]

> More often than not the killing of the victim—was . . . a means to an end—that is, of accomplishing ultimate possession of the victim, so to speak.[276]

> I think we see a point reached—slowly perhaps—where the control, the possession aspect, came to include the, within its demands, the necessity . . . for purposes of gratification . . . the killing of the victim.[277]

He likened his behavior to that of the hunter who goes out and shoots animals: "And that's the way some guys may approach killing their fellow human beings."[278]

But Bundy was also a compulsive gambler. The more he killed, the more he showed himself in control, the greater risks he was driven to take:

> There's control. Yeah, you're right. We can say there's more control because the M.O., the modus operandi, became more familiar —but on the other hand, we see that with the greater incidence of—the greater success this person had—the more likely that part of him that required that sort of stimulation would be to want *more* of that kind of stimulation. And with the security of having, quote, successfully carried it off, there would be a greater, the urge to do it, we'd expect, would become more frequent.[279]

Finally he raised the stakes too high. What finally did him in, and led to his arrest, was an invasion, at night, of a Florida sorority during which he clubbed two girls to death and seriously wounded two others.

Is There a Cure?

A correct appreciation of the role of the "irresistible impulse" is essential to understanding the violent aspects of the post-encephalitic syndrome.

It is a neurologic impulse and thus, by definition, *irresistible*— a "discharge-like neural event" identical in nature to the tics and grunts of the Tourette Syndrome patient.[280] Probably no amount of exhortation, punishment, or retraining will teach, pursuade, or in any other way induce these individuals to restrain the fulfillment of such impulses.

This is a hard lesson for Americans to learn, with our tendency to sentimental optimism, our belief that every condition has its cure. It is especially hard for psychologists and psychiatrists with their unwavering determination to seek "emotional" factors behind every behavioral act. But it will have to be learned if any remedy is to be found for our plague of social violence.

Seeking an "emotional" basis for the uncontrollable impulse is a futile waste of time.

No medicinal treatment, technique of behavioral modification, or psychiatric counseling has succeeded in retraining individuals with this violently impulsive behavior. An account of one such program, in Washington State, for juvenile sex offenders, describes the difficulties.

> Once they are involved in treatment, Echo Glen offenders sign off on a two-step individual plan to prevent future offenses. For every warning signal, they are taught, there is a preventive measure.
>
> The prevention plan of one boy at Echo Glen begins with an admission: he says he gets turned on by "helpless powerless-looking kids/boys/girls." His matching prevention calls for him to say a prayer [!!] or have a talk with himself if his mind wanders in that direction.
>
> When the boy feels "like I want to rape, molest, or hurt," he promises to "go lift weights, say a prayer, do push-ups, read a book, help a friend." He has agreed to avoid what he considers high-risk situations, including the zoo [??], shops, and killing bugs and animals.
>
> Therapists call the trick "mind over testicles." They don't know if such gauzy promises keep the boys from temptation when they leave the institution. The boys themselves speak only of one day at a time.[281]

No one could possibly have any confidence in the success of such a program. After the prayers and gauzy promises these adolescents will one day be released from Echo Glen to become future Ted Bundys—or future Earl Shriners:

> Shriner [now thirty-nine] was in state institutions for much of his life after being implicated as a juvenile in the death of one teenage girl and convicted as an adult of kidnapping and assaulting two others.
>
> Shriner was considered mildly retarded, but his IQ was too high and his past too violent for him to get help from the state's system for the developmentally disabled. A psychiatrist labelled him a sexual psychopath, and officials tried unsuccessfully to have him committed to Western State from prison. The law just doesn't allow someone to be committed on the basis of what they have threatened to do; they have to be judged a danger to themselves or others.[282]

Shriner's constitutional rights were safeguarded. He was let out, and shortly afterwards cut off the penis of a seven-year-old boy. Now he is back in for good.

Chapter V Notes

1. Kissel, S.J., 1986, 153.
2. Check, W. A., 1985, 721, Kelley, D., 1985, 55. Federal Bureau of Investigation, 1981-1988.
3. Federal Bureau of Investigation, 1981-1988.
4. Fineman, K.R., 1980, 483.
5. Federal Bureau of Investigation, 1981-1988.
6. Check, W.A., 1985, 721.
7. Kissel, S.J.,1986, 155.
8. *The Washington Post*, Sept. 3, 1988, B-2.
9. Check, W.A., 1985, 727-728.
10. *The Washington Post*, Sept. 10, 1988, B-1.
11. *Ibid.*, Sept. 2, 1988, C-3.
12. Kissel, S.J., 1986, 155. *The New York Times*, November 6, 1987, 1; November 9, 1987, B-1.
13. *The Washington Post*, April, 14, 1988, A-23.
14. Auletta, Ken, 1981, 162.
15. *The Washington Post*, September 20, 1988, B-1.
16. *Ibid.*, December 17, 1985, A-1, 12.
17. *Ibid.*, April 27, 1989, A-1, 34.
18. *Ibid.*, March 22, 1988, D-5.
19. *The Seattle Times*, October 5, 1989, 1.
20. *Loc. cit.*
21. *The International Herald Tribune*, February 5, 1987.
22. *The New York Times*, December 5, 1987, B-1.
23. Bond, E.D. and Appel, K.E., 1931, 14-15.
24. Elliott, Frank R., 1983, 87.
25. Lurie, L.A. *et al.*, 1947, 177-178.
26. Ward, C.D., 1986, 220.
27. Ford, Frank R., 1937, 360-361.
28. Lurie, L.A. and Levy, Sol, 1942, 891.
29. Bond, E.D. and Appel, K.E., 1931, 14-15.
30. Kennedy, Roger, 1924, 171.
31. Holt, W.L., 1937, 1142-1143. Gibbs, C.E., 1929/1930, 622, 624. Neal, Josephine A., 1942, 364.
32. Neal, Josephine A., 1942, 364.

33. Ford, Frank R., 1937, 356. Hill, T.R., 1928, 5-7. Grossman, M., 1922, 961. Bakwin, Harry, 1949, 272.
34. Mawson, D. *et al.*, 1985.
35. Cowart, V.S., 1988(b), 2647.
36. Maletzky, B.M., 1973, 180.
37. Monroe, R.R., 1978, 21.
38. *Loc. cit.* Elliott, Frank, A., 1982, 682. Kelley, David, 1985, 58. Auletta, Ken, 1981, 180.
39. Rimland, B. and Larson, G.E., 1981, 56.
40. Lewis, Dorothy O., ed., 1981, 57.
41. *Loc. cit.*
42. *Ibid.*, 58.
43. *The International Herald Tribune*, March 5, 1986.
44. *The New York Times*, October 31, 1988, B-1.
45. Bryant, E.T. *et al.*, 1984, 323-324.
46. Cowart, V.S., 1988(b), 2647.
47. American Psychiatric Association, 1987, 53.
48. Wender, Paul H., 1971, 204-211, 215-216.
49. American Psychiatric Association, 1987, 53. Hartsough, C.S. and Lambert, N.M., 1987. Workman-Daniels, K.L. *et al.*, 1987.
50. American Psychiatric Association, 1980, 318.
51. *Ibid.*, 1987, 343.
52. *People*, July 11, 1988, 40-43.
53. Lewis, D.O., 1981, 28.
54. Hollander, H.A. *et al.*, 1985, 225.
55. Satterfield, J.H. *et al.*, 1982, 795.
56. Lewis, Dorothy O., ed., 1981, 28. See also, Menkes, M.M. *et al.*, 1967.
57. Lewis, Dorothy O., ed., 1981, 28.
58. *Ibid.*, 27.
59. Weiss, Gabrielle *et al.*, 1985, 219.
60. Aman, Michael, 1984, 51-52. Elliott, Frank A., 1984, 117.
61. Simeon, Jovan, 1978, 1224. Wood, D.R., 1976, 1453.
62. Mendlewicz, J., 1978, 1229. Kelley, D., 1985, 56.
63. Auletta, Ken, 1981, 164.
64. *The New York Times*, October 31, 1988, Op-Ed page. Auletta, Ken, 1981, 92, 95.
65. Robins, Lee N., 1966, 303.
66. Hollander, H.E. and Turner, F.D., 1985, 221.
67. *The New York Times*, October 31, 1988, B-1.
68. White, R. *et al.*, 1964. Lapin, J.B., 1943, 19.
69. Hopkins, A., 1987, 11.

70. Benatar, S.R., 1986, 424. Evans, R. *et al.*, 1987, 655.
71. Geschwind, N., 1982, 20.
72. Pasamanick, B. and Knobloch, H., 1960, 299. National Center for Health Statistics, 1986, *passim*. Pasamanick, B. and Knobloch, H., 1966. Niswander, K., ed., 1972, 126.
73. Moyer, K.F., 1976, 36.
74. Commission for the Control of Epilepsy, 1977, Vol.II, Part I, 822.
75. Elliott, Frank A., 1982, 684.
76. Lewis, Dorothy O., ed., 1981, 50.
77. Lewis, Dorothy O., *et al.*, 1988. Also Climent, C.E., 1977. *The Washington Post*, July 19, 1988. "Health," 12.
78. Heffron, W.M. *et al.*, 1987.
79. Elliott, Frank A., 1982, 680.
80. *The New York Times*, September 17, 1985, C-1, 3.
81. Moyer, K.E., 1976, 40. Simeon, J., 1978, 1225. Elliott, Frank A., 1982, 685. Monroe, R.R., 1978, 16ff., 34ff. Serafetinides, E.A., 1980, 31.
82. Woods, S.M., 1961, 1348-1349.
83. Moyer, K.E., 1976, 42.
84. Kellaway, P. *et al.*, 1959, 582.
85. Woods, S.M., 1961.
86. Treiman, D.M., 1986, S78. Moyer, K.E., 1976, 42-44.
87. Maletsky, B.M., 1973, 184. Also Lewis, Dorothy O., ed., 1981, 30.
88. Hollander, H.E. and Turner, F.D., 1985, 225. Monroe, R.N., 1978, 20. Bach-y-Rita, G. *et al.*, 1474. Elliott, Frank A., 1976, 299. Heilbrun, A.B. *et al.*, 1985.
89. Elliott, Frank A., 1982, 683.
90. *Loc. cit.*
91. *Loc. cit.*
92. Kelley, David, 1985, 55. Simeon, J., 1978, 1226.
93. Tartar, R.E. *et al.*, 1985. Elliott, F.A., 1982, 682.
94. Tartar, R.E. *et al.*, 1985. Yuedall, L.T. and Fromm-Auch, D. 1979.
95. Hellman, D.S. and Blackman, N., 1966. Wood, D.R. *et al.*, 1976, 1457.
96. Fineman, K.R., 1980, 483.
97. *Ibid.*, 487.
98. *Ibid.*, 493.
99. *Ibid.*, 487, 491.
100. Elliott, Frank A., 1982, 684. Fineman, K.R., 1980, 490. Maletzky, B.M., 1973, 182.
101. Wood, D. R. *et al.*, 1976, 1453. Kupfer, D.J. *et al.*, 1975, 75. Robins, L.N., 1966, 121.

102. Simeon, J., 1978, 1225. Monroe, R. R., 1978, 32. Maletzky, B.M., 1973, 179, 181.
103. Monroe, R.R., 1978, 32. Elliott, Frank A., 1982, 681.
104. Climent, C.J. *et al.*, 1977.
105. Monroe, R.R., 1978, 17, 32. Robins, L.N., 1966, 120, 121. Woods, S.M., 1961, 1348.
106. West, D.J., 1980, 624.
107. Cleckley, H., 1976, 346.
108. *Ibid.*, 348.
109. Elliott, F.A., 1982, 682.
110. *Loc. cit.* Cleckley, H., 1976, 350. Monroe, R. R., 1978, 144.
111. McPherson, M., 1989, 196.
112. Auletta, Ken, 1981, 170. Cleckley, H., 1976, 341. McPherson, M., 1989, 188, 190.
113. Monroe, R. R., 1978, 32.
114. Mawson, D. *et al.*, 1985, 567.
115. Auletta, Ken, 1981, 162.
116. *Ibid.*, 167.
117. Woods, S.M., 1961, 1349.
118. *The Washington Post*, December 18, 1985, A-26.
119. Monroe, R.R., 1978, 16.
120. Kelley, D., 1985, 58. Cleckley, H., 1976, 352.
121. Kelley, D., 1985, 58. Michaud, S.G. and Aynesworth, H., 1989, 3, 4.
122. Serafetinides, E.A., 1980, 34. Kelley, D., 1985, 58.
123. Lewis, Dorothy O., 1981, 63.
124. Auletta, Ken, 1981, 167.
125. Monroe, R.R., 1978, 23. Bach-y-Rita, G., 1971, 1477. Tanke, E.D. *et al.*, 1985, 1410.
126. Monroe, R.R., 1978, 29.
127. Cleckley, H., 1976, 364.
128. Elliott, F.A., 1982, 682.
129. Cleckley, H., 1976, 345.
130. *Ibid.*, 341.
131. Kelley, D., 1985, 59.
132. Monroe, R.R., 1978. 16.
133. Woods, S.M., 1961, 1348-1349.
134. *Loc. cit.* American Psychiatric Association, 1980, 46.
135. Check, W., 1985, 730.
136. Bach-y-Rita, G. *et al.*, 1971, 1477.
137. *Ibid.*, 1476.
138. Pfeffer, C.R. *et al.*, 1985, 775.
139. Auletta, Ken, 1981, 159-160.

140. Cleckley, H., 1976, 364.
141. *Ibid.*, 343.
142. Monroe, R.R., 1978, 17. Tanke, E.D. *et al.*, 1985. Maletzky, B.M.. 1973, 184. Maletzky, B.M., 1976. Bland, R. and Orn, H., 1966.
143. McPherson, M., 1989, 142.
144. Elliott, F.A., 1982, 685. Elliott, F.A., 1984, 115.
145. Pfeffer, C.R. *et al.*, 1985, 775. Maletzky, B.M., 1973, 181.
146. Levine, M.D. *et al.*, 1984, 366.
147. Monroe, R.R., 1978, 83. Cleckley, H., 1976, 350.
148. Cited in Check, W.A., 1985, 728.
149. Monroe, R.R., 1978, 83.
150. Climent, C.E. *et al.*, 1977.
151. American Psychiatric Association, 1987, 343.
152. West, D.J., 1980, 624.
153. Cleckley, H., 1976, 359ff., 363, 364. Elliott, F.A., 1976, 299.
154. McPherson, M., 1989, 190.
155. *Loc. cit.*
156. American Psychiatric Association, 1987, 343.
157. Von Economo, 1931, 129.
158. Bach-y-Rita, G. *et al.*, 1971, 1476.
159. Fedio, Paul, 1986, 273. Elliott, F.A., 1976, 299.
160. Bach-y-Rita, G. *et al.*, 1477.
161. Maletzky, B.M., 1973, 181.
162. American Psychiatric Association, 1987, 342.
163. Wood, David R. *et al.*, 1976, 1458.
164. Heffron, W.M. *et al.*, 1987, 385.
165. Check, William A., 1985, 721.
166. Cowart, V.S., 1988(b), 2647.
167. *The Los Angeles Times*, January 22, 1988, 22. Kelley, D., 1985, 56.
168. *The New York Times*, November 15, 1988, C-3.
169. Volkmar, F.R. *et al.*, 1985, 49, 52. Ritvo, E. *et al.*, 1988.
170. Lerner, J.A. *et al.*, 1985, 46. Weiss, G. *et al.*, 1985, 212, 219. Tartar, R.E. *et al.*, 1977. Hartsough, C.S. *et al.*, 1987.
171. Tartar, R.E. *et al.*, 1977.
172. Workman-Daniels, K.L. *et al.*, 1987. Wood, D.R. *et al.*, 1458.
173. Wood, D.R. *et al.*, 1453. Routh, D.K., 1977, 419. Lewis, D.O. ed., 1981, 29. Daniel, A.E. *et al.*, 1981. Simeon, J., 1979, 1224.
174. Robins, L.N., 1966, 302. Lewis, D.O. ed., 1981, 22. Kelley, D., 1985, 56. West, D.J., 1980, 623. American Psychiatric Association, 1980, 46, 318.
175. Monroe, R.R., 1978, 83.
176. *Ibid.*, 35. Maletzky, B.M., 1976.

177. Elliott, F.A., 1984, 115,122. Bach-y-Rita, G. *et al.*, 1971, 1475. Elliott, F.A., 1976, 299.
178. Maletzky, B.M., 1976, 681. Cleckley, H., 1976, 356.
179. Elliott, F.A., 1983, 89.
180. Michaud, S.G. and Aynesworth, H., 1989, 71, 121, 260.
181. *Ibid.*, 107.
182. Cowart, V.S., 1988(a), 2522.
183. Elliott, F.A., 1986, 229. Campbell, M, 1973. Laufer, M.W. and Denhoff, E., 1957, 470. Laufer, M.W., Denhoff, E., and Solomons, G., 1957.
184. *Physicians' Desk Reference* 1985, 1959.
185. Aman, M.G., 1982, 393.
186. Laufer, M.W. and Denhoff, E., 1957, 470.
187. *Ibid.*, 471. Lewis, D.O., 1981, 30. Wender, P.O., 1971, 203. Gastfriend, D.R. *et al.*, 1985, 144.
188. *Physicians' Desk Reference*, 1982, 1794. American Academy of Pediatrics, 1987. August, G.T. *et al.*, 1984, 604. Aman, M.T., 1982, 393.
189. Campbell, M., 1973, 350. Aman, M.G., 1982, 393. Campbell, M. *et al.*, 1984, 311.
190. Gastfriend, D.R. *et al.*, 1985, 144.
191. Laufer, M.W. and Denhoff, E., 1957, 471.
192. *Loc. cit.* American Academy of Pediatrics, 1987.
193. *The New York Times*, November 9, 1983.
194. Gastfriend, D.R., *et al.*, 144. American Academy of Pediatrics, 1987.
195. American Academy of Pediatrics, 1987. Sankar, D.V.S., 1968, 510. Julien, R.M., 1978, 127.
196. Monroe, R.M., 1978, 20. Miller, D., 1986, 593.
197. Bach-y-Rita, G. *et al.*, 1971, 1475.
198. McGinniss, J., 1989, 610.
199. Julien, R.M., 1978, 74.
200. Cowart, V.S., 1988(a), 2521. Avery, M.E. and First, L.R., 1989, 72. Behrman, R.E. *et al.*, 1987, 94.
201. *Physician's Desk Reference*, 1985, 865.
202. Julien, R.M., 1978, 81-82.
203. Millichap, J.G., 1976, 64.
204. *Physicians' Desk Reference*, 1985, 865.
205. Cowart, V.S., 1988(a), 2523.
206. Whalen, C.K. *et al.*, 1984, 412-413.
207. Wender, P.H., 1971, 202. American Academy of Pediatrics, 1987.
208. Gastfriend, D.R. *et al.*, 1985, 144.

209. *Physicians' Desk Reference*, 1985, 865. American Academy of Pediatrics, 1987.
210. *The Wall Street Journal*, February 11, 1971.
211. Elliott, F.A., 1986, 229.
212. *Physicians' Desk Reference*, 1985, 1977. Julien, R.M., 1978, 128.
213. Laufer, M.W. and Denhoff, E., 1957, 472.
214. *Loc. cit.* Wender, P.H., 1971, 203.
215. Schmidt, W.R. *et al.*, 1966. *Physicians' Desk Reference*, 1985, 1977 (Thorazine), 2014 (Prolixin), 1877 (Permitil), 1201 (Haldol).
216. Tepper, S.J. *et al.*, 1979.
217. Schmidt, W.R. *et al.*, 1966, 373.
218. DeVeaugh-Geiss, J., 1979, 59.
219. Kane, J.M. *et al.*, 1985, 136. Perry, R. *et al.*, 1985, 140. Campbell, M. et al., 1984, 309. Tepper, S.J. *et al.*, 1979. DeVeaugh-Geiss, J., 1979.
220. Denckla, M.B. *et al.*, 1976.
221. Schmidt, W.R. *et al.*, 1966, 369.
222. Lidsky,T.I. *et al.*, 1981, 1190.
223. *The Washington Post*, Sept. 20, 1988, A-8. *The New York Times*, November 12, 1988, 7. See Breuning, Stephen E. and Poling, Alan D., 1982.
224. Check, W.A., 1988(a), 2583.
225. Maletzky, B.M., 1973, 180. Elliott, F.A., 1976, 311.
226. Campbell, M., 1973, 355.
227. Campbell, M. 1973, 350. Laufer, M.W. and Denhoff, E., 1957, 473.
228. Ornitz, E.M. *et al.*, 1976, 617. Ritvo, E.R. *et al.*, 1984, 304. Campbell, M., 1973, 357.
229. Wender, P.H., 1971, 203, 217.
230. *Physicians' Desk Reference*, 1985, 969.
231. *Ibid.*, 1970, 657. Julien, R.M., 1978, 125.
232. Laufer, M.W. and Denhoff, E., 1957, 473.
233. Schrag, P. and Divoky, D., 1975 (reviewed in *J. Autism* 6:2 [1976], 203-205). Cowart, V.S., 1988a, 2522.
234. Cowart, V.S., 1988(a), 2522.
235. *Loc. cit.*
236. *Ibid.*, 2521.
237. Ward, C.D., 1986, 218.
238. Golden, G.S., 1984, 95.
239. Bruun, R.D. and Shapiro, A.K., 1972, 330.
240. *Loc. cit.*
241. Woods, S.M., 1961, 1349. See, also, Gibbs, C.E., 1929/1930, 623-

624.
242. McPherson, M., 1989, 196.
243. Michaud, S.G. and Aynesworth, H., 1989, 257, 292.
244. *Ibid.*, 13, 14, 24.
245. *Ibid.*, 13.
246. *Ibid.*, 15.
247. *Ibid.*, 23-24.
248. *Ibid.*, 60.
249. *Ibid.*, 63.
250. *Ibid.*, 250.
251. *Ibid.*, 65-66.
252. *Ibid.*, 133.
253. *Ibid.*, 203.
254. *Ibid.*, 192.
255. *Ibid.*, 247.
256. *Ibid.*, 179.
257. McPherson, M., 1989, 148-149.
258. Michaud, S.G. and Aynesworth, H., 1989, 66-67.
259. *Ibid.*, 73.
260. *Loc. cit.*
261. *Ibid.*, 75.
262. *Ibid.*, 77.
263. *Ibid.*, 65.
264. *Ibid.*, 67.
265. *Ibid.*, 194.
266. *Ibid.*, 258.
267. *Ibid.*, 62.
268. *Ibid.*, 123.
269. *Ibid.*, 124-125.
270. *Ibid.*, 256.
271. *Ibid.*, 264.
272. Kelley, D., 1985, 58.
273. Michaud, S.G. and Aynesworth, H., 1989, 125.
274. *Ibid.*, 202.
275. *Loc. cit.*
276. *Ibid.*, 127.
277. *Ibid.*, 123.
278. *Ibid.*, 186.
279. *Ibid.*, 248.
280. Monroe, R.R., 1978, 21.
281. *The Seattle Times*, October 5, 1989, A-14.
282. *Loc. cit.*

VI

Medical Hubris and its Consequences*

This book advances the perhaps startling thesis that childhood vaccination programs cause a wide range of neurologic disabilities, and that these disabilities yield the bulk of the autistics, minimally brain-damaged, and sociopaths who have undermined the American educational system and American society, giving this country during the past two decades the highest crime rate in its history.

The most cogent evidence for this is found in the symptomatic parallels among the five conditions described: vaccine damage, the post-encephalitic syndrome, autism, minimal brain damage, and the sociopathic personality.

We have stressed these symptomatic parallels since they are the foundation of the analysis.

And they are the justification for the assumption that certain individuals presented here as examples—Tommy Colella, the Central Park "wolfpack," the Bolden brothers, and Ted Bundy—are truly cases of post-encephalitic syndrome.

It would, of course, have been preferable to present comprehensive medical records on each of these individuals. But this is a task for the public authorities, who have the necessary legal powers and financial resources. The purpose of this book has been to provide a reasoned and substantiated hypothesis based largely upon symptomatic and epidemiologic evidence.

---

*Hubris—"wanton insolence or arrogance resulting from excessive pride or from passion."

Hypotheses serve the function of opening new vistas for future research. Efforts should be made to confirm or refute the hypothesis presented in these pages.

Some will criticize our essentially symptomatic approach. The main reason for adopting it has been that no unambiguous anatomical, physiological, or biochemical indicator of vaccine damage exists. Careful symptomatic descriptions are ultimately the best evidence of the parallels among the neurologic disabilities discussed.

As we have shown, the variety of symptoms from vaccine damage is greater than is found in any single individual. Each victim manifests only a part of the overall symptom pattern. This fact will create methodological problems for future researchers accustomed to thinking of diseases as discrete entities separated from one another in watertight compartments.

There is no such compartmentalization in the post-encephalitic syndrome, and future research must take this into consideration.

But all the neurologically damaged show the "delayed development" that is the common denominator of these symptoms. And they react to it in the same way—by aggressive, impulsive, unreflective, irrational behavior.

A British physician in 1928 noted that "changes in morals and character" in patients who have had encephalitis reveal a "curious uniformity."[1] This same "curious uniformity" stamps the autistic, the minimally brain damaged, and the sociopath.

This book has stressed the essential identity of autism, minimal brain damage, and the sociopathic personality. They represent a continuum of neurologic damage due to encephalitis which in the overwhelming majority of cases is from vaccination.

To quote the wise Leo Kanner one more time: "In medicine . . . any illness may appear in different degrees of severity, all the way from the so-called *forme fruste* to the most fulminant manifestation."

Differences are only of degree. Behavior which in its milder form seems merely peculiar or idiosyncratic becomes criminality at the extreme end of the spectrum.

The moderate autistic whose sex life is "performed with no

feelings" is the neurologic ally of the sociopath whose sex life is "impersonal, trivial, and poorly integrated." This increasingly widespread feature of contemporary sexuality is behind the extraordinary contemporary surge in rapes and other sexual crimes. When combined with the "precocious puberty" of the post-encephalitic, the outcome is the phenomenon of violent sexual offenses committed by boys as young as six.

The radical alienation of the autistic is seen in a milder form in the sociopathic criminal—who treats his victims as objects, not as human beings. The "spitting tic" of the post-encephalitic, or the Tourette Syndrome victim's compulsion to utter obscenities, exemplify the same uncontrollable urge which drove Ted Bundy to commit his series of murders.

The autistic child with "temper tantrums" and "rage" becomes the sociopathic criminal in whom "control by rage is absolute." The autistic boy, Tony W., who killed the guinea pig at the Yale Child Study Center, is manifesting the same behavior as the Central Park "wolfpack" which attacked an innocent jogger.

The autistic's paranoia, tendency to put on weight, and developmental delay, when writ large, reflect several prominent features of contemporary American society and are due to the same causal factor.

The parallels could be multiplied indefinitely.

Adolescents with the post-encephalitic syndrome are often drawn to drugs and alcohol by the need to calm their hyperactivity or by a subliminal realization that they are not entirely normal, unable to cope with ordinary stresses, less worthy than others. When they behave disruptively in school, they are systematically dosed with amphetamines and other behavior-modifying substances. Can it really be astonishing that this neurologically damaged group ultimately graduates into full-fledged alcoholism and drug addiction?

Quite recently physicians have started to blame drug addiction in the mother for minimal brain damage in the child, specifying such symptoms in the child as inability to concentrate, learning disabilities, "needing a strict structure," "overwhelmed by tasks easily performed by others their age," and even "smaller head circumferences."[2] While exposure to cocaine or heroin *in utero* is obviously not conducive to later good health and rapid development, the symptoms mentioned are precisely the ones which have been encountered for the past thirty years, and it is unclear why this should now be blamed on drug-addiction in the mother.

At the very least, thought should be given to the impact of vaccinating children who are already weakened and impaired by being born to drug-addicted mothers.

The mere recognition that autism and minimal brain damage are consequences of encephalitis should be convincing evidence that the childhood vaccination program is responsible. Vaccination, after all, is known to cause encephalitis, and no other candidate is in sight.

If there is pervasive subclinical encephalitis in the U.S. population, it must come from the vaccination program.

Subliminal awareness that discussing autism and minimal brain damage in terms of encephalitis leads to questioning the rationale of childhood vaccination has probably kept physicians and other researchers away from this explosive issue.

A favorite scapegoat has been the family—usually the poor mother who is held up to censure because she has a job, does not go to church on Sundays, is divorced from her husband, does not devote enough attention to her children, etc., and thereby, as it were, generates autism and learning disabilities and contributes to juvenile delinquency:

> Dear Ann Landers:
> I have been blasted by yet another one of your blanket rules and prepackaged diagnoses. Again its "blame the parent."
> I have read the same reason for alcohol and drug abuse. Recently a TV evangelist credited his children's love of God to his wife staying home to raise the children. Strange. I also stayed home to raise the children.
> I was the perennial homeroom mother, went on field trips, slept on lumpy cots next to hospital beds, and never went to sleep until all the kids were in the house. While they didn't turn out to be Hell's Angels, I harbor no illusions about their sexual behavior and involvement with drugs.

Is it possible that exposure to steamy sex on TV and in the movies, commercials that glamorize sensuality, and the barnyard behavior of stars and athletes whom our kids idolize has something to do with the way they behave?

Frankly, I'm sick to death of all the "experts" and their "answers." Never has a group tried so hard and been blamed so much as today's parents.

Let's face it. Our kids are living in a sick society that loves violence and greed and demands instant gratification.[3]

But blaming the family, or society, for our troubles misses the point. While the family shapes us, it does not subsist in a vacuum, and its fate is not determined only by the emotional interaction among its members. These are all structures which we ourselves build. The individual is prior both to the family and to society.

Children are the building blocks of the family, and later of society. If these are defective from infancy, the development of both family and society will be distorted and denatured.

When ten or twenty percent of all children are minimally brain-damaged, how can family life be normal? When ten or twenty percent of high-school graduates have never learned to read, how can they not watch television during most of their waking hours? When over a million children every day are legally receiving amphetamines and other drugs in school to suppress hyperactivity, how can there not be a drug culture?

The family and society are both victims—of vaccination programs forced on them by state legislatures which are entirely too responsive to medical opinion and medical organizations. Committee chairmen who unhesitatingly criticize economists, ecologists, city-planners, and manufacturers become uncharacteristically meek when confronting a medical expert.

These programs have spawned the profusion of twisted and distorted individuals who have created the American family and the American society we know today.

Over and above the symptomatic parallels among these various diseased states, the chronology of their emergence is highly suggestive of an origin in the vaccination programs.

The pertussis vaccination program was only sporadic in the 1920s and 1930s, becoming widespread during and after World War II. The appearance of autism and learning disabilities reflects the concomitant growth of this vaccination program.

Autism is diagnosed during the first years of life; so vaccinations yielded the first autistics in the early 1940s. Learning disabilities emerged eight or ten years later, when the children of this same generation were seen to have chronic difficulties in school. The learning-disabled children of the early 1950s were the brothers and sisters of the autistics of the early 1940s.

But these children, of course, kept growing into adolescence and adulthood. The generation born in 1945, and thus exposed for the first time to widespread vaccination, came of age in 1963.

Any analysis of 1960s radicalism at once discloses the themes which have already figured in our discussion of the sociopathic, post-encephalitic syndrome. For example, *Roots of Radicalism*, by Stanley Rothman and S. Robert Lichter, touches upon: ego weakness, feelings of worthlessness, childish egotism, impulsive violence, impatience, narcissism, the need to be in control, megalomania, alienation, lack of meaning, rage, paranoia, ambivalent hostility to authority, unfocussed aggression, the search for experience and sensation, inability to form intimate relations combined with sexual licentiousness, anxiety, depression, pyromania ("Burn, baby, burn!!"), sociopathy, alcoholism, and drug abuse.[4]

The "liberation" for which these young people were striving takes on new and poignant meaning when it is realized that many were seeking to be freed from their own feelings of neurologic weakness and instability.

These personality traits and their impact on society, designated the "social issue," were behind Richard Nixon's electoral victories in 1968 and 1972.

The legacy of the 1960s is still with us: a 1984 survey of the mental health of Americans found that rates of sociopathic personality and of other mental illness (anxiety, depression, "schizophrenia," and alcohol or drug abuse) are much higher in those born in 1940 or later than in those born prior to 1940.[5]

In California a Task Force to Promote Self-Esteem was created by the legislature in 1986.

And psychologists are finding that Americans remain adolescent longer than they used to. "Adolescence doesn't really end until the late twenties," stated one university professor in 1988.[6] The author of a 1986 book on this subject wrote: "It now takes another decade to grow up in our culture" — developmental delay with a vengeance.[7]

The year 1963, when children born in 1945 reached the age of eighteen and when John F. Kennedy was assassinated, marked the start of the 1960s turmoil. It also marked the start of a decline in the American IQ.

Childhood vaccinations cause various types of mental retardation ranging from a slight drop in IQ to total idiocy; they also generate dyslexia and other reading disabilities. It is no coincidence, therefore, that when the 1945 generation took the examinations in 1963 for entry into college or into the army, they gave notice of an incipient decline in the American intelligence.

This was measured, for instance, by the Scholastic Aptitude Tests taken by college-bound high-school seniors. In 1963 the average SAT verbal score was at its highest since the commencement of testing—478, while the average methematics score was 502. Thereafter it declined until by 1980 the verbal score had dropped 54 points to 424, and the math score 36 points to 466. The scores today are the lowest in the sixty-year history of these tests.

And since the tests themselves have actually become easier, other researchers conclude that the IQ decline is fifty percent worse.[8]

The American College Testing (ACT) Program, similar to the SAT program, has also reported a consistent test-score decline since the mid-1960s.[9]

Tests given to military recruits in the 1970s showed their mental capacity to be significantly inferior to that of recruits in 1941–1945.

In 1977 a Blue-Ribbon Panel was convened to ascertain the reasons for the IQ decline, and seventy-nine hypotheses were advanced. None proved satisfactory. The possibility of a relationship with vaccine damage was not discussed.[10]

A national study in 1988 found that mathematical ability has virtually vanished in American adolescents. Nearly half of seventeen-year olds cannot perform math problems normally taught in junior high school; one third of eleventh-graders do not normally even understand what the teacher is saying; twenty-seven percent of thirteen-year olds cannot perform mathematics problems normally assigned in elementary school. The average Japanese high-school student outperforms the top five percent of Americans in college preparatory courses.[11]

Rimland and Larson state that "the level of science and mathematics taught to Russian students is so much higher than the level taught to American students that comparisons between Russian and American students are meaningless." Their conclusion: "Exceptions and irregularities notwithstanding, the overall trend appears to represent a real and unexplained decline in ability, a decline that has serious implications . . . for our whole society."[12]

A 1986 survey by the Census Bureau found that nine percent of adults twenty to forty years old (i.e., born between 1946 and 1966) whose native language is English are illiterate—a total of about ten million. Thirty-six million cannot read at the eighth grade level, while seventy million cannot read at the eleventh grade level. The Bureau found that forty percent of U.S. adults cannot read a road map, while eighty percent cannot calculate a tip in a restaurant or understand a bus schedule.[13]

The survey, covering 3400 adults, took the form of a 26-question multiple-choice test. It could hardly be described as difficult. One problem read: "The patient has the right to ask for information about his sickness." The testee had to pick a synonym for "sickness" from the following: "benefits, business, expenses, illness."

The situation is bound to deteriorate still further as persons who are functional illiterates take their places in the teaching profession! This is no idle fear. Examinations given since 1976 by the School Board of Pinellas County, Florida, reveal that half the applicants (all college graduates) cannot read at the tenth grade level or solve eighth-grade problems in mathematics.[14]

Society's increasing production of neurologic defectives has caused a remarkable upsurge in violent crime. The start of this rise can be dated precisely to the early 1960s.

It was preceded by increasing levels of violence among children and adolescents. This is well illustrated by two surveys of adolescent boys in Philadelphia: one of 10,000 boys in 1945 and the second of 13,000 from the same background and neighborhoods in 1958. The authors found that in both groups one third had been arrested at least once by age eighteen. What is more, in both groups most of the crime was committed by a small minority: six percent in 1945 and 7.5 percent in 1958. Inexplicable, however, was the much greater tendency to violence of the 1958 group. One of the authors called this "escalation of violent criminality" a "fearful sign for the public."[15]

The authors of the study could perceive no epidemiologic difference between the 1945 and the 1958 generations. They did not think that the second group was largely vaccinated against diphtheria, pertussis, tetanus, poliomyelitis, and smallpox, while the first group would have had only the smallpox shot.

Rimland and Larson have called attention to "the striking, almost mirror-image correlation, starting about 1963, between the curves showing the decline in SAT scores and the upsurge in violent crime," suggesting "the existence of one or more common causal factors."[16]

The vaccination program was given a boost in 1965 when Congress passed the Immunization Assistance Act. In the following years more and more states extended their vaccination programs and made them obligatory.[17]

Four or five years thereafter physicians encountered a whole new group of neurologically defective four- and five-year-olds. A 1986 National Health Interview Survey found that between 1969 and 1981 the prevalence of "activity-limiting chronic conditions" in persons younger than seventeen increased by an inexplicable forty-four percent—from 2,680/100,000 to 3,848/100,000; almost all the increase occurred between 1969 and 1975.[18]

Most of these "activity-limiting chronic conditions" are readily seen to be associated with the post-encephalitic syndrome. Childhood "respiratory diseases" increased forty-seven percent, childhood asthma sixty-five percent, and deaths from asthma in children aged five and older also increased; "mental and nervous system disorders" increased eighty percent, personality and other nonpsychotic mental disorders (including behavioral disorders, drug abuse, and hyperactivity) went up 300 percent, and diseases of the eyes and ears—especially otitis media—120 percent; reported cases of hearing loss in both ears rose 129 percent.[19]

The increase was virtually identical in high-income and low-income families, excluding poverty as a major cause.[20]

Conditions not associated with vaccine damage—injuries, genito-urinary disorders, diseases of the circulatory system, infective or parasitic diseases, and deformities—remained stationary during this time or actually declined.

By 1980 the overall number of disabled children (many, of course, with multiple conditions) had more than doubled. Over two million children in the U.S. had some "limitation of activity," up from one million in 1960.[21]

In percentage terms, two percent of children had some limitation in the early 1960s and four percent in 1981; one percent had a "severe handicap" in the early 1960s, two percent in 1981.

But both figures have continued to rise: in 1985 the rate for all degrees of limitation was over five percent, and for "severe handicap"—3.7 percent.[22]

Today about three million children are born every year in the United States. Of them 150,000 develop a less severe handicap, 110,000 a more severe one. Every year 250,000 of them achieve the age of eighteen and graduate into adulthood.

Aside from the heartbreak to the families, these handicapped persons are a major expense to society. They must be provided with special ramps, elevators, curricula, and teachers. The Education of the Handicapped Act, adopted by Congress in 1975, allocated $1 billion annually for this purpose.[23]

As seems to be universal in every vaccine-associated condition, the authorities profess ignorance of the causes: "The reasons for the increases are generally not well understood."[24] But pediatricians pay tribute to this phenomenon, calling it the "new morbidity," defined as "learning difficulties and school problems, behavioral disturbances, allergies, speech difficulties, visual problems, and the problems of adolescents in coping and adjusting"—which are "today the most common concerns about children."[25]

The physician is irresistibly impelled to characterize the "new morbidity" as "emotional," or perhaps "congenital," because these disabilities can then be blamed on the child or the parents. In fact, the responsibility should be placed squarely at the physician's own door. The vaccination program is intrinsically dangerous, which was never recognized or admitted, and has been implemented across the board in a careless way—without due concern for contraindications.*

The outcome has been the almost infinite series of disorders detailed in the preceding chapters.

The price for physicians' mistakes and misjudgments is being paid by the parents:

If someone had told me four years ago that this is where I'd be at today, I'd have said, "No way!" I could never have handled it. But every day you do cope. You just take it one day at a time. If it's a good day, you're glad. And if it's a bad day, you hope tomorrow will be better.

This book has shown, in particular, that the vaccination programs are the root cause of our ongoing epidemic of social violence.

We realize, of course, that violent crime is also caused by ignorance, poverty, child abuse, broken families, alcoholism, drug addiction, and the like. When sociologist Talcott Parsons interprets aggressive adolescent sexuality by young males from matriarchal households as a repudiation of their feminine identification, he may be on to something.[26] But the present book is about the contribution of the post-encephalitic syndrome. The fact that these other factors may, and do, play a certain role does not detract from the role of encephalitis. And before attempting to ascertain the scope of "social" factors such as poverty, illiteracy, child abuse, broken families, racial tension, violence, alcoholism, and drug addiction—or "emotional"

---

*On physician failure to observe contraindications in administering vaccines see Coulter, H. and Fisher, B., Chapter 13.

factors such as repudiation of their feminine identification by adolescent males—the role of vaccine-damage should be studied and analyzed. For this syndrome, now into its second generation, makes its own notable contribution to poverty (hyperactive adolescents cannot keep jobs), illiteracy (dyslexic children cannot study), child abuse (hyperactive young adults have little tolerance for hyperactivity in their children), broken families (the stresses and strains of minimal brain damage lead to marital breakdowns), social violence (uneducated youth without jobs have nothing else to do), racial tension (black children may be affected disproportionately by vaccination), alcoholism, and drug addiction (adolescents and adults with neurologic disorders must find escape somewhere).

While "emotional" disorders and disabilities may make a contribution here and there, most often they are *reactions* to neurologic defects generated by vaccination and the concomitant problem of getting along in the world.

When the input of vaccine damage has been evaluated in its entirety, and the necessary corrective measures taken, these "social" and "emotional" causative factors may seem less intractable. Some of them, indeed, will perhaps already have disappeared.

*   *   *

The catastrophe of childhood vaccinations is due above all to professional hubris—the physician's desire (often with the best motives!) to seize control over forces of nature and bend them to his will.

The consequence can only be called a pollution of our internal environment similar to the pollution of the external environment with which we are only too lamentably familiar. The hubris of physicians resembles that of the oil and chemical companies who have also felt they could violate nature without paying a price.

But, as the Greek dramatists knew, nature cannot be challenged in this way without exacting retribution. And the retribution has indeed been prompt and devastating, even though not yet generally acknowledged.

"Hubris" is overweening self-confidence, and the hubris of physicians reflects the dominant political position they have held since the 1920s.

In that decade nearly all state legislatures adopted the laws known as "Medical Practice" acts which granted virtual monopoly status and monopolistic powers to the medical profession and its representative organizations.

Claiming a monopoly over medical "science," the profession demanded, and received, a monopoly over medical practice and "health care."

This was the first step in the emergence and triumph of the medical-industrial complex we know today.

In this way the profession was induced to assume a role for which it is not suited—that of judge and arbiter of all that pertains to health.

This is too great a responsibility for a mere professional group. The inability of physicians to cope with it has brought on the tragedy described in these pages.

The bureaucratic transformation of medicine strengthened the power of professional organizations and lessened that of the practitioner. It has insulated medicine from both internal and external criticism.

The possibility of whistle-blowing from within the ranks of practitioners has been almost entirely stifled. The physician who sees first-hand the disastrous consequences of vaccination can rarely make his voice heard, and can never prevail against professional bureaucrats. So the juggernaut rolls on and on.

Any blaming of physicians voiced in this book is, in fact, a rebuke directed against its bureaucratic structure, which has prevented many well-meaning practitioners, who understood the potential dangers of vaccination, from speaking out.

Medical bureaucracies are also largely insulated from external criticism.

Medicine has powerful allies in business and politics. And it has even coopted a part of the press which, while willing enough to censure the highest officials in the land, is often timid and subservient before the self-confidently dogmatic physician.

Protected on all sides, medical organizations were able to press forward with one vaccination program after another, ignoring the evidence that these were exacting a toll in ruined lives.

Once the dimensions of the vaccination catastrophe have been adequately appreciated, corrective action should be taken. If the errors of the past—the wrong decisions and wrong actions taken in relation to vaccination programs—are seen to reflect the medical profession's monopoly position in all matters relating to health, the cure should be sought in a curtailment of these monopoly powers.

Power corrupts in medicine as elsewhere. In granting absolute power to medical organizations we have made them candidates for absolute corruption.

If organized medicine is permitted to retain its present dominance over the health of the citizenry, tragedies similar to the one described in this book will inevitably recur in the future.

Organized medicine's claim to preeminence in medical science should be scrutinized. What kind of "science" is it that inflicts neurologic damage on several hundred thousand children a year?

The first corrective measure, which should be taken at once, is to suspend all childhood vaccinations pending an investigation of their true impact on the public health. When and if these programs are resumed, the "shots" should be voluntary, not compulsory.

Immunization will always involve a risk, however many improvements are made in the design and manufacture of vaccines. Hence it is intolerable that families should be compelled by the government to subject their children to this threat. Decisions which affect the individual's health and life should not be forced upon him by self-appointed groups of experts who are not even in a position to take responsibility for their errors.

The errors of physicians are being paid for by thousands and thousands of American families. What have they done to deserve such a fate?

Our authorities should be mindful of the fact that in Western Europe only the tetanus and the oral poliomyelitis vaccinations are obligatory. They should heed the words of Justus Stroem, the prominent Swedish vaccine specialist, who stated, "The modern infant must receive a large number of injections, and a reduction in their number would be a distinct advantage."[27]

"The most immunized child in history" should disappear into history.

Chapter VI Notes

1. Hill, T.R., 1928, 2.
2. *The Washington Post*, October 24, 1989, Health, 5.
3. *Ibid.*, September 19, 1988, B-8: Ann Landers.
4. Rothman, S. and Lichter, S.R., 1982, passim.
5. Time, October 15, 1984, 80.
6. *The New York Times*, November 8, 1988, C-1.
7. Review of Susan Littwin, *The Postponed Generation: Why America's Grown-Up Kids are Growing Up Later* (New York: Morrow, 1986) in *The International Herald Tribune*, February 20, 1986.
8. Rimland, B. and Larson, G.E., 1981, 31–33.
9. *Ibid.*, 33.
10. *Loc. cit.* Wharton, Y.L., 1977.
11. *The Washington Post*, June 8, 1988, A-6.
12. Rimland, B. and Larson, G.E., 1981, 34.
13. *The New York Times*, October 30, 1986: Op-Ed page; April 21, 1986, 1, B-7.
14. Rimland, B. and Larson, G.E., 1981, 36.
15. *The New York Times*, September 17, 1985, C-1, C-3.
16. Rimland, B. and Larson, G.E., 50.
17. Coulter, H. and Fisher, B., 1985, 339.
18. Newacheck, P.W. *et al.*, 1986, 180.
19. *Ibid.*, 181. Evans, R. *et al.*, 1987, 65S.
20. Newacheck, P.W., *et al.*, 1986, 179.
21. *Loc. cit.* Newacheck, P.W. *et al.*, 1984, 236.
22. Kirchner, C., 1988, 4. Newacheck, P.W., *et al.*, 1986, 178.
23. *The Washington Post.*, September 1, 1988, 13.
24. Newacheck, P.W., *et al.*, 1984, 232.
25. Newacheck, P.W. *et al.*, 1986, 183.
26. Lewis, D.O., 1981, 91.
27. Stroem, J., 1960, 1186.

Appendix:
The Interviews

The materials upon which this book is based include three sets of interviews.

Series One consists of more than 100 interviews which Barbara Fisher conducted for our earlier book, *DPT: A Shot in the Dark*. These were families who suspected that their child might have been vaccine-damaged and who contacted Dissatisfied Parents Together, the organization of families of vaccine-damaged children. These interviews averaged two to three typewritten pages in length and, in most cases, were limited to a description of the baby's acute reaction to the vaccine.

Nearly all the children covered by this first set of interviews were younger than six.

While the information already presented in *DPT: A Shot in the Dark* has not been repeated, this early set of interviews contained much additional data which could be used in these pages.

Series Two consists of thirty-one in-depth interviews conducted by myself—three by telephone, the rest at the homes of children with moderate-to-severe neurologic damage (autism, epilepsy, learning disabilities, hyperactivity). The families in most cases did not suspect a connection with vaccination, and the purpose of the interview was to try to pinpoint such a connection.

The families were located through parents' organizations of autistic, learning-disabled, and other neurologically damaged children. Their children were older than those in the first group—ranging in age from six to late adolescence.

A few of the parents in Series Two remained unconvinced that the sudden or insidious onset of their child's disability was connected with vaccination. This was especially true where no severe acute reaction had been noted. One family asked specifically that their reservation in this respect be noted here.

265

However, as has been discussed in the text, an acute reaction to the shots is not needed for subsequent development of a neurologic disability. If the child developed the symptoms of the post-encephalitic syndrome, we assumed that this was due to an encephalitis. And, in the absence of a medical history of encephalitis from some other source, the child was assumed to have suffered a vaccine reaction. We have at all times been guided by similarity between the symptom-picture of the child and that of the post-encephalitic syndrome.

Series Three consists of twenty-eight questionnaires answered by parents of neurologically damaged children who had heard about the preparations for this book and wanted their own children's stories to be included. The interviews covered the child's reaction to vaccinations and subsequent development. The age range was the same as in Series Two.

As mentioned in the footnote on page two above, quotations in italics—with a few exceptions which are clear from the context (e.g., page 167)—represent statements by parents from one or another of these Series.

Not all of the interviews conducted in preparation for this book have been included. Five cases were adjudged not to be vaccine-related. And, in three cases, the parents refused to give permission to use the interview materials.

As mentioned in the Introduction, the interview materials have been used to reinforce the basic argument—which is itself drawn from the specialized literature on autism, minimal brain damage, learning disabilities, encephalitis, and vaccine-damage.

Bibliography

Adams, R.D. and M.Victor. *Principles of Neurology.* Second Edition. New York: McGraw-Hill, 1981.

Akerley, M.S. "Reactions to 'Employing Electric Shock with Autistic Children.'" *J. Autism* 6:3 (1976), 289–294.

————. "Springing the Tradition Trap." *J. Autism* 5:4 (1975), 373–380.

Aman, M.G. "Hyperactivity: Nature of the Syndrome and its Natural History." *J. Autism* 14:1 (1984), 39–56.

————. "Stimulant Drug Effects in Developmental Disorders and Hyperactivity—Toward a Resolution of Disparate Findings." *J. Autism* 12:4 (1982), 385.

American Academy of Pediatrics. Committee on Children with Disabilities. Committee on Drugs. "Medication for Children with an Attention Deficit Disorder." *Pediatrics* 80:5 (1987), 758–760.

American Psychiatric Association. *Diagnostic and Statistical Manual of Mental Disorders.* First Edition, Washington, D.C., 1951. Second Edition, Washington, D.C. 1968. Third Edition, Washington, D.C., 1980. Third Edition-Revised, Washington, D.C., 1987.

Amiel-Tison, C. "Neurologic Disorder in Neonates Associated with Abnormalities of Pregnancy and Birth." *Current Problems of Pediatrics* III:3 (January 1973), 3–37.

Annell, Anna-Lisa. "Pertussis in Infancy—A Cause of Behavioral Disorders in Children." *Acta Societatis Medicorum Upsaliensis* LVIII, Supp. 1 (1953).

Arnason, B. Editorial: "Neuroimmunology." *New England J. Med.* 316:7 (1987), 406–408.

Askin, J.A. and H.M. Zimmerman. "Encephalitis Accompanying Whooping Cough." *A.J. Diseases of Children* 39 (1929), 97–102.

Auden, G.A. "Behavior Changes Supervening Upon Encephalitis in Children." *Lancet* (October 28, 1922), 901–904.

August, G.A. and L.H. Lockhart. "Familial Autism and the Fragile-X Chromosome." *J. Autism* 14:2 (1984), 197–204.

————, M.A. Stewart, and L. Tsai. "The Incidence of Cognitive Disabilities in the Siblings of Autistic Children." *British J. Psychiatry* 138 (1981), 416–422.

267

Auletta, Ken. "A Reporter at Large. The Underclass-I." *The New Yorker* (November 16, 1981), 63–181.

Avery, M.E. and L.R. First. *Pediatric Medicine*. Baltimore: Williams and Wilkins, 1989.

Bach-y-Rita, G., J.R. Lion, C.E. Climent, and F.R. Ervin. "Episodic Dyscontrol: A Study of 130 Violent Patients." *A.J. Psychiatry* 127:11 (1971), 1473–1478.

Backman, Z. "The Relationship Between Learning Disabilities and Behavioral Manifestations with Toxicity and Cerebral Allergy." *The Digest of Chiropractic Economics* (May/June, 1985), 18–19.

Baker, A.B. "The Central Nervous System in Infectious Diseases of Childhood." *Postgraduate Medicine* 5 (1949), 1–12.

Baker, S.M. "Diagnostic and Therapeutic Strategies in an Autistic Child with a Positive Response to Taurine." In *Proceedings, 1984 Annual Conference of the National Society for Children and Adults with Autism*. Washington, D.C., 1984, 8–23.

Bakwin, H. "Cerebral Damage and Behavior Disorders in Children." *J. Pediatrics* 34 (1949) 371–382.

_____. "Early Infantile Autism." *J. Pediatrics* 45 (1954), 492–497.

Bannister, R. *Brain's Clinical Neurology*. Fifth Edition. Oxford: University Press, 1978.

Bartak, L. and M. Rutter. "Differences Between Mentally Retarded and Normally Intelligent Autistic Children." *J. Autism* 6 (1976), 109–120.

_____. "Language and Cognition in Autistic and 'Dysphasic' Children." In Neil Connor, ed., *Language, Cognitive Defects, and Retardation*. London and Boston: Butterworths, 1975.

Baumann, E., R.R. Binder, W.Falk, E.G.Huber, R.Kurz, and K. Rosanelli. "Development and Clinical Use of an Oral Heat-Inactivated Whole Cell Pertussis Vaccine." *Develop. Biol. Standard.* 61 (1985), 511–516.

Beavers, D.*J. Autism: Nightmare Without End*. Port Washington, N.Y.: Ashley Books, 1982. Reviewed in *J. Autism* 15:1 (1985), 113–119.

Behrman, R.E., V.C. Vaughan, III, and W.E. Nelson. *Nelson's Textbook of Pediatrics*. Thirteenth Edition. New York: W.B. Saunders, 1987.

_____ and R. Kliegman. *Nelson Essentials of Pediatrics*. Philadelphia: Saunders, 1989.

Bemporad, J. "Adult Recollections of a Formerly Autistic Child." *J. Autism* 9:2 (1979), 179–197.

Benatar, S.R. "Fatal Asthma." *New England J. Med.* 314:7 (February 13, 1986), 423–427.

Bender, Lauretta. "Burn Encephalopathies in Children." *Arch. Pediatrics* 60 (1943), 75–87.

_____. "The Goodenough Test (Drawing a Man) in Chronic Encephalitis in Children." *J. Nervous and Mental Disease* 91:3 (1940), 277–286.

Benson, D.F. "Interictal Behavior Disorders in Epilepsy." *Psychiatric Clinics of North America* 9:2 (June 1986), 283–292.

Bergman, P. and S.R. Escalona. "Unusual Sensitivities in Very Young Children." *Psychoanalytic Study of the Child* 3–4 (1949), 333–352.

Bettelheim, Bruno. *A Home for the Heart.* New York: Knopf, 1974. Reviewed in *J. Autism* 6 (1976), 193–205.

_____. "A Problem Learner." *Parents Magazine* 35:3 (May 1960), 52.

Betz, B.J. "A Study of Tactics for Resolving the Autistic Barrier in the Psychotherapy of the Schizophrenic Personality." *A.J. Psychiatry* 104 (1947), 267–273.

Bille, B. "Migraine in School Children." *Acta Paediatrica* 51 (1962), Supplement 136.

Bland, R. and H.Orn. "Family Violence and Psychiatric Disorder." *Canadian Journal of Psychiatry* 31 (March 1986), 129–137.

Bond, E.D. and K.E. Appel. *The Treatment of Behavior Disorders following Encephalitis.* New York: The Commonwealth Fund, 1931.

_____ and G.E. Partridge. "Post-Encephalitic Behavior Disorders in Boys and Their Management in a Hospital." *A.J. Psychiatry* VI (1926/1927), 25–80.

_____ and L.H. Smith. "Post-Encephalitic Behavior Disorders: A Ten-Year Review of the Franklin School." *A.J. Psychiatry* 92:1 (1935), 17–33.

Breuning, S.E. and A.D. Poling, eds. *Drugs and Mental Retardation.* Springfield: Thomas, 1982.

Brown, W.T., E.C. Jenkins, E. Friedman, J. Brooks, K. Wisniewski, S. Raguthu, and J. French. "Autism is Associated with the Fragile-X Syndrome." *J. Autism* 12:3 (1982), 303–308.

Bruun, R.D. and A.K. Shapiro. "Differential Diagnosis of Gilles de la Tourette's Syndrome." *J. Nervous and Mental Disease* 155:4 (1972), 328–334.

Bryant, E.T., M.L. Scott, C.J. Golden, and C.D. Tori. "Neuropsychological Deficits, Learning Disability, and Violent Behavior." *J. Consulting and Clinical Psychology* 52:2 (1984), 323–324.

Byers, Randolph K. and F.C. Moll. "Encephalopathies Following Prophylactic Pertussis Vaccine." *Pediatrics* 1:4 (1948), 439–457.

_____ and N.D. Rizzo. "A Follow-Up Study of Pertussis in Infancy." *New England J. Med.* 242:23 (June 8, 1950), 887–891.

Campbell, M. "Biological Interventions in Psychoses of Childhood." *J. Autism* 3 (1973), 347–373.

_____. "Psychopharmacological Treatment of Children with the Syndrome of Autism." *Pediatric Annals* 13:4 (1984), 309–318.

Cappon, D. "Clinical Manifestations of Autism and Schizophrenia in Childhood." *Canadian Medical Association Journal* 69 (1953), 44–49.

Carlson-Leavitt, J. "The Importance of Choice." *J. Autism* 8 (1978), 243–245.

Charlton, M.H. "Infantile Spasms." In Maurice H. Charlton, ed., *Myoclonic Seizures*. Amsterdam: Excerpta Medica/American Elzevier, 1975.

Check, W.A. "Homicide, Suicide, Other Violence Gain Increasing Medical Attention." *J. Amer. Med. Assoc.* 254:6 (August 9, 1985), 721–730.

Cherry, James D., Philip A. Brunell, Gerald S. Golden, and David T. Karzon. "Report of the Task Force on Pertussis and Pertussis Immunization." *Pediatrics* 81:6 Part II (June 1988). Supplement.

_____ and W.D. Shields. "Recurrent Seizures After Diphtheria, Tetanus, and Pertussis Immunization." *A.J. Dis. Children* 138 (October 1984), 904–907.

Chess, Stella. "Autism in Children with Congenital Rubella." *J. Autism* 1 (1971), 33–47.

_____. "Follow-Up Report on Autism in Congenital Rubella," *J. Autism* 7 (1977), 69–81.

Chevrie, J.J. and J. Aicardi. "Convulsive Disorders in the First Year of Life: Etiologic Factors." *Epilepsia* 18:4 (1977), 489–497.

Christian, H.A. *Principles and Practice of Medicine*. New York: Appleton-Century, 1947.

Churchill, D.W. "The Relation of Infantile Autism and Early Childhood Schizophrenia to Developmental Language Disorders of Childhood." *J. Autism* 2 (1972), 182–197.

Ciaranello, R. "Neurochemical Models of Infantile Autism." *Proceedings, 1981 International Conference of the National Society for Children and Adults with Autism*. Washington, D.C., 1981, 178–188.

_____, S.R. VandenBerg, and T.F. Anders. "Intrinsic and Extrinsic Determinants of Neuronal Development: Relation to Infantile Autism," *J. Autism* 12:2 (1982), 115–139.

Clark, P. and M. Rutter, "Compliance and Resistance in Autistic Children." *J. Autism* 7 (1977), 33–47.

Cleckley, H. *The Mask of Sanity*. St. Louis: Mosby, 1976.

Clements, S.D. and J.E. Peters. "Syndromes of Minimal Brain Dysfunction." In P. Black, ed., *Brain Dysfunction in Children: Etiology, Diagnosis, and Management*. New York: Raven, 1981.

Climent, C.E., R. Plutchik, F.R. Ervin, and A. Rollins. "Parental Loss, Depression, and Violence. III. Epidemiological Studies of Female Prisoners." *Acta Psychiatr. Scand.* 55 (1977), 261–268.

Cohen, D.J. "The Pathology of the Self in Primary Childhood Autism and Gilles de la Tourette Syndrome." *Psychiatric Clinics of North America* 3:3 (December 1980), 383–402.

Cole, Blanche E. "The Problem of Social Adjustment Following Epidemic Encephalitis in Children." *Mental Hygiene* 8 (1924), 977–1023.

Coleman, Mary, ed. *The Autistic Syndromes.* Amsterdam: North Holland Publishing Company, 1976.

————. "New Research Findings and Concepts in Autism." *Proceedings, 1980 Annual Meeting and Conference of the National Society for Autistic Children.* Washington, D.C., 1980, 8–19.

———— and J.P.Blass. "Autism and Lactic Acidosis." *J. Autism* 15:1 (1985), 1–8.

Commission for the Control of Epilepsy. *Plan for a Nationwide Action on Epilepsy.* Unpublished materials, 1977.

Connaught Laboratories, Inc. *Diphtheria and Tetanus Toxoids and Pertussis Vaccine Adsorbed USP (for Pediatric Use). Physicians' Desk Reference,* 1989.

Coulter, Harris L. and Barbara Fisher. *DPT: A Shot in the Dark.* New York: Harcourt Brace Jovanovich, 1985.

Cowart, V.S. "Attention-Deficit Hyperactivity Disorder: Physicians Helping Parents Pay More Heed." *J. Amer. Med. Assoc.* 259:18 (May 13, 1988), 2647–2652. (b)

————. "The Ritalin Controversy: What's Made This Drug's Opponents Hyperactive?" *J. Amer. Med. Assoc.* 259:17 (May 6, 1988), 2521–2523. (a)

Creak, M., K. Cameron, and V. Cowie. "Schizophrenic Syndrome in Childhood: Progress Report of the Working Party." *Cerebral Palsy Bulletin* 3 (1961), 501–504.

———— and G. Pampiglione. "Clinical and EEG Studies on a Group of 35 Psychotic Children." *Dev. Med. Child Neurology* 11 (1969), 218–227.

Damasio, A.R. and R.G. Maurer. "A Neurologic Model for Childhood Autism." *Arch. Neurology* 35 (1978), 777–786.

Daniel, A.E. and P.W. Harris. "Female Offenders Referred for Pre-Trial Psychiatric Evaluation." *Bull. Amer. Acad. Psychiatry and the Law* 9 (1981), 40–47.

Darr, G.C. and F.G. Worden. "Case Report Twenty-Eight Years After an Infantile Autistic Disorder." *A.J. Orthopsychiatry* 21 (1951), 559–568.

DeLong, G.R., S.C. Bean, and F.R. Brown. "Acquired Reversible Autistic Syndrome in Acute Encephalopathic Illness in Children." *Arch. Neurology* 38 (1981), 191–194.

DeMyer, M.K. *Parents and Children in Autism.* Washington, D.C.: W.H. Winston, 1979. Reviewed in *J. Autism* 10 (1980).

272   *Bibliography*

_____, S. Barton, W.E. DeMyer, J.A. Norton, J. Allen, and R. Steele. "Prognosis in Autism: A Followup Study." *J. Autism* 3 (1973), 199–246.

DeMyer, W. and M. "Infantile Autism." *Neurologic Clinics* 2:1 (1984), 139–152.

Denckla, M.B., J.R. Bemporad, and M.C. MacKay. "Tics Following Methylphenidate Administration: A Report of 20 Cases." *J. Amer. Med. Assoc.* 235:13 (March 29, 1976), 1349–1351.

Deslauriers, A.M. "The Cognitive-Affective Dilemma in Early Infantile Autism: the Case of Clarence." *J. Autism* 8 (1978), 219–232.

Despert, J. Louise. "Some Considerations Relating to the Genesis of Autistic Behavior in Children." *A.J. Orthopsychiatry* 21 (1951), 335–350.

DeVeaugh-Geiss, J. "Neuroleptic Drugs: How to Reduce the Risk of Tardive Dyskinesia." *Geriatrics* (July 1979), 59–66.

Dewey, M. and M. Evarard. "The Near-Normal Autistic Adolescent." *J. Autism* 4 (1974), 348–356.

Deykin, E.Y. and B. Macmahon. "Viral Exposure and Autism." *A.J. Epidemiology* 109:6 (1979), 628–638.

Diamond, E.F. "Sudden Infant Death in Five Consecutive Siblings." *Illinois M.J.* 170:1 (1986), 33–34.

Dickey, L.D., ed. *Clinical Ecology*. Springfield: Thomas, 1976.

Dietrich, R.B., W.G. Bradley, E.J. Zaragoza, R.J. Otto, R.K. Taira, G.H. Wilson, H. Kangarloo. "MR Evaluation of Early Myelination Patterns in Normal and Developmentally Delayed Infants." *AJR* 150 (April, 1988), 889–896.

Dobbing, John. "Effects of Experimental Undernutrition on Development of the Nervous System." In N.S. Scrimshaw and J.E. Gordon, ed., *Malnutrition, Learning, and Behavior*. Cambridge: MIT Press, 1968.

Dohan, F.V. "Coeliac Disease and Schizophrenia." *Lancet* (April 25, 1970), 897–898.

_____. "Is Celiac Disease a Clue to the Pathogenesis of Schizophrenia?" *Mental Hygiene* 53:4 (1969), 525–529.

Easson, W.M. "The Early Manifestations of Adolescent Thought Disorder." *J. Clinical Psychiatry* (November, 1979), 469–475.

Egger, J., C.M. Carter, P.J. Graham, D. Gumley, and J.F. Soothill. "Controlled Trial of Oligoantigenic Treatment in the Hyperkinetic Syndrome. *Lancet* (March 9, 1985), 540–545.

Eisenberg, Leon. "The Autistic Child in Adolescence." *A.J. Psychiatry* 112 (January-June, 1956), 607–612.

Elliott, Frank A. "Biological Roots of Violence." *Proceedings of the American Philosophical Society* 127:2 (1983), 84–93.

————. "The Episodic Dyscontrol Syndrome and Aggression." *Neurologic Clinics* 2:1 (February 1984), 113–125.

————. "Historical Perspective on Neurobehavior," *Psychiatric Clinics of North America* 9:2 (June 1986), 225–239.

————. "Neurological Factors in Violent Behavior." *Bull. Amer. Acad. Psychiatry and the Law* 4 (1976), 297–315.

————. "Neurological Findings in Adult Minimal Brain Dysfunction and the Dyscontrol Syndrome." *J. Nervous and Mental Disease* 170:11 (1982), 680–687.

Evans, R. *et al.* "National Trends in the Morbidity and Mortality of Asthma in the US. Prevalence, Hospitalization and Death from Asthma Over Two Decades." *Chest* 91:6 (June, 1987), Supplement, 65S–74S.

Everard, M.P. "Mildly Autistic Young People and Their Problems." Unpublished. National Society for Autistic Children, Huntington, West Virginia. (n.d.)

————. "The National Society for Autistic Children in Britain." *J. Autism* 3 (1973), 278–279.

Federal Bureau of Investigation. *Uniform Crime Reports for the United States.* Washington, D.C.: U.S. Dept. of Justice, 1981–1988.

Fedio, P. "Behavioral Characteristics of Patients with Temporal Lobe Epilepsy." *Psychiatric Clinics of North America* 9:2 (June 1986), 267–281.

Fejn, D., B. Skoff, and A.F. Mirsky, "Clinical Correlates of Brainstem Dysfunction in Autistic Children." *J. Autism* 11:3 (1981), 303–315.

Ferrari, M. and W.S. Mathews. "Self-Recognition Deficits in Autism: Syndrome-Specific or General Developmental Delay?" *J. Autism* 13:3 (1983), 317–324.

Ferry, P.C., W. Banner, and R.A. Wolf, *Seizure Disorders in Children.* New York: J.B.Lippincott, 1986.

Fields, Mr. and Mrs. M. "The Relationship Between Problem Behavior and Food Allergies: One Family's Story." *J. Autism* 6:1 (1976), 75–91.

Fineman, K.R. "Firesetting in Childhood and Adolescence." *Psychiatric Clinics of North America.* 3:3 (December 1980), 483–500.

Finley, K.H. "Pathogenesis of Encephalitis Occurring with Vaccination, Variola, and Measles." *AMA Archives of Neurology and Psychiatry* 39 (1938), 1047–1054.

Firestone, P. and S.Peters. "Minor Physical Anomalies and Behavior in Children: A Review." *J. Autism* 13:4 (1983), 411–425.

Folstein, S. and M.L. Rutter. "Autism: Familial Aggregation and Genetic Implications." *J. Autism* 18:1 (1988), 3–26.

Ford, Frank R. *Diseases of the Nervous System in Infancy, Childhood, and Adolescence*. Springfield: C.C. Thomas, 1937.

Forness, S.R. and K.A. Kavale. "Autistic Children in School: The Role of the Pediatrician." *Pediatric Annals* 13:4 (April 1984), 319–328.

Foxx, R. "Working with the Self-Abusive Individual." *Proceedings, 1980 Annual Meeting and Conference of the National Society for Autistic Children*. Washington, D.C., 1980, 47–60.

Freeman, B.J. and E.R. Ritvo. "The Syndrome of Autism: Establishing the Diagnosis and Principles of Management." *Pediatric Annals* 13:4 (April 1984), 284–296.

Freeman, S.W., *Does Your Child Have a Learning Disability?* Springfield: Thomas, 1974.

Friend, M.R. "On Sleep Disturbances in Children." *J. American Psychoanalytical Association* 4 (1956), 514–525.

Fritz, G.K. and J. Armbrust. "Enuresis and Encopresis." *Psychiatric Clinics of North America* 5:2 (August 1982), 283–296.

Gastaut, H., B. Zifkin, and M. Rufo. "Compulsive Respiratory Stereotypies in Children with Autistic Features: Polygraphic Recording and Treatment with Fenfluramine." *J. Autism* 17:3 (1987), 391–405.

Gastfriend, D.R., J. Biederman, and M.S. Jellinek. "Desipramine in the Treatment of Attention Deficit Disorder in Adolescents." *Psychopharmacology Bulletin* 21:1 (1985), 144–145.

Geraghty, Kevin C. *DPT-Gate: Reagan's Baby*. El Cerrito, California, 1987.

———, A.C. Zahalsky, and A. Novotny. "Histamine Sensitization and its Consequences in Genetic Strains of Mice" (to be published).

Geschwind, Norman. "Why Orton Was Right." *Annals of Dyslexia* XXXII (1982), 13–30.

——— and Peter Behan. "Left-handedness: Association with immune disease, migraine, and developmental learning disorder." *Proc. National Academy of Sciences USA* 79 (August, 1982), 5097–5100.

Gibbs, Charles E. "Behavior Disorders in Chronic Epidemic Encephalitis." *A.J. Psychiatry* IX (1929–1930), 619–636.

Gillberg, Christopher. "Are Autism and Anorexia Nervosa Related?" *B.J. Psychiatry* 143 (April, 1983), 428. (a)

———. "Autism and Anorexia Nervosa: Related Conditions?" *Nord. Psykiatr. Tidsskr.* 39 (1985), 307–312. (a)

———. "Asperger's Syndrome and Recurrent Psychosis—A Case Study." *J. Autism* 15 (1985), 389–397. (b)

———. "Identical Triplets with Infantile Autism and the Fragile X Syndrome." *B.J. Psychiatry* 143 (1983), 25–26. (b)

_____. "Onset at Age 14 of a Typical Autistic Syndrome: A Case Report of a Girl with Herpes Simplex Encephalitis." *J. Autism* 16:3 (1986), 369–375.

_____. "The Sex Chromosomes—One Key to Autism? An XYY Case of Infantile Autism." *Applied Research in Mental Retardation* 5 (1984), 353–360.

_____. Gunilla Carlstroem, and Peder Rasmussen. "Hyperkinetic Disorders in Seven-Year Old Children with Perceptual, Motor, and Attentional Deficits." *J. Child Psychol. Psychiatr.* 24:2 (1983), 233–236.

_____ and H. Schaumann. "Social Class and Infantile Autism." *J. Autism* 12:3 (1982), 223–228.

_____. "Epilepsy Presenting as Infantile Autism? Two Case Studies." *Neuropediatrics* 14 (1983), 206–212.

_____and S. Steffenburg. "Outcome and Prognostic Factors in Infantile Autism and Similar Conditions: A Population-Based Study of 46 Cases Followed Through Puberty." *J. Autism* 17:2 (1987), 273–287.

Globus, J.H. and J.L. Kohn. "Encephalopathy Following Pertussis Vaccination Prophylaxis." *J. Amer. Med. Assoc.* 141:8 (1949), 507–509.

Godfrey, S. "What is Asthma?" *Arch. Dis. Childhood* 60 (1985), 997–1000.

Golden, Gerald S. "Psychologic and Neuropsychologic Aspects of Tourette's Syndrome." *Neurologic Clinics of North America* 2:1 (February 1984), 91–102.

Goodwin, Mary Stewart and W. Campbell. "In a Dark Mirror." *Mental Hygiene* 53:4 (October 1969), 550–563.

_____ and M.A. Cowan. "Malabsorption and Cerebral Dysfunction: A Multivariate and Comparative Study of Autistic Children." *J. Autism* 1 (1971), 48–62.

Green, J.B. and R.A. Mercille. "Psychiatric Complications of Epilepsy." *Neurologic Clinics* 2:1 (February 1984), 103–112.

Greenebaum, J.V. and Louis A. Lurie. "Encephalitis as a Causative Factor in Behavior Disorders of Children." *J. Amer. Med. Assoc.* 136:14 (April 3, 1948), 922–930.

_____, B. Leichentritt, and F.M. Rosenthal. "Effects of Encephalitis Occurring During Childhood on Behavior and Personality: A Study of 50 Cases." *Ohio State M.J.* 4 (1945), 1018–1021.

Greenough, A. and J.A. Davis. "Encephalitis Lethargica: Mystery of the Past or Undiagnosed Disease of the Present?" *Lancet* (April 23, 1983), 922–923.

Grossman, M. "Late Results in Epidemic Encephalitis." *Arch. Neur. and Psych.* 5 (1921) 580–587.

_____. "Sequels of Acute Epidemic Encephalitis." *J. Amer. Med. Assoc.* 78 (1922), 959–962.

Guilleminault, C., "Obstructive Sleep Apnea Syndrome." *Psychiatric Clinics of North America* 10:4 (December 1987), 607–621.

Gwirtsman, H.E. and R.H. Gerner. "Neurochemical Abnormalities in Anorexia Nervosa: Similarities to Affective Disorders." *Biological Psychiatry* 16:10 (1981), 991–995.

Hall, Arthur J. "The Mental Sequelae of Epidemic Encephalitis in Children." *Brit. Med. J.* (January 17, 1925), 110–111.

Halmi, K.A. "Pragmatic Information on the Eating Disorders." *Psychiatric Clinics of North America* 5:2 (August, 1982), 371–377.

Harper, J. and S. Williams. "Age and Type of Onset and Critical Variables in Early Infantile Autism." *J. Autism* 5 (1975), 24–36.

_____. "Early Environmental Stress and Infantile Autism." *M.J. Australia* (March 9, 1974), 341–346.

Hartsough, C.S. and N.M. Lambert. "Pattern and Progression of Drug Use Among Hyperactives and Controls: A Prospective Short-Term Longitudinal Study." *J. Child Psychiatr.* 28:4 (1987), 543–553.

Hawkins, D. and L. Pauling, eds. *Orthomolecular Psychiatry: Treatment of Schizophrenia.* San Francisco: W.H. Freeman, 1973.

Heffron, W.M., C.A. Martin, R.J. Welsh, P. Perry, and C.K. Moore. "Hyperactivity and Child Abuse." *Canadian J. Psychiatry* 32 (June 1987), 384–386.

Heilbrun, A.B. and M.R. "Psychopathy and Dangerousness: Comparison, Integration, and Extension of Two Psychopathic Typologies." *Brit. J. Clin. Psychology* 24 (1985), 181–195.

Hellman, D.S. and N.Blackman. "Enuresis, Firesetting and Cruelty to Animals: A Triad Predictive of Adult Crime." *A.J. Psychiatry* 122 (June 1966), 1431–1435.

Hemachudha, T., D.E. Griffin, J.J. Giffels, R.T. Johnson, A.B. Moser, and P. Phanuphak. "Myelin Basic Protein as an Encephalitogen in Encephalomyelitis and Polyneuritis Following Rabies Vaccination." *New England J. Med.* 316:7 (1987), 369–374.

Hetzler, B.E. and J.L. Griffin. "Infantile Autism and the Temporal Lobe of the Brain." *J. Autism* 11:3 (1981), 317–330.

Hier, D.B., M. LeMay, and P.B. Rosenberger. "Autism and Unfavorable Left-Right Asymmetries of the Brain." *J. Autism* 9:2 (1979), 153–159.

Hill, T.R. "The Problem of Juvenile Behavior Disorders in Chronic Epidemic Encephalitis." *J. Neurology and Psychopathology* 9:33 (1928), 1–10.

Hirtz, D.G., K.B. Nelson, and J.H. Ellenberg. "Seizures Following Childhood Immunizations." *J. Pediatrics* 102:1 (January, 1983), 14–18.

Hoffer, A. "Hyperactivity, Allergy, and Megavitamins." *Canadian Psychiatric Association Journal* 19 (1974), 124–125.

Hollander, H.E. and F.D. Turner. "Characteristics of Incarcerated Delinquents: Relationship Between Development Disorders, Environmental and Family Factors, and Patterns of Offense and Recidivism." *J. Amer. Acad. Child Psychiatry* 24:1 (1985), 221–226.

Holm, Vanja A. "The Causes of Cerebral Palsy." *J. Amer. Med. Assoc.* 247:10 (March 12, 1982), 1473–1477.

Holt, W.J. "Epidemic Encephalitis: A Follow-Up Study of Two Hundred and Sixty-Two Cases." *Arch. Neurology and Psychiatry* 38:6 (1937), 1135–1144.

Hopkins, A. *Epilepsy.* New York: Demos, 1987.

Hsu, L.K.G., K. Wisner, E.T. Richey, and C. Goldstein. "Is Juvenile Delinquency Related to an Abnormal EEG? A Study of EEG Abnormalities in Juvenile Delinquents and Adolescent Psychiatric Inpatients." *J. Amer. Acad. Child Psychiatry* 24:1 (1985) 310–315.

Hurley, A.D. and R. Sovner. "Anorexia Nervosa and Mental Retardation: A Case Report." *J. Clinical Psychiatry* (November, 1979), 480–481.

Ironside, Redvers. "Discussion on the Neurological Complications of the Acute Specific Fevers." *Proc. Royal Soc. Med.* 49 (1956), 139–146.

Iwasa, Saburo, I.Setsuji, and K.Akama. "Swelling of the Brain in Mice Caused by Pertussis Vaccine—Its Quantitative Determination and the Responsible Factors in the Vaccine." *Japan. J. Med. Sci. Biol.* 38 (1985) 53–65.

Jacob, J. and F. Mannino. "Increased Intracranial Pressure After Diphtheria, Tetanus, and Pertussis Immunization." *A. J. Dis. Children* 133 (February, 1979), 217–218.

James, A. and R.J. Barry. "Developmental Effects in the Cerebral Lateralization of Autistic, Retarded, and Normal Children." *J. Autism* 13:1 (1983), 43–56.

Jeavons, P.M. and B.D. Bower. *Infantile Spasms: A Review of the Literature and a Study of 112 Cases.* London: The Spastics Society, 1964.

_____. "Infantile Spasms." In P.J. Vinken and G.W.Bruyn, *Handbook of Clinical Neurology,* Volume 15 (1973), 219–234.

Johnson, C. "The Syndrome of Bulimia: Review and Synthesis." *Psychiatric Clinics of North America* 7:2 (June 1984), 247–273.

Johnson, D.H. and L.J. *Learning Disabilities.* Wash., D.C.: National Educational Association, 1978.

Johnston, I.D.A., H.R. Anderson, H.P. Lambert, and S. Patel. "Reading Attainment and Physical Development After Whooping Cough." *J. Epid. and Community Health* 39 (1985), 314–319.

Julien, R.M. *A Primer of Drug Action.* San Francisco: W.H. Freeman, 1978.

Kahn, Eugen and Louis H. Cohen. "Organic Drivenness: A Brain-Stem Syndrome and an Experience." *New England J. Med.* 210:14 (April 5, 1934), 748–756.

Kandt, R.S. "Neurologic Examination of Children with Learning Disorders." *Pediatric Clinics of North America* 31:2 (April 1984), 297–315.

Kane, J.M. *et al.* "The Prevalence of Tardive Dyskinesia." *Psychopharmacology Bulletin* 21:1 (1985), 136–139.

Kanner, Leo. "Autistic Disturbances of Affective Contact." *The Nervous Child* II (1942–1943), 217–250.

_____. "The Concept of Wholes and Parts in Early Infantile Autism." *J. Pediatrics* 108 (1951), 23–26.

_____. "Early Infantile Autism." *J. Pediatrics* 25 (1944), 211–217.

_____. "Follow-Up Study of Eleven Autistic Children Originally Reported in 1943." *J. Autism* 1 (1971), 119–145.

_____. "Problems of Nosology and Psychodynamics of Early Infantile Autism." *A.J. Orthopsychiatry* 19 (1949), 416–426.

_____. "To What Extent is Early Infantile Autism Determined by Constitutional Inadequacies?" In *Genetics and the Inheritance of Integrated Neurological and Psychiatric Patterns* (Baltimore: Williams and Wilkins, 1954), being Vol. 33 of the Proceedings of the Association for Research in Nervous and Mental Disease.

_____ and Leon Eisenberg. "Early Infantile Autism: 1943–1955." *Psychiatric Research Reports* 7 (1957), 55–65.

_____ and L.I. Lesser. "Early Infantile Autism." *Pediatric Clinics of North America* (August 1958), 711–730.

Kaplan, B.J., J. McNicol, R.A. Conte, and H.K. Moghadam. "Physical Signs and Symptoms in Preschool-Age Hyperactive and Normal Children." *Developmental and Behavioral Pediatrics* 8:6 (December 1987), 305–309.

_____. "Sleep Disturbance in Preschool-Aged Hyperactive and Nonhyperactive Children." *Pediatrics* 80:6 (December 1987), 839–844.

Karlin, Isaac. "Congenital Verbal-Auditory Agnosia." *Pediatrics* 7 (1951), 60–68.

_____. "A Psychosomatic Theory of Stuttering." *J. Speech Disorders* 12 (1947), 319–322.

Katz, Donald R. "The Kids with the Faraway Eyes." *Rolling Stone* (March 8, 1979). Institute for Child Behavior Research, Publication #44.

Kellaway, P., J.W. Crawley, and N. Kagawa. "A Specific Electroencephalographic Correlate of Convulsive Equivalent Disorders in Children." *J. Pediatrics* 55 (1959), 582–592.

Kelley, David. "Stalking the Criminal Mind." *Harpers* (August 1985), 53–59.

Kennedy, R.L.J. "The Prognosis of Sequelae of Epidemic Encephalitis in Children," *A.J. Dis. Children* 28 (1924) 158–172.

Kirschbaum, W.R. "Excessive Hunger as a Symptom of Cerebral Origin." *J. Nervous and Mental Disease* 113:2 (1951), 95–114.

Kirschner, C. "Recent Trends and Prevalence Rates and Numbers of Blind and Visually Handicapped School children." American Foundation for the Blind, 1988. (unpublished)

Kissel, S.J. "Violence in America: An Emerging Public Health Problem." *Health and Social Work* 11:2 (Spring 1986), 153–155.

Kolata, Gina. "Math Genius May Have Hormonal Basis." *Science* 222 (December 23, 1983), 1312.

Komoto, J. and J. Hirata. "Infantile Autism and Affective Disorder." *J. Autism* 14:1 (1984), 81–84.

———, S. Usui, S. Otsuki, and A. Terao. "Infantile Autism and Duchenne Muscular Dystrophy." *J. Autism* 14:2 (1984), 191–195.

Konstantareas, M.M. and S. Homatidis. "Brief Report: Ear Infections in Autistic and Normal Children." *J. Autism* 17:4 (1987), 585–593.

Kringelbach, J. and J. Senstius. "Hypsarrhythmia efter triplevakcination." *Nordisk Medicin* 76:49 (December 8, 1966), 1435–1436.

Kulenkampff, M., J.S. Schwartzman, and J. Wilson. "Neurological Complications of Pertussis Inoculation." *Arch. Disease in Childhood* 49:1 (January 1974), 46–49.

Kupfer, D.J., T.P. Detre, and J. Koral. "Relationship of Certain Childhood 'Traits' to Adult Psychiatric Disorders." *A.J. Orthopsychiatry* 45:1 (1975), 74–80.

Lapin, Joseph H. *Whooping Cough.* Springfield and Baltimore: Thomas, 1943.

Lasch, Christopher. *The Culture of Narcissism.* New York: Warner Books, 1979.

Laufer, M.W. and E. Denhoff. "Hyperkinetic Behavior Syndrome in Children." *J. Pediatrics* 50 (1957), 463–474.

——— and G. Solomons. "Hyperkinetic Impulse Disorder in Children's Behavior Problems." *Psychosomatic Medicine* 19:1 (1957), 38–49.

Lerner, J.A., T.S. Inui, E.W. Trupin, and E. Douglas. "Preschool Behavior Can Predict Future Psychiatric Disorders." *J. Amer. Academy Child Psychiatry* 24:1 (1985), 42–48.

Levine, M.D. and B.G. Zallen. "The Learning Disorders of Adolescence: Organic and Nonorganic Failure to Strive." *Pediatric Clinics of North America* 31:2 (April 1984), 345–369.

Levine, M.I. "Autism—An Unsolved Pediatric Problem." *Pediatric Annals* 13:4 (1984), 279–281.

Leviton, A. "Do Learning Handicaps and Headache Cluster?" *J. Child Neurology* 1 (October 1986), 372–377.

Lewis, Dorothy O., ed. *Vulnerabilities to Delinquency.* New York: SP Medical and Scientific Books, 1981.

————, *et al.* "Neuropsychiatric, Psychoeducational, and Family Characteristics of Fourteen Juveniles Condemned to Death in the United States." *A.J. Psychiatry* 145:5 (May, 1988), 584–589.

Lewis, S.R. and S. van Ferney. "Early Recognition of Infantile Autism." *J. Pediatrics* 56:4 (April, 1960), 510–512.

Lidsky, T.I., T. Labuszewski, and F.M. Levine. "Are Movement Disorders the Most Serious Side Effects of Maintenance Therapy with Antipsychotic Drugs?" *Biological Psychiatry* 16:12 (1981), 1189–1194.

Littwin, S. *The Postponed Generation: Why America's Kids are Growing Up Later.* New York: Morrow, 1986.

Litvak, A.M., H. Gibel, S.E. Rosenthal, and P. Rosenblatt. "Cerebral Complications in Pertussis." *J. Pediatrics* 32 (1948), 357–379.

Long, K.A. and D.V. McQueen. "Detection and Treatment of Emotionally Disturbed Children in Public Schools: Problems and Theoretical Perspectives." *J. Clinical Psychology* 40:1 (January 1984), 379–390.

Lotter, V. "Epidemiology of Autistic Conditions in Young Children." *Social Psychiatry* 1 (1966/1967), 124–137.

Low, N.L. "Electroencephalographic Studies Following Pertussis Immunizations." *J. Pediatrics* 47 (1955), 35–39.

Lurie, L.A., J.V. Greenebaum, B. Leichentritt, and F.M. Rosenthal. "Late Results Noted in Children Presenting Post-Encephalitic Behavior." *A.J. Psychiatry* 104 (1947), 171–179.

———— and Sol Levy. "Personality Changes and Behavior Disorders of Children Following Pertussis." *J. Amer. Med. Assoc.* 120:12 (November 21, 1942), 890–894.

MacPherson, Myra. "The Roots of Evil." *Vanity Fair* (May 1989), 142–149, 188–196.

Maletsky, B.M. "The Diagnosis of Pathological Intoxication." *J. Studies on Alcohol* 37:9 (1976), 1215–1227.

————. "The Episodic Dyscontrol Syndrome." *Diseases of the Nervous System* (March 1973), 178–185.

Manclark, C. *et al.* "Pertussis." In R. Germanier, ed., *Bacterial Vaccines.* New York: Academic Press, 1984.

Markowitz, P.I. "Autism in a Child with Congenital Cytomegalovirus Infection." *J. Autism* 13:3 (1983), 249–253.

Maurer, R.G. "Neuropsychology of Autism." *Psychiatric Clinics of North America* 9:2 (1986), 367–380.

_____ and A.R. Damasio. "Childhood Autism from the Point of View of Behavioral Neurology." *J. Autism* 12:2 (1982), 195–205.

Mawson, D., A. Grounds, and D. Tantam. "Violence and Asperger's Syndrome: A Case Study." *B.J. Psychiatry* 147 (1985), 566–569.

McCann, B.S. "Hemispheric Asymmetries and Early Infantile Autism." *J. Autism* 11:4 (1981), 401–411.

McGinniss, J. *Fatal Vision.* New York: Signet Books, 1989.

Melchior, J.C. "Infantile Spasms and Early Immunization Against Whooping Cough." *Arch. Dis. in Childhood* 52 (1977), 134–137.

_____. "Infantile Spasms and Immunization in the First Year of Life." *Neuropaediatrie* 3 (1971/1972), 3–10.

_____. "Infantile Spasmer og Vaccinationer." *Ugeskr. Laeg.* 131:17 (1969), 748.

Mendlewicz, J. "Genetic Factors of Human Violent Behavior." In J. Obiols, C. Ballus, E. Gonzalez Monclus, and J. Pujol, eds., *Biological Psychiatry Today.* Elsevier/North Holland Biomedical Press, 1979, 1229–1231.

Menkes, John H. *Textbook of Child Neurology.* Philadelphia: Lea and Febiger, 1980.

Menkes, M.M., J.S. Rowe, and J.H. Menkes. "A Twenty-Five Year Follow-Up Study on the Hyperkinetic Child with Minimal Brain Dysfunction." *Pediatrics* 39 (1967), 393–399.

Menolascino, F.J. and M.L. Egger. *Medical Dimensions of Mental Retardation.* Lincoln: University of Nebraska Press, 1978.

Merritt, H. H. *Textbook of Neurology.* Sixth Edition. Philadelphia: Lea and Febiger, 1979.

Meryash, D. L., L.S. Szymanski, and P.S. Gerald. "Infantile Autism Associated with the Fragile-X Syndrome." *J. Autism* 12:3 (1982), 295–301.

Michaud, Stephen G. and Hugh Aynesworth. *Ted Bundy: Conversation with a Killer.* New York: Signet Books, 1989.

Miller, D. "Affective Disorders and Violence in Adolescents." *Hospital and Community Psychiatry* 37:6 (June 1986), 591–596.

Miller, D.L., E.M. Ross, R. Alderslade, M.H. Bellman, and N.S.B. Rawson. "Pertussis Immunization and Serious Acute Neurological Illness in Children." *British M.J.* 282 (May 16, 1981), 1595–1599.

Miller, H.G. and J.B.Stanton. "Neurological Sequelae of Prophylactic Inoculation." *Q.J. Medicine* 24:89 (1954), 1–27.

Millichap, J.G. "The Hyperactive Child." *Practitioner* 217 (1976), 61–65.

Milman, D.H. "Minimal Brain Dysfunction in Childhood: Outcome in Late Adolescence and Early Adult Years." *J. Clin. Psychiatry* 40 (1979), 371–380.

Mitler, M.M., S. Nelson, and R. Hajdukovic. "Narcolepsy: Diagnosis, Treatment, and Management." *Psychiatric Clinics of North America* 10:4 (December 1987), 593–606.

Mnukhin, S.S. and D.N. Isaev. "On the Organic Nature of Some Forms of Schizoid or Autistic Psychopathy." *J. Autism* 5 (1975), 99–108.

Money, J., N. Bobrow, and F.C. Clarke. "Autism and Autoimmune Disease: A Family Study." *J. Autism* 1 (1971), 146–160.

Monroe, R.R. *Brain Function in Aggressive Criminals*. Lexington, Massachusetts: Lexington Books, 1978.

Moyer, K.E. *The Psychobiology of Aggression*. New York: Harper and Row, 1976.

Murphy, J.V., L.D. Sarff, K.M. Marquardt. "Recurrent Seizures After Diphtheria, Tetanus, and Pertussis Vaccine Immunization." *A.J. Dis. Children* 138 (October, 1984), 908–911.

Myklebust, H.R., J. Killen, and M. Bannochie. "Emotional Characteristics of Learning Disability." *J. Autism* 2 (1972), 151–159.

National Center for Health Statistics. *Maternal Weight Gain and the Outcome of Pregnancy: United States, 1980*. Washington, D.C.: GPO, 1986.

National Society for Children and Adults with Autism. Form Letter Regarding Megavitamin Therapy for Autism and Related Disorders (Publication 39b).

Neal, Josephine B. *Encephalitis: a Clinical Study*. New York: Grune and Stratton, 1942.

———. "Types of Epidemic Encephalitis: A Comparison of the Cases Seen in St. Louis in 1933 with Those Seen in New York City." *A.J. Public Health* 23 (1933), 1144–1154.

Nelson, K. and J.H. Ellenberg. "Antecedents of Seizure Disorders in Early Childhood." *A.J. Dis. Children* 140 (October 1986), 1053–1061.

Newacheck, P.W., P.B. Budetti, and P. McManus. "Trends in Childhood Disability." *A.J. Public Health* 74:3 (March 1984), 232–236.

——— and N. Halfon. "Trends in Activity-Limiting Chronic Conditions Among Children." *A.J. Public Health* 76:2 (February 1986), 178–184.

Niswander, K., ed. *The Women and Their Pregnancies. Collaborative Perinatal Study of the National Institute of Neurological Diseases and Stroke*. Washington, D.C.: USDHEW PHS NIH, 1972.

Nomura, Y., M. Segawa, and M. Hasegawa. "Rett Syndrome—Clinical Studies and Pathophysiological Consideration." *Brain and Development* 6:5 (1984), 475–486.

Nyhan, W.L. "Clinical Features of the Lesch-Nyhan Syndrome." *Arch. Internal Medicine* 130 (August 1972), 186–192.

_____. "Behavior in the Lesch-Nyhan Syndrome." *J. Autism* 6 (1976), 235–252.

O'Banion, D., B. Armstrong, R.A. Cummings, and J. Stange. "Disruptive Behavior: A Dietary Approach." *J. Autism* 8 (1978), 325–337.

O'Brien, J. "School Problems: School Phobia and Learning Disabilities." *Psychiatric Clinics of North America* 5:2 (August, 1982), 297–307.

O'Connell, T.S. "The Musical Life of an Autistic Boy." *J. Autism* 4 (1974), 223–229.

O'Reilly, D.E. and J.E. Walentynowicz. "Etiological Factors in Cerebral Palsy: an Historical Review." *Developmental Medicine and Child Neurology* 23 (1981), 633–642.

Ornitz, E.M. "The Modulation of Sensory Input and Motor Output in Autistic Children." *J. Autism* 4 (1974), 196–215.

_____ and E. Ritvo. "The Syndrome of Autism: A Critical Review." *A.J. Psychiatry* 133:6 (June 1976), 609–621.

Palkes, H. and M. Stewart. "Intellectual Ability and Performance of Hyperactive Children." *A.J. Orthopsychiatry* 42 (1972), 35–39.

Park, Clara Claiborne. Review of D.J.Beavers, *Autism: Nightmare Without End. J. Autism* 15:1 (1985), 113–119.

_____. *The Siege.* New York: Harcourt Brace, 1967.

_____. "The Limits of Normalization." *J. Autism* 7:3 (1977), 301–302.

Pasamanick, B. and H. Knobloch. "Brain Damage and Reproductive Casualty." *A.J. Orthopsychiatry* 39 (1960), 299–305.

_____. "Early Feeding and Birth Difficulties in Childhood Schizophrenia: An Explanatory Note." *J. Psychology* 56 (1963), 73–77.

_____. "Retrospective Studies on the Epidemiology of Reproductive Casualty: Old and New." *Merrill-Palmer Quarterly* (December 12, 1966), 7–26.

Perry, R. *et al.* "Neuroleptic-Related Dyskinesias in Autistic Children: A Prospective Study." *Psychopharmacology Bulletin* 21:1 (1985), 140–143.

Petty, L.K., E.M. Ornitz, J.D. Michelman, E.G. Zimmerman. "Autistic Children Who Become Schizophrenic." *Arch. General Psychiatry* 41 (February 1984), 129–135.

Pfeffer, C.R., G. Solomon, R. Plutchik, M.S. Mizruchi, and A. Weiner. "Variables that Predict Assaultiveness in Child Psychiatric Inpatients." *J. Amer. Acad. Child Psychiatry* 26:6 (1985), 775–780.

Physicians' Desk Reference (various years)

Piacente, G.J. "Aggression." *Psychiatric Clinics of North America* 9:2 (1986), 329–339.

Pingree, C.B. "Parents vs. Autism: Our Pediatrician, the Coach." *Pediatric Annals* 13:4 (1984), 330–338.

Pittman, Margaret and C.B. Cox. "Pertussis Vaccine Testing for Freedom-from-Toxicity." *Applied Microbiology* 13:3 (May 1965), 447–456.

Plaut, T.F. *Children with Asthma: A Manual for Parents.* Amherst: Pedipress, 1984.

Pontius, A.A. and K.F. Ruttiger. "Frontal Lobe System Maturational Lag in Juvenile Delinquents Shown in Narratives Test." *Adolescence* 11:44 (1976), 509–518.

Poser, C.M. "Neurologic Syndromes That Arise Unpredictably." *Consultant* (January 1987), 45–55.

Prensky, A.L. "History of Convulsions and Use of Pertussis Vaccine" (editorial). *J. Pediatrics* 107:2 (August 1985), 244–246.

_____. "Time—A Fourth Dimension for Encephalopathies." *New England J. Med.* 310:23 (1984), 1527–1528.

Quitkin, F. and D.F. Klein. "Two Behavioral Syndromes in Young Adults Related to Possible Minimal Brain Dysfunction." *J. Psychiatric Research* 7 (1969), 131–142.

Randolph, Theron G. and Ralph W. Moss. *Allergies: Your Hidden Enemy.* Wellingborough, Northamptonshire: Turnstone Press, 1981.

Rapp, Doris J. *Allergies and the Hyperactive Child.* New York: Sovereign Books, 1979.

_____ with Bamberg, D.L. *The Impossible Child: in School, at Home.* Buffalo: Practical Allergy Research Foundation, 1986.

Ravenholt, R.T. and W.H. Foege. "1918 Influenza, Encephalitis Lethargica, Parkinsonism." *Lancet* (October 16, 1982), 860–864.

Realmuto, G.M. and B. Main. "Coincidence of Tourette's Disorder and Infantile Autism." *J. Autism* 12:4 (1982), 367–372.

Reichler, R.J. "Diagnosis and its Implications." *Proceedings. 1980 Annual Meeting and Conference of the National Society for Autistic Children.* Washington, D.C., 1980, 95–112.

Reiser, J. "Asthma in Childhood." *B.J. Hospital Medicine* (April 1985), 196–204.

Rimland, Bernard. "High-Dosage Levels of Certain Vitamins in the Treatment of Children with Severe Mental Disorders." In D. Hawkins and L. Pauling, eds. *Orthomolecular Psychiatry: Treatment of Schizophrenia.* San Francisco: W.H. Freeman, 1973.

_____. *Infantile Autism: The Syndrome and Its Implications for a Neural Theory of Behavior.* New York: Appleton Century Crofts, 1962.

_____ and G.E. Larson. "The Manpower Quality Decline: An Ecological Perspective." *Armed Forces and Society* 8:1 (Fall 1981), 21–78.

Ritvo, E.R. "Evidence for Autosomal Recessive Inheritance in 46 Families with Multiple Incidences of Autism." *A.J. Psychiatry* 142:2 (February 1985), 187–192.

———. "Genetic and Immunohematologic Factors in Autism." *J. Autism* 12:2 (1982), 109–114.

——— and B.J. Freeman. "A Medical Model of Autism: Etiology, Pathology, and Treatment." *Pediatric Annals* 13:4 (1984), 298–305.

———, B.J. Freeman, A. Mason-Brothers, A. Mo, and A.M. Ritvo. "Concordance for the Syndrome of Autism in 40 Pairs of Afflicted Twins." *A.J. Psychiatry* 142:1 (January 1985), 74–77.

———, A.M. Brothers, B.J. Freeman, C. Pingree. "Eleven Possibly Autistic Parents." *J. Autism* 18:1 (1988), 139–145.

Rivers, Thomas M. and F.F. Schwentker. "Encephalomyelitis Accompanied by Myelin Destruction Experimentally Produced in Monkeys." *J. Exp. Med.* 61 (1935), 689–702.

Robins, Lee N. *Deviant Children Grown Up.* Baltimore: Williams and Wilkins, 1966.

Robison, Caroline. "A Troubled Child." *Parents Magazine* 35:3 (May 1960) 53.

Rodier, P.M. "Chronology of Neuron Development: Animal Studies and their Clinical Implications." *Dev. Med. Child Neurology* 22 (1980), 525–545.

Rosenberg, G. "Meningoencephalitis Following an Influenza Vaccination." *New England J. Med.* 283 (1970), 1209–1211.

Rosenblum, S.M., J.R. Arick, D.A. Krug, E.G. Stubbs, N.B. Young, and R.O. Pelson. "Auditory Brainstem Evoked Responses in Autistic Children." *J. Autism* 10:2 (1980), 215–225.

Rothman, S. and S.R. Lichter. *Roots of Radicalism: Jews, Christians and the New Left.* New York and Oxford: Oxford University Press, 1982.

Routh, D.K. Book Reviews in *J. Autism* 7 (1977), 417–422.

Rutter, M. "Brain-Damage Syndromes in Childhood: Concepts and Findings." *J. Child Psychol. Psychiatr.* 18 (1977), 1–21.

———. "Childhood Schizophrenia Reconsidered." *J. Autism* 2 (1972), 315–337.

———. "Syndromes Attributed to 'Minimal Brain Dysfunction' in Childhood." *A.J. Psychiatry* 139:1 (January 1982), 21–33.

——— and E. Schopler. "Autism and Pervasive Developmental Disorders: Concepts and Diagnostic Issues." *J. Autism* 17:2 (1987), 159–186.

———, D. Shaffer, and M. Shepherd. *A Multi-Axial Classification of Child Psychiatric Disorders.* Geneva: World Health Organization, 1975.

Sadler, J.E. Jr. "Childhood Asthma from the Point of View of the Liaison

Child Psychiatrist." *Psychiatric Clinics of North America* 5:2 (August 1982), 333–343.

Sadler, W.S. *Theory and Practice of Psychiatry*. St.Louis: Mosby, 1936.

Sankar, D. V. S., ed. *Schizophrenia: Current Concepts and Research*. Hicksville, N.Y.: PJD Publications, Inc., 1969.

Sargent, J. and R. Liebman. "Outpatient Treatment of Anorexia Nervosa." *Psychiatric Clinics of North America* 7:2 (June 1984), 235–245.

Satterfield, J.H., C.M. Hoppe, and A.M. Schell. "A Prospective Study of Delinquency in 110 Adolescent Boys with Attention Deficit Disorder and 88 Normal Adolescent Boys." *A.J. Psychiatry* 139:6 (1982), 795–798.

Satz, P., H.V. Soper, D.L. Orsini, R.R. Henry, and J.C. Zvi. "Handedness Subtypes in Autism." *Psychiatric Annals* 15:7 (July 1985), 447–449.

Sauvage, D., I. Leddet, L. Hameury, and C. Barthelemy. "Infantile Rumination: Diagnosis and Follow-up Study of Twenty Cases." *J. Amer. Acad. Child Psychiatry* 24:1 (1985), 197–203.

Schachar, R., M. Rutter, and A. Smith. "The Characteristics of Situationally and Pervasively Hyperactive Children: Implications for Syndrome Definition." *J. Child Psychology and Psychiatry* 22:4 (1981), 375–392.

Schain, R.J. *Neurology of Childhood Learning Disorders*. Second Edition. Baltimore: Williams and Wilkins, 1977.

———— and H. Yannet. "Infantile Autism: An Analysis of 50 Cases and a Consideration of Certain Relevant Neurophysiologic Concepts." *J. Pediatrics* 57:4 (1960), 560–567.

Schmidt, W.R. and L.W. Jarcho. "Persistent Dyskinesias Following Phenothiazine Therapy." *Arch. Neurology* 14 (April 1966), 369–377.

Schopler, E. "Convergence of Learning Disability, Higher-Level Autism, and Asperger's Syndrome." *J. Autism* 15:4 (1985), 359.

————. "The Stress of Autism as Ethology." *J. Autism* 4:3 (1974), 193–195.

————, S. Chess, and L. Eisenberg. "Memorial to Leo Kanner." *J. Autism* 11:3 (1981), 258–269.

———— and M. Rutter. "Editorial: Change of Journal Scope and Title." *J. Autism* 9:1 (1979), 1–10.

Schrag, Peter and Diane Divoky. *The Myth of the Hyperactive Child*. New York: Pantheon, 1975.

Serafetinides, E.A. "Epilepsy, Cerebral Dominance, and Behavior." In M. Girgis and L.G. Kiloh, eds., *Limbic Epilepsy and the Dyscontrol Syndrome*. Amsterdam: Elsevier/North Holland Biomedical Press, 1980.

Shaywitz, S.E. and B.A. "Diagnosis and Management of Attention Deficit Disorder: A Pediatric Perspective." *Pediatric Clinics of North America* 31:2 (April 1984), 429–457.

_____. "Current Status of the Neuromaturational Examination as an Index of Learning Disability." *J. Pediatrics* 104:6 (June 1984), 819–825.

Shea, V. and G.B. Mesibov. "Brief Report: The Relationship of Learning Disabilities and Higher-Level Autism." *J. Autism* 15 (1985), 425–435.

Sherwin, A.C. "Reactions to Music of Autistic (Schizophrenic) Children." *A.J. Psychiatry* 109 (1953), 823–839.

Sholevar, G.P., R.M. Benson, and B.L. Blinder, *Emotional Disorders in Children and Adolescents*. NY and London: SP Scientific Books, 1980.

Silva, P.A., S. Williams, and R. McGee. "A Longitudinal Study of Children with Developmental Language Delay at Age Three: Later Intelligence, Reading, and Behavior Problems." *Dev. Med. and Child Neurology* 29 (1987), 630–640.

Simeon, J. "Biology and Therapy of Violent Behavior in Children." In J. Obiols, C. Ballus, E. Gonzalez Monclus, and J. Pujol, eds., *Biological Psychiatry Today*. Amsterdam: Elsevier/North Holland Biomedical Press, 1979, 1223–1231.

Simons, J.M. "Observations on Compulsive Behavior in Autism." *J. Autism* 4 (1974), 1–10.

Smith, D.E.P., S.D. Miller, M. Stewart, T.L. Walter, and J.V. McConnell. "Conductive Hearing Loss in Autistic, Learning-Disabled, and Normal Children." *J. Autism* 18:1 (1988), 53–64.

Smith, Martin H. "National Childhood Vaccine Injury Compensation Act." *Pediatrics* 82:2 (August 1988), 264–269.

Steg, J.P. and J.L. Rapoport. "Minor Physical Anomalies in Normal, Neurotic, Learning Disabled, and Severely Disturbed Children." *J. Autism* 5 (1975), 299–307.

Steinman, L., S. Sriram, N.E. Adelman, S. Zamvil, H.O. McDevitt, and H. Urich. "Murine Model for Pertussis Vaccine Encephalopathy: Linkage to H-2." *Nature* 299 (October 21, 1982), 738–740.

Stevenson, L.D. and E.C. Alvord. "Allergy in the Nervous System." *A.J. Medicine* 3 (1948), 614.

Stewart, Gordon T. "Re: 'Whooping Cough and Whooping Cough Vaccine: The Risks and Benefits Debate.'" *A.J. Epidemiology* 119:1 (1984), 135–137.

_____. "Vaccination Against Whooping Cough: Efficacy versus Risks." *Lancet* (January 29, 1977), 234–237.

Stewart, M.A., C. Cummings, S. Singer, and C.S. DeBlois. "The Overlap Between Hyperactive and Unsocialized Aggressive Children." *J. Child Psychology and Psychiatry* 22 (1981), 35–45.

Stiver, R.L. and J.P. Dobbins. "Treatment of Atypical Anorexia Nervosa in the Public School: An Autistic Girl." *J. Autism* 10:1 (1980), 67–73.

Stokes, K.S. "Planning for the Future of a Severely Handicapped Autistic Child." *J. Autism* 7:3 (1977), 288–298.

Stores, G., J. Hart, and N. Piran. "Inattentiveness in Schoolchildren with Epilepsy." *Epilepsia* 19 (1978), 169–175.

Strauss, Alfred A. and Laura E. Lehtinen. *Psychopathology and Education of the Brain-Injured Child*. New York: Grune and Stratton, 1947.

Stroem, Justus. "Is Universal Vaccination Against Pertussis Always Justified?" *British M.J.* (October 22, 1960), 1184–1186.

Strother, C.R. "Minimal Brain Dysfunction: A Historical Overview." *Annals N.Y. Academy of Sciences* 205 (1973), 6–17.

Stubbs, E. G. "Autistic Children Exhibit Undetectable Hemagglutinin-Inhibition Antibody Titers Despite Previous Rubella Vaccination." *J. Autism* 6 (1976), 269–274.

————. "Autistic Symptoms in a Child with Cytomegalovirus Infection." *J. Autism* 8 (1978), 37–43.

————, E. Ash, and C.P.S. Williams. "Autism and Congenital Cytomegalovirus." *J. Autism* 14:2 (1984), 183–189.

————, M.L. Crawford, D.R. Burger, and A.A. Vandenbark. "Depressed Lymphocyte Responsiveness in Autistic Children." *J. Autism* 7 (1977), 49–55.

———— and R.E. Magenis. "HLA and Autism." *J. Autism* 10:1 (1980) 15–19.

Student, M. and H. Sohmer. "Evidence from Auditory Nerve and Brainstem Evoked Responses for an Organic Brain Lesion in Children with Autistic Traits." *J. Autism* 8 (1978), 13–20.

Sullivan, Ruth Christ. "The Burn-Out Syndrome." *J. Autism* 9:1 (1979), 112–126.

————. "Hunches on Some Biological Factors in Autism." *J. Autism* 5:2 (1975), 177–186.

————. "Siblings of Autistic Children." *J. Autism* 9:2 (1979), 287–298.

————. "What Does Deinstitutionalization Mean for Our Children?" *J. Autism* 11:3 (1981), 347–355.

————"Why Do Autistic Children?" *J. Autism* 10:2 (1980), 231–241.

Taft, L.T. and H.J. Cohen. "Hypsarrhythmia and Infantile Autism: A Clinical Report." *J. Autism* 1 (1971), 327–336.

Tanguay, P.E. and R.M. Edwards. "Electrophysical Studies of Autism: The Whisper of the Bang." *J. Autism* 12:2 (1982), 177–184.

Tanke, E.D. and J.A. Yesavage. "Characteristics of Assaultive Patients Who Do and Do Not Provide Visible Clues of Potential Violence." *A.J. Psychiatry* 142:12 (1985), 1409–1413.

Tartar, R.E., H. McBride, N. Buonpane, D.U. Schneider. "Differentiation of Alcoholics." *Arch. Gen. Psychiatry* 34 (July 1977), 761–768.

———, A.M. Hegedus, N.E. Winsten, and A.I. Alterman. "Intellectual Profiles and Violent Behavior in Juvenile Delinquents." *J. Psychology* 119:2 (1985), 125–128.

Tepper, S.J. and J.F. Haas. "Prevalence of Tardive Dyskinesia." *J. Clin. Psychiatry* 40 (1979), 508–516.

Thorpy, M.J. and P.B. Glovinsky. "Parasomnias." *Psychiatric Clinics of North America* 10:4 (December 1987), 623–639.

Tinbergen, Nikolaas. "Ethology and Stress Diseases." *Science* (July 5, 1974), 20–23.

Torisky, Constance. "The Hostage Parent: A Life-Style or a Challenge?" *J. Autism* 8 (1978), 234–240.

———, Dan and Connie. "Sex Education and Sexual Awareness Building for Autistic Children and Youth: Some Viewpoints and Considerations." *J. Autism* 15:2 (1985), 213–227.

———, Jesse A. "My Brother, Eddie." *J. Autism* 9:2 (1979), 288–293.

Treiman, D.M. "Epilepsy and Violence: Medical and Legal Issues." *Epilepsia* 27 (1986). Supplement 2, S77-S104.

Trollfors, B. "Bordetella Pertussis Whole Cell Vaccines —Efficacity and Toxicity." *Acta Paediatrica Scand.* 73 (1984), 417–425.

Tsai, Luke. "Brief Report: The Developent of Hand Laterality in Infantile Autism." *J. Autism* 14:4 (1984), 447–450.

———. "Brief Report: Handedness in Autistic Children and Their Families." *J. Autism* 12:4 (1982), 421–423.

———. "The Relationship of Handedness to the Cognitive, Language, and Visuo-Spatial Skills of Autistic Patients." *B.J. Psychiatry* 142 (1983), 156–162.

———. "The Development of Sex Differences in Infantile Autism." *B.J. Psychiatry* 142 (1983), 373–378.

———. "Social Class Distribution of Fathers of Children Enrolled in the Iowa Autism Program." *J. Autism* 12:3 (1982), 211–221.

Tsaltas, M. "A Pilot Study on Allergic Responses." *J. Autism* 16:1 (1986), 91–92.

Tudor-Hart, J. "Wheezing in Young Children: Problems of Measurement and Management." *J. Royal College of General Practitioners* (February 1986), 78–81.

U.S. Department of Health and Human Services. Public Health Service. National Institutes of Health. "Facts About Childhood Hyperactivity." Reprinted from *Children Today* (July-August 1984).

Van Bourgondien, M.E. and G.B. Mesibov. "Humor in High-Functioning Autistic Adults." *J. Autism* 17:3 (1987), 417–424.

Van den Berg, B. and J. Yerushalmy. "Studies on Convulsive Disorders in Young Children." *Pediatr. Res.* 3 (1969) 298–304.

Van Krevelen, A. "Critica Sobre el Diagnostico del Autismo Infantil Precoz." *Revista de Psiquiatria y Psicologia Medica* II:4 (1955), 318–325.

──────. "Early Infantile Autism and Autistic Psychopathy." *J. Autism* 1 (1971), 82–86.

Vaughan, Warren T., J.C. Sullivan, and F. Elmadjian. "Immunity and Schizophrenia: A Survey of the Ability of Schizophrenic Patients to Develop an Active Immunity Following the Injection of Pertussis Vaccine." *Psychosomatic Medicine* 11 (1949), 327–333.

Verhees, B. "A Pair of Classically Early Infantile Autistic Siblings." *J. Autism* 6 (1976), 53–59.

Vinken, P.J. and G.W. Bruyn. *Handbook of Clinical Neurology*. Volume 15. Amsterdam: North Holland Publishing Co., 1973.

Volkmar, F.R. and D.J. Cohen. "The Experience of Infantile Autism: A First-Person Account by Tony W." *J. Autism* 15:1 (1985) 47–54.

──────, and R. Paul. "The Use of 'Asperger's Syndrome.'" *J. Autism* 15 (1985), 437–439.

Von Economo, Constantine. *Encephalitis Lethargica: its Sequelae and Treatment*. London: Oxford University Press, 1931.

Wakabayashi, S. "The Present Status of an Early Infantile Autism First Reported in Japan Thirty Years Ago." *Nagoya M.J.* 46 (1984), 35–39.

Walker, A.M., H. Jick, D.R. Perera, T.A. Knauss, and R.S. Thompson. "Neurologic Events Following Diphtheria-Tetanus-Pertussis Immunization." *Pediatrics* 81:3 (March 1988), 345–349.

Ward, C.D. "Encephalitis Lethargica and the Development of Neuropsychiatry." *Psychiatric Clinics of North America* 9:2 (1986), 215–224.

Warren, R., N.C. Margaretten, N.C. Pace, and A. Foster. "Immune Abnormalities in Patients with Autism." *J. Autism* 16:2 (1986), 189–197.

Warren, W.R. "Encephalopathy Due to Influenza Vaccine." *AMA Archives Int. Med.* 97 (1956), 803–805.

Weiss, G., L. Hechtman, T. Milroy, and T. Perlman. "Psychiatric Status of Hyperactives as Adults: A Controlled Prospective 15-Year Follow-up of 63 Hyperactive Children." *J. Amer. Acad. Child Psychiatry* 24:1 (1985), 211–220.

Weizman, A., R. Weizman, G.A. Szekely, H. Wijsenbeek, and E. Livni. "Abnormal Immune Response to Brain Tissue Antigen in the Syndrome of Autism." *A.J. Psychiatry* 139:11 (1982), 1462–1465.

Wender, Paul H. *Minimal Brain Dysfunction in Children*. New York: Wiley Interscience, 1971.

West, D.J. "The Clinical Approach to Criminology." *Psychological Medicine* 10 (1980), 619–631.

Westall, F.C. and R.C. Root-Bernstein. "Suggested Connection Between Autism, Serotonin, and Myelin Basic Protein." *A.J. Psychiatry* 140:9 (1983), 1260–1261.

Whalen, C.K. and B. Henker. "Hyperactivity and the Attention Deficit Disorders: Expanding Frontiers." *Pediatric Clinics of North America* 31:2 (April 1984), 397–427.

Wharton, Y.L. *List of Hypotheses Advanced to Explain the SAT Scores Decline.* New York: College Entrance Examination Board, 1977.

White, R., L. Finberg, and A. Tramer. "The Modern Morbidity of Pertussis in Infants." *Pediatrics* 33 (1964), 705–710.

Whitehouse, D. and J.C. Harris. "Hyperlexia in Infantile Autism." *J. Autism* 13:3 (1984), 281–289.

Wilbur, C.W. "One of the Lucky Ones." *J. Autism* 7:3 (1977), 298–299.

Wing, Lorna. "Asperger's Syndrome: a Clinical Account." *Psychological Medicine* 11 (1981), 115–129.

———. "Clarification on Asperger's Syndrome." *J. Autism* 16:4 (1986), 513–515.

Wintrobe, M. *Clinical Hematology.* Eighth Edition. Philadelphia: Lea and Febiger, 1981.

Witt, E.D., C. Ryan, and L.K. George Hsu. "Learning Deficits in Adolescents with Anorexia Nervosa." *J. Nervous and Mental Disease* 173:3 (1985), 182–184.

Wolf, L. and B. Goldberg. "Autistic Children Grow Up: An Eight to Twenty-Four Year Follow-up Study." *Canadian J. Psychiatry* 31 (1986), 550–555.

Wolf, S.M. and A. Forsythe. "Behavior Disturbance, Phenobarbitol, and Febrile Seizures." *Pediatrics* 61:5 (May 1978), 728–731.

Wolfe, Tom. "The 'Me' Decade and the Third Great Awakening." *New York* (August 23, 1976), 26–40.

Wood, David R., F.W. Reimherr, P.H. Wender, and G.E. Johnson. "Diagnosis and Treatment of Minimal Brain Dysfunction in Adults." *Arch. Gen. Psychiatry* 33 (1976), 1453–1460.

Woodcock, J.H. "A Neuropsychiatric Approach to Impulse Disorders." *Psychiatric Clinics of North America* 9:2 (1986), 341–352.

Woods, C.A. "Encephalopathy Due to Influenza Vaccine." *J. Pediatrics* 65 (1964), 745–748.

Woods, Sherwyn M. "Adolescent Violence and Homicide: Ego Disruption and the 6 & 14 Dysrhythmia. *Proceedings of the Third World Congress of Psychiatry, Montreal, 1961,* II, 1348–1352.

Woody, R.C. and M.E. Blaw. "Ophthalmoplegic Migraine in Infancy." *Clinical Pediatrics* 25:2 (February 1986), 82–84.

Workman-Daniels, K.L. and V.M. Hesselbrock. "Childhood Problem Behavior and Neuropsychological Functioning in Persons at Risk for Alcoholism." *J. Studies on Alcohol* 48:3 (1987), 187–193.

Yamazuki, K., Y. Saito, F. Okada, T. Fujieda, and I. Yamashita, "An Application of Neuroendocrinological Studies in Autistic Children and Heller's Syndrome." *J. Autism* 5:4 (1975), 323–332.

Yates, A. "Autism: the Case for Left Hemispheric Damage." *Arizona Medicine 16 (1984), 395–397.*

Yearbook of Pediatrics, 1971. Chicago: Yearbook Publishers, 436–439.

Yeudall, L.T. and D. Fromm-Auch. "Neuropsychological Impairments in Various Psychopathological Populations." In J. Gruzelier and P. Flor-Henry,, *Hemisphere Asymmetries of Function in Psychopathology.* Amsterdam: Elsevier/North Holland Biomedical Press, 1979, 401–428.

Younes, R.P., B. Rosner, and G. Webb. "Neuroimmaturity of Learning-Disabled Children: A Controlled Study." *Dev. Med. and Child Neurology* 25:5 (October 1983), 574–580.

Yudkovitz, E. "Book Review of Books on Autism." *J. Autism* 7 (1977), 417–425.

Index

abdominal pain (see: gastrointestinal pain)
abstractions, abstract thought 25-27, 78, 114, 131, 207-209 (see: fragmented thinking, use of symbols)
abuse
—of animals 88, 180, 188-190, 203, 229
—child 91, 171, 174, 175, 178, 180, 212-216, 260
adjuvant effect of pertussis vaccine 159
aggression, aggressiveness 37, 40-46, 86-89, 134-138, 141, 144, 181, 196, 202, 254 (see: violence)
alcoholism 144, 178, 186, 187, 192, 195, 202, 211, 214-218, 221, 254, 259, 260 (see: "St. Louis Triad")
alienation 1-2, 7, 24-28, 37, 82-83, 128, 144, 195, 196, 232, 233, 251, 254 (see: loneliness, anomie)
allergy 102, 103, 151-167, 203, 224, 259 (see: hypersensitivity)
—milk 152, 153 (see: colic)
ambidexterity (see: left-handedness)
American Academy of Pediatrics (AAP) xii, xvi, 228
American College Testing (ACT) Program 255
American Medical Association (AMA) xii, xvi
American Psychiatric Association (APA) xiii, 81, 83, 89, 158, 228
—*Diagnostic and Statistical Manual (DSM)* xiii, 33, 62, 86
amnesia (see: memory)
amphetamines 64, 166, 212, 219 221, 224, 226, 227, 251, 253
anemia, pernicious 154
animals, cruelty to (see: abuse of animals)
ankle clonus 17
Ann Landers 84, 87, 107, 109
Annell, Anna Lisa 102, 114, 118, 120, 121, 125, 159
anomie 37 (see: alienation, loneliness)
anorexia 28-30, 64, 65, 73, 102, 108-110, 144, 220
anti-conceptual thinking (see: abstractions)

anxiety 5-7, 27, 28, 75, 81, 127-129, 186, 190, 203, 214, 217, 218, 226, 233, 254
—separation 38-39, 75, 83
apnea 102, 103, 106
—sleep 66, 74
appetite disorders 28-30, 64, 108-110, 115, 204 (see: rumination)
argumentativeness (see: stubbornness, resisting change)
arm-biting (see: self-mutilation)
arson 88, 136, 140, 173, 180, 186, 189, 190, 192, 200, 203, 222, 254
arthritis, rheumatoid 154
Asperger's Syndrome 31, 35, 36, 78, 181-182, 206
assault 172-173, 178, 193, 202
asthma 23, 69-70, 73, 108, 197, 257 (see: respiratory disorders)
Atarax 226
attention-deficit disorder 61, 62, 69, 79, 86, 103, 111, 114, 129, 183, 186, 191, 208, 215, 219, 251
authority, resisting 41, 86-87, 134-135, 212-213 (see: oppositional disorder)
autism xiii-xvi, 1-53, 70, 76, 82, 85, 91, 93-94, 99, 100, 106, 114, 115, 119, 122, 123, 127, 129, 131, 143, 153-155, 160-166, 171, 181, 182, 190, 197, 200, 202, 204, 207, 210, 216-219, 223-229, 249-254, 265, 266
—in Austria 35, 50
—in Chile 50
—in England 50
—in France 50, 155
—in Holland 50
—in Japan 50
—in Scandinavia 50
—in the USA 49-50
—in the USSR 30, 47
autoimmune diseases 151, 154, 155, 161
avoidant disorder 83, 91

back-arching 30, 105
Bakwin, Harry 125, 131
balance, inability to 62
Bannister, Roger 121, 160
barbiturates 166
Behan, P. 31, 63, 66